HOW GOD BECAME JESUS

HOW GOD BECAME JESUS

THE REAL ORIGINS OF BELIEF
IN JESUS' DIVINE NATURE—
A RESPONSE TO BART EHRMAN

Michael F. Bird
Craig A. Evans
Simon J. Gathercole
Charles E. Hill
Chris Tilling

ZONDERVAN

How God Became Jesus
Copyright © 2014 by Michael F. Bird, Craig A. Evans, Simon J. Gathercole,
Charles E. Hill, Chris Tilling

This title is also available as a Zondervan ebook.
Visit www.zondervan.com/ebooks.

Requests for information should be addressed to:

Zondervan, 3900 *Sparks Drive SE, Grand Rapids, Michigan 49546*

Library of Congress Cataloging-in-Publication Data

    How God became Jesus : the real origins of belief in Jesus' divine nature--a response
to Bart Ehrman / Michael F. Bird, Craig A. Evans, Simon J. Gathercole, Charles E. Hill,
Chris Tilling.
        pages cm
    ISBN 978-0-310-51959-1 (softcover)
    1. Jesus Christ—Divinity—History of doctrines—Early church, ca. 30-600.
2. Ehrman, Bart D. How Jesus became God. 3. Jesus Christ. 4. Jesus Christ—Historicity.
5. Jesus Christ—Person and offices. I. Bird, Michael F.
BT216.3.H69 2014
232—dc23   2014003073

Cover design: Jeffrey Thomson
Interior design & composition: Greg Johnson/Textbook Perfect

Printed in the United States of America

HB 01.23.2024

CONTENTS

Editor's Preface

The purpose of this volume is to offer a critical response to Bart Ehrman's book *How Jesus Became God: The Exaltation of a Jewish Preacher from Galilee*. Ehrman is something of a celebrity skeptic. The media attraction is easy to understand. Ehrman has a famous deconversion story from being a fundamentalist Christian to becoming a "happy agnostic." He's a *New York Times* bestselling author, having written several books about the Bible, Jesus, and God with a view to debunking widely held religious beliefs as based on a mixture of bad history, deception, and myth. He's a publicist's dream since in talk shows and in live debates he knows how to stir a crowd through hefty criticism, dry wit, on the spot recall of historical facts, and rhetorical hyperbole. He also has a global audience. In fact, if I can offer a personal anecdote, on two occasions I've received emails from Christians in the Middle East asking how to respond to local Muslims who have been reading Ehrman's writings and are quoting them at Christians as evidence that the Christian Bible has been corrupted, and that Islam is the only religion with a pure set of sacred writings. So there is more at stake here than being the resident religious skeptic on the Colbert Report—much more!

As to why Ehrman's works have been so popular, well, I have my own theory. For conservative Christians, Ehrman is a bit of a bogeyman, the Prof. Moriarty of biblical studies, constantly pressing an attack on their long-held beliefs about God, Jesus, and the Bible. Conservatives buy his books if only for the purpose of keeping their disgust with him fresh and to find out what America's favorite skeptic is up to now. For secularists, the emerging generation of "nones" (i.e., the growing number of people who list their religion as "none" even if they are not committed to either atheism or agnosticism),

Ehrman is a godsend. He provides succor and solace that one need not take Jesus too seriously, confirming that religion is the opiate of the masses and that the whole God thing might be just a big mistake. In any event, Ehrman is worth addressing, since his skill as a textual critic is widely acknowledged and his showmanship as a public intellectual can hardly be denied. Such a pity then that he is almost always wrong!

In the recent book *How Jesus Became God*, Ehrman proffers the view that belief in Jesus' divinity emerged gradually in a messy process that ebbed and flowed from exaltation to incarnation. If this were so, recognition of Jesus as God was not so much a result of divine revelation as it was a human process, a process that struggled for legitimacy even within the church. We, the contributors, do not dispute that christological development took place and the theological controversies that followed were indeed messy. We dispute, however, whether Ehrman's account and explanation for this development is historically accurate.

Not everything Ehrman says about the origins of belief in Jesus' divinity is wrong. Some things are quite true, some things we'd agree with but say differently, some things we'd suggest need better nuance, and other things we contend are just plain out of sync with the evidence. While Ehrman offers a creative and accessible account of the origins of Jesus' divinity in Christian belief, at the end of the day, we think that his overall case is about as convincing as reports of the mayor of Chicago, Rahm Emanuel, sitting in a Chick-Fil-A restaurant, wearing a Texan-style cowboy hat, while reading Donald Trump's memoire — which is to say, not convincing at all. But you'll have to read the rest of the book to find out why!

There are several people who need to be thanked for getting this volume out in a quick-fire fashion. First, our contributors, Craig A. Evans (Acadia Divinity College), Simon Gathercole (Cambridge University), Chuck Hill (Reformed Theological Seminary – Orlando), and Chris Tilling (St. Mellitus College). These fellas did a cracking good job of writing robust and readable responses to Ehrman over the Christmas break of 2013. They worked to a deadline that was positively draconian and did not disappoint in the quality of the arguments they mustered together. Second, the editorial team at Zondervan, especially Katya Covrett, Jesse Hillman, and Verlyn Verbrugge, dropped what they were doing in the midst of the snowpocalypse of 2013 and despite office moves across town, so that we could get this book released simultaneously with Ehrman's book. I think I nearly broke them, but it's turned out to be a cool project in the end. Third, I'm grateful for the good folk at HarperOne for releasing Ehrman's manuscript to us well in advance of its publication.

Michael F. Bird
15th of January 2014
The Holy Birthday Feast of St. Katya of Гранд Рапидс

ABBREVIATIONS

AsTJ	*Asbury Theological Journal*
BNTC	Black's New Testament Commentary
BTB	*Biblical Theology Bulletin*
ca.	circa
CIJ	*Corpus Inscriptionum Iudaicarum*
CITM	Christianity in the Making
COQG	Christian Origins and the Question of God
DJG	*Dictionary of Jesus and the Gospels*
ed.	edition, edited
EDEJ	*Eerdmans Dictionary of Early Judaism*
eds.	editors
IEJ	*Israel Exploration Jurnal*
JBL	*Journal of Biblical Literature*
JSHJ	*Journal for the Study of the Historical Jesus*
JSNT	*Journal for the Study of the New Testament*
JSNTSup	Journal for the Study of the New Testament Supplement
LNTS	Library of New Testament Studies
NCCS	New Covenant Commentary Series
NETS	New English Translation of the Septuagint
NDIEC	*New Documents Illustrating Early Christianity*
NIGTC	New International Greek Testament Commentary
NSBT	New Studies in Biblical Theology
NTS	*New Testament Studies*
OGIS	*Orientis Graeci Inscriptiones Selectae*
P.Oxy	Papyrus Oxyrhynchus
SBLSS	Society of Biblical Literature Symposium Series
SBLSP	*Society of Biblical Literature Seminar Papers*
SNTS	Society of New Testament Studies
trans.	translator
TT	*Theology Today*
WUNT	*Wissenschaftliche Untersuchungen zum Neuen Testament*
ZNW	*Zeitschrift für die neutestamentliche Wissenschaft*

CHAPTER 1

The Story of Jesus as the Story of God

Michael F. Bird

So exactly "when" did Jesus become God? To be honest, let's recognize that this is a loaded question as it assumes that there was a time when Jesus was *not* God at all. Accordingly, for some, like Professor Bart Ehrman, Jesus was a human being who lived a human life and died an ordinary human death. It was through the incrementally increasing religious devotion of his followers after his death that he was eventually elevated to the status of a divine being equal to the God of Israel. On a divine–human spectrum, Ehrman has a low view of Jesus. "The Christians exalted him to the divine realm in their theology, but in my opinion," Ehrman confesses, "he was, and always has been, a human."[1] Suffice to say, Ehrman's view of Jesus is low, so low in fact that it could probably win a limbo contest against a leprechaun.

Such an approach to the historical origins of belief in Jesus' deity is essentially evolutionary—with beliefs about Jesus mutating over time shaped by various internal and external influences. This view begins, as Charlie Moule said years ago, "with a Palestinian Rabbi and ends with the divine Lord of Hellenistic Saviour-cult."[2] None of this is particularly innovative or new; others have said much of the same thing before. However, Ehrman is the latest proponent to prosecute the idea that belief in Jesus' divinity and worship of him as a divine figure was a gradual process that developed as time went on.

I have my own view as to "when" Jesus became God. It was not by virtue of the evolution of belief, nor as the result of any ecumenical committee; rather, I think I can articulate the answer by way of a quotation from John the Evangelist: "In the beginning was the Word, and the Word was with God, and the Word was God" (John 1:1). Jesus' deity did not spring forth from the resolution of any church council, but rests in eternity past. So he never *became* God; he was always God, and he *became* human, the man Jesus of Nazareth. The testimony of John the Evangelist is that Jesus is the Logos, the preexistent Word of God, Israel's Messiah, Son of God and Son of Man, equal to God, one with the Father, and the Father's agent for the restoration of Israel and for the renewal of creation. John's claim is on any level extravagant and even offensive to the monotheistic sensibilities of many Jews and Muslims. And yet it is a programmatic claim for the entire gospel. C. K. Barrett, a distinguished British biblical scholar, once said: "John intends that the whole of his gospel shall be read in light of this verse. The deeds and words of Jesus are the deeds and words of God; if this be not true the book is blasphemous."[3]

I entirely admit that such a claim about Jesus' divine identity is a confessional one, borne of religious devotion and justified by the theological claims of a believing community. I admit too that the gospel of John's precise articulation of the identity of Jesus is disputed, as is the continuity between John's image of Jesus and other images of Jesus in the rest of the New Testament. Then there is question of whether John the Evangelist is even correct. Is Jesus really God?

Whether Jesus of Nazareth really is God, as Christians of all varieties have historically claimed, can only be answered as a matter of faith. It comes down to whether one believes the early church's testimony to Jesus attested by Holy Scripture that he is the Son of God. I belong to a community that does, and I am not ashamed to identify myself in that way. However, exactly when, where, and why Christians first began to make such elevated claims about Jesus' heavenly origins and divine nature is a *historical* question and one that can only be answered through a concerted investigation of the evidence. Such an enquiry can be responsibly pursued by mapping out the christological claims and religious devotion of early Christian writings in the first four centuries of the Common Era. This is the area in which we wish to critically engage the work of Ehrman directly. For he claims "that Jesus was not originally considered to be God in any sense at all, and that he eventually became divine for his followers in some sense before he came to be thought of as equal with God Almighty in an absolute sense. But the point I stress is that this was, in fact, a development."[4]

THE EARLY HIGH CHRISTOLOGY CLUB

In contrast to the thesis of Ehrman and others that a "high Christology," which identified Jesus as a fully divine figure, was an evolutionary development, a cohort of scholars has argued for something more akin to a "big bang" approach to the origins of a fully divine Christology.[5] Several scholars have asserted that the first few decades of the church saw the rise of a form of devotion and types of christological confession that clearly placed Jesus within the orbit of the divine identity. The cast of scholars who have done the most to promote this paradigm of an early and relatively strong identification of Jesus with the God of Israel is known within scholarly circles as the EHCC, or, "Early High Christology Club." The names Martin Hengel, Richard Bauckham, and Larry Hurtado are associated with this "club." This group is far from monolithic and agreed on every aspect about Christian origins and devotion to Jesus. However, they are in full accord that a "high Christology" emerged very early.

The late Martin Hengel exposed many of the tenuous arguments put forward for an evolutionary process of christological development. He argued: "The time between the death of Jesus and the fully developed Christology which we find in the earliest Christian documents, the letters of Paul, is so short that the development which takes place within it can only be called amazing."[6] If that is the case, then "more happened in this period of less than two decades than in the whole next seven centuries, up to the time when the doctrine of the early church was completed."[7]

Hengel surgically dismantled the view held by the old "history of religions" school about how belief in Jesus as God emerged. On their account there were a number of separate and insulated Christian communities comprised of Jewish Christian, Hellenistic Jewish Christian, and Gentile Christian tiers, each of which represented a separate developmental phase in the formation of beliefs about

Jesus. This development began with Jesus as the "Son of Man" in Palestinian communities to a fully divinized "Lord" influenced by mystery cults in Greek-speaking centers. However, as Hengel ably pointed out, the earliest evidence indicates that Aramaic-speaking and Greek-speaking believers existed side by side from the beginning. They coexisted in Jerusalem and elsewhere, such as Caesarea, Damascus, Antioch, and Rome. The movements of key persons like Barnabas, John Mark, Silas/Silvanus, Paul, and Peter—known from Paul's letters and the Acts of the Apostles—demonstrates how these linguistic groups interpenetrated each other and were mutually influential on each other's beliefs. Therefore, confession of Jesus as the divine Lord was *not* the result of faith in Christ encountering Greek religion and philosophy.

Hengel also contended that Paul's letters, written mostly in the 50s, use traditional and stereotyped formulations for talking about Jesus' identity and divine status (e.g., Rom 1:3–4; 1 Cor 8:6; Gal 4:4; Phil 2:5–11; etc.), and go back to his earliest missionary activities in the eastern Mediterranean in the 40s. These texts make outstandingly elevated claims about Jesus, including his preexistence, his divine nature, and his mediation of creation and salvation. Hengel does not deny that development did occur. The later Logos Christology of the John the Evangelist at the end of the first century and Justin Martyr in the mid-second century represent a genuine development that attempts to flesh out Jesus' divine functions and to explain them in terms relatable to Greek metaphysics. Yet these developments are based on a logical fusion of Jesus' preexistent sonship with Jewish wisdom traditions, and so they are not derived from an interface with pagan sources.

According to Hengel, the key influences for the church's beliefs about Jesus were not Hellenistic mystery cults or a Gnostic redeemer myth, but a mixture of experience and scriptural exegesis. The sending of the Son had a close analogy with Jewish wisdom traditions about the descent and ascent of wisdom into the world as sent from God. Confessions of Jesus as "Son of God" and "Lord" were stimulated by reflection on Psalms 2 and 110. Going even earlier, the germinal roots of the Christology of the early church can be traced to: (1) the impact of Jesus on his closest followers; and (2) after Jesus' crucifixion, the experience of visions of the risen Christ to his followers and the experience of the Spirit soon after. These two factors set off a "unique dynamic and creative impulse" among Jesus' followers, which expressed itself in devotion toward him as the exalted Lord and God.[8]

Larry Hurtado has argued that the devotional practices of the early Christians were foundational for their doctrinal developments.[9] So rather than focus on a study of the major christological titles found in the New Testament, Hurtado addresses instead the worship patterns in the early church and what they tell us about the divine status of Jesus. His conclusion is that early Christian worship shows a clear veneration of Jesus as the God of Israel in human form. Jesus was treated as a recipient of devotion and was associated with God in often striking ways. Such devotion to Jesus as divine "erupted suddenly and quickly, not gradually and late, among first-century circles of followers" and exhibited "an unparalleled intensity and diversity of expression."[10]

Hurtado situates this phenomenon of Jesus devotion within the context of Jewish monotheism. While maintaining that Jewish monotheism was a characteristically strict monotheism, Hurtado contends that the crucial indicator of divinity was the giving or withholding of worship. The worship of Jesus, in prayer and by other means, is a sure pointer to his divine status in the eyes of devotees—so much so that the Christian God could be properly identified as the Old Testament deity, who had created all things, who had spoken through Moses and the prophets, and who was now revealed more fully and decisively through Jesus.

Richard Bauckham is a British scholar who has devoted much attention to Jewish monotheism as the context for early Christian claims about Jesus (and yet his work is entirely ignored by Ehrman!). According to Bauckham, Jewish authors focused on several salient elements to identify the uniqueness of God. God was known as the one and only God through his relationship to Israel as the one who reveals the divine name, YHWH, but also, and more importantly, through God's relationship to all of reality as the sole Creator and highest sovereign over all things. In the New Testament, Bauckham argues, Jesus is also regarded as a divine figure since his relationship to Israel and to the whole of reality is configured in a similar way. As such, Bauckham declares: "When New Testament Christology is read with this Jewish theological context in mind, it becomes clear that, from the earliest post-Easter beginnings of Christology onwards, early Christians included Jesus, precisely and unambiguously, within the unique identity of the one God of Israel" so that "the earliest Christology was already the highest Christology."[11]

For Bauckham a focus on intermediary figures as precedents for Jesus' divinity fails because the intermediary figures are either (a) created beings distinct from the divine identity (e.g., archangels, patriarchs, etc.), or (b) personifications of God and part of the divine identity (e.g., Word and Wisdom). The accent in New Testament christological texts falls squarely on Jesus' divine identity as a participant in creation, possessing the divine name, sharing God's throne, and receiving worship. This Christology of divine identity shows that Jesus Christ was regarded as being intrinsic to the unique and eternal identity of the God of Israel. The theological reflection of the church fathers did not so much develop this theme as transpose it into a conceptual framework to be readily explored in terms of essences and natures.

I do not mean to say that the EHCC (i.e., Hengel, Hurtado, and Bauckham) represents some kind of infallible triumvirate about the emergence of belief in Jesus. Each of the contributors to this volume will have his own assessment of their claims and arguments.[12] However, it would be fair to say that our team is broadly supportive of the EHCC approach to mapping the emergence of a fully blown "christological monotheism," where the one God is known as and identified with Jesus the Christ.

Furthermore, if the EHCC is correct, two things follow. First, belief in the divinity of Jesus emerged surprisingly early. While the coherence and grammar of "incarnation" still had to be worked out, there was an immediate regard for Jesus as belonging to the God-side of the ledger in our earliest sources. Second, it also means that later creedal claims about Jesus' divine personhood are not wildly innovative. The creedal formulations find their theological DNA within the devotional practices and theological confessions of the primitive church. In other words, the Niceno-Constantinopolitan creeds of the fourth century are not purely politically driven and radically innovative statements of faith. They are, instead, contextualized clarifications of New Testament teaching.

THE GOSPEL ACCORDING TO EHRMAN

The claims of the EHCC and our own cohort of contributors can be contrasted with the thesis that Ehrman sets forth in his book *How Jesus Became God: The Exaltation of a Jewish Preacher from Galilee.*[13]

For Ehrman, ancient monotheism was not particularly strict. In his reading of ancient texts, Ehrman posits a pyramid of power, grandeur, and deity that could be shared with creatures to some degree. There was no absolute divide between the divine and human realms; it was more like a continuum, where divine beings could become human, and humans could become divine. The many mythical stories about intermediary figures, like heavenly angels who become human or powerful kings who become divine, provide a way of understanding what the early Christians meant when they regarded Jesus as a "god."

In addition, according to Ehrman, Jesus was not regarded as God by anyone during his own lifetime. Jesus did not think of himself as God. Rather, Jesus was an apocalyptic prophet who looked for God's dramatic intervention in the world.[14] Jesus had set his hopes on a mysterious and heavenly figure called the "Son of Man," whom God would use to usher in his kingdom in the immediate future. Explicit claims to Jesus' divinity in the gospel of John are secondary and inventive accretions to the tradition, which have been projected back into Jesus' career.

What is more, the gospel accounts of Jesus' resurrection are highly contradictory and are not historically accurate. Although Jesus was definitely crucified, he was not buried by Joseph of Arimathea, nor was his tomb found empty. Instead, reports of his resurrection emerged when his disciples had visionary experiences of him as still alive. These visionary experiences were transformative for his disciples, and they thereafter began to talk of Jesus in elevated categories, as a human exalted to heaven. Then later others began to think of Jesus as a preexistent being who became human.

As such, Ehrman identifies two primary ways in which Jesus was divinized by the early church. First, and the earliest version, was "exaltation Christology," whereby Jesus was a man who was made divine at his resurrection or baptism. Second was "incarnation Christology," whereby Jesus was a preexistent being who became human.

Applying this paradigm to the New Testament, the gospel of Mark understands Jesus in terms of an exaltation Christology, while the gospel of John reflects an "incarnation Christology. In the case of Paul, Ehrman believes that Paul thought of Jesus as an angel who became human and was then exalted to a position beside God.

Finally, Ehrman describes the various controversies about the nature of Christ that were waged in the churches in the succeeding centuries, climaxing is the Nicene Creed in the fourth century. There he maintains that what was the earliest form of Christology, namely, exaltation Christology, was deemed heretical or unorthodox by the church in the second century. Among the many repercussions of the Nicene Christology was the increase in anti-Semitism. In the mind of Christians, if Jesus was God and if the Jews killed Jesus, then the Jews had killed their own God. According to Ehrman, the Christ of Nicea is a far cry from the historical Jesus of Nazareth. Despite the innovations that took place in the twenty or so years after Jesus' death, where followers believed him to be a preexistent being who became human only temporarily before he was made Lord of the universe, still, it was only at Nicea that Jesus became fully God.

A SUMMARY OF OUR CASE AGAINST EHRMAN

In chapter 2, Michael Bird addresses Ehrman's account about intermediary figures whose divinization is said to provide a way of understanding what people meant when they began to describe Jesus as "God." Several problems abound on Ehrman's approach to this subject. First, Ehrman overemphasizes the similarities between ancient views about intermediary figures with Christian views about Jesus as divine without properly recognizing the often tangible differences. Second, Christian beliefs about Jesus as divine were not based on ripping off ideas in these sources about intermediary figures, as much as they were based on a "christological monotheism." By that I mean, Jesus was regarded part of God's own identity but without thereby compromising the strict nature of Jewish monotheism. In the end, mighty angels and exalted persons serve God, but they do not share his rule, nor do they receive his worship, but Jesus does. Thus, Ehrman has not accounted for the genuine innovation that typified early views about Jesus.

In chapter 3, Michael Bird contests Ehrman's treatment of Jesus' self-understanding. According to Bird, it is probable that Jesus understood himself as a divine agent who uniquely shared in divine prerogatives, embodied God's sovereignty, and identified his work with God's action in the world. Also, if Jesus is located against the backdrop of Jewish restoration hopes for the future, including the hope for the Lord's return to Zion, then Jesus probably believed that in his own person this return was actually happening. Amidst Jesus' kingdom message and kingdom work, God was becoming king and coming to redeem his people. Such a conviction enables us to make sense of several sayings and symbolic actions where Jesus indicated that he spoke and acted for and even as God. In addition, Jesus undoubtedly did refer to himself as the Son of Man. The cohort of sayings about a future Son of Man is best understood with Jesus as the intended subject. On top of that, since Jesus spoke Aramaic, his use of *son of man* amounts to a Semitic idiom that, when used in a definite sense, is a form of self-reference. Finally, Jesus also appears to have understood himself as the figure in Daniel 7:13–14, who would be enthroned beside God on God's own throne.

In chapter 4, Craig Evans contests Bart Ehrman's claims that the story of the burial of Jesus in a known tomb is a late fiction and that therefore there probably was no tomb discovered by his followers. He further claims that Jesus in all probability was not buried, according to Roman law and custom, and that the empty tomb in any event probably played no role in early Christianity's understanding of the resurrection of Jesus. Evans responds that these arguments are not persuasive, for Roman law in fact did permit burial of the executed, including the crucified. Moreover, there is compelling literary and archaeological evidence that Roman authority in Israel in the time of Jesus did respect Jewish law and burial traditions, in which all dead, including the crucified, were buried before nightfall. It is further argued that Jesus' followers would not have spoken of Jesus' resurrection had the body of Jesus remained in the tomb.

In chapter 5, Simon Gathercole examines evidence for the christological claims of the Synoptic Gospels and the "tunnel period" of preliterary sources running roughly 30 to 50 CE. According to Gathercole, the Synoptic Gospels do have a Christology of divine identity in a strong sense, as well as one of preexistence. Their Christology of preexistence is exemplified in the "I have come" sayings, where Jesus' "coming" implies a journey from a heavenly abode to earth because such sayings are closely analogous, not to the opening remarks by biblical prophets, but to statements given by angels as to the purpose of their earthly visitation in the Old Testament. Moreover, other elements in the Synoptics indicate that Jesus shares the identity of God, not least that he performs activities and possesses prerogatives thought to be exclusive privileges of God according to the Old Testament. The evidence from the "tunnel period" in texts like Romans 1:4 and Acts 2:36 does not provide evidence that Jesus was made something that he was not. Instead, it shows that Jesus entered into new roles appropriate to his divine person in a postincarnation exalted state. The "changes" that took place in Jesus' exaltation are about Jesus' relationship to the church and the world rather than to his relationship to God the Father.

In chapter 6, Chris Tilling subjects Ehrman's conception of monotheism and Christology to rigorous scrutiny. He engages in a critical discussion of Ehrman's interpretive approach, such as his understanding of "monotheism," his postulation of two alternative Christologies of "exaltation" and "incarnation," and the claim that a text like Galatians 4:14 supports an "angel Christology." Tilling argues that these interpretive judgments, which appear throughout Ehrman's argument, cannot account for the data that they seek to explain and are therefore artificially imposed. As a consequence, they signal Ehrman's profound interpretive confusion.

In chapter 7, Tilling continues his critique by examining Ehrman's understanding of incarnational Christology, principally in Paul's letters. Tilling sets out what is actually involved in understanding the apostle's Christology. Tilling demonstrates that doing the work of a historian involves examining a few explanatory conditions, and this—in turn—shows Paul's Christ as fully divine in the sense of sharing the transcendent uniqueness of the one God of Israel. Second, Tilling turns to assessing Ehrman's actual exegesis, and his verdict is far from sympathetic. Tilling claims that Ehrman's textual analysis is deficient on the grounds that it focuses on just one passage from Paul's letters and does not demonstrate any substantial awareness of a wider swath of scholarship. While Ehrman's book might be given some latitude since it is a popular level work, in any case, Ehrman's study appears distinctly uninformed and even superficial. The upshot is that Ehrman simply misconstrues Paul's Christology and so undermines his entire project. Thereafter, Tilling closes by looking at a few problems in Ehrman's reading of the gospel of John and the letter to the Hebrews, which prove to be equally as dissatisfying as his reading of Paul.

In chapter 8, Charles Hill takes a look at what happened in the early church after the books of the New Testament were written. Hill reviews what Ehrman says about a number of christological "dead ends" (i.e., adoptionism, docetism, Gnosticism) and about what he calls "hetero-orthodoxies," that is, christological views that affirmed both the humanity and deity of Christ, but were ultimately rejected. This chapter reminds readers of the resolutely biblical orientation of the orthodox theologians and tests some of Ehrman's more questionable claims about the Ebionites, the Modalists, and Tertullian in particular.

In chapter 9, Charles Hill continues narrating the story of people and movements in the early church and how they handled the paradox of Jesus being both God and man, and the paradox of the Trinity consisting of one God in three persons. He reviews and deconstructs Ehrman's newly-coined term "ortho-paradox." Ehrman's chronology of christological development is shown to be not the conclusion of historical study, but rather a presupposition that determines the outcome of historical study in advance. Finally, Hill takes up and contests Ehrman's charge that the mistreatment of Jews in the fourth and fifth centuries is directly attributable to the belief that Jesus was divine.

Not everything Ehrman says is wrong. Much we accept, and other scholars may side with him on issues here and there. However, our overall verdict is that Ehrman has not extended or enhanced our knowledge of Christian origins. Therefore, we hope to put up a rival perspective to Ehrman by critiquing his arguments and by offering a better model for understanding the origins of belief in Jesus' divine nature. In doing so, we aim to give a historically informed account as to why the Galilean preacher from Nazareth was hailed as "the Lord Jesus Christ" and how he became the object of worship in the early church. We believe, in short, that God became Jesus!

CHAPTER 2

Of Gods, Angels, and Men

Michael F. Bird

INTRODUCTION

So what counts as a "god" these days?[1]

Such a question reminds me of the 1984 blockbuster movie *Ghostbusters*. In one scene from the movie, the Sumerian deity Gozer appears on top of a New York building, amidst much paranormal activity, and is confronted by the four ghostbusters. Gozer, who appears as a woman, challenges them by asking, "Are you a god?" Ray Stantz (Dan Aykroyd) replies, "No." Gozer responds, "Then die!" and she nearly blasts them off the top of the building. As they pick themselves up, one of the other ghostbusters turns to Ray and says, "Ray, when someone asks you if you're a god, you say 'yes!'" But don't worry. The ghostbusters defeat Gozer in the end. Fair to say, though, that the ghostbusters had a fairly loose definition of what counts as a god.

So when the early church claimed that Jesus was "God," what did they mean by that claim? Did they mean that he was the one and only God? Or were they making a slightly lesser claim, that Jesus was divine, like an angel, or perhaps like a king who was deified after death? Ehrman knows full well that the early church regarded Jesus as "God," but he seeks to determine in what sense they meant it (see the excursus at the end of the chapter for examples of intermediary figures like angels and divinized kings).[2]

In his book, Ehrman argues that in antiquity there was originally no concept of God as the sole and supreme sovereign, who was up in heaven, far above and beyond all earthly life. Such a notion of "God," as an exclusive and absolute deity, came much later and was a creation of the church in the fourth century, some three hundred years after Jesus. Instead, Ehrman contends that the ancients did not imagine a sovereign God up in heaven separated by a huge chasm from lowly sinners toiling down below. In Ehrman's reading of ancient sources, there was a continuum of existence from the human to the divine. Not only that, but within the divine realm there were numerous deities, ranked within a graded pyramid of power and grandeur.[3]

Ehrman spends the first two chapters of his book talking about Greco-Roman and Jewish sources that depict divine figures who become human or humans who become divine. These writings provide the "first step in seeing how Jesus came to be thought of in these terms" as divine in the early church.[4] Jesus could be "god" in the same sense that the Roman Emperor Augustus was deified after his death according to Suetonius, or that Enoch was transformed into an angel as depicted in 2 Enoch, or that Moses was declared to be a god by the Jewish philosopher Philo. In other words, to say that Jesus is "god" does not require that he be part of an absolute and singular divine reality, which is infinitely removed from the world and utterly beyond all earthly reality. Jesus could be a "god" in this broader sense of a lesser being who traverses the divine and human realms, but not "God Almighty" in an infinite sense.

For Ehrman, rather than thinking of Jesus as the one and only true God, a much better analogy for Jesus' divinity is in the stories of chief angels who visited earth and humans who later became angels. He writes: "In other words, if humans could be angels (and angels humans), and if angels could be gods, and if in fact the chief angel could be the Lord himself—then to make Jesus divine, one simply needs to think of him as an angel in human form."[5] There we have it, Jesus the angel! Gosh darn it, could Oprah and the Jehovah's Witnesses actually be right?

A NOTE ON METHOD

The sources Ehrman cites might strike some modern readers as shocking since they make fantastic claims about deified kings, divine men, horny gods, misbehaving angels, an exalted Enoch, a mysterious Melchizedek, and even Moses gets some divine majesty of his own. All of this could well grate against the convictions of anyone with monotheistic sensibilities. However, it is worth remembering that the New Testament authors were perfectly aware of this world. It is evident that they not only read about it, but they even experienced it in the marketplace of religions and philosophies in the ancient world. Part of the challenge of the early church was to negotiate a way within this religiously diverse context in order to make converts to the faith and to strengthen churches that faced manifold challenges pertaining to their beliefs.

As evidence of early Christian awareness of this environment, the apostle Paul wrote to the church in Corinth: "For even if there are so-called gods, whether in heaven or on earth (as indeed there are many 'gods' and many 'lords'), yet for us there is but one God, the Father, from whom all things came and for whom we live; and there is but one Lord, Jesus Christ, through whom all things came and through whom we live" (1 Cor 8:5–6). As to what these "gods" were, Paul seems to think of them as somewhere between nonentities and demons (see 1 Cor 8:4; 10:20–21). Paul and Barnabas also had the amusing, though soon problematic, experience of being confused with the gods Zeus and Hermes in Pisidian Antioch (Acts 14:12–13).

In Paul's letter to the Colossians, there is also a warning against the worship of angels, a presumably hot issue in the smelting pot of religions in the interior of Asia Minor (Col 2:18). Jude also quotes writings such as *1 Enoch* and the *Assumption of Moses* in his letter to churches, encountering strange teachings and immoral behaviors (Jude 9, 14). The idea of the Logos, the governing rational principle of the universe in Stoic philosophy, was utilized by John the Evangelist in his prologue as a way of describing the incarnation of the preexistent Jesus as God's self-communication. John the Seer devotes much of his Apocalypse to confronting the problem of how Christians in Asia Minor are to respond to the imperial cult with its demands for worship of the emperor. For anyone who had lived and travelled around the Mediterranean basin, the stories of gods becoming human or humans becoming gods would hardly be new. The question is how this all relates to the divine nature of Jesus according to early Christian sources.

Ehrman assumes that these sources explain how or in what sense Jesus was regarded as divine. So for Ehrman, Augustus was hailed as a son of God, and Jesus was hailed as a Son of God, so they might be saying the same thing with only minor variations on a theme. Moses became an angel, Enoch became an angel, so maybe Jesus became an angel too. Well, there are obvious relevancies with such comparisons, but it might not be so simple as A = B. It's kind of like saying, "Butternut squash and butterscotch pudding, they are all made of butter, aren't they?" Alas, no, they are not the same thing! So a few comments are in order.

First, Ehrman risks the error of relying too heavily on parallels with ancient sources to provide an explanation for Christian claims about Christ. The problem here is that for a long time scholars have been aware of a fallacious line of argumentation that Samuel Sandmel called "parallelomania." This is what happens when scholars find words and concepts in one document and allege that they mean the same thing in another document. The parallels are then said to show that the same idea is shared by both sources or that there is a literary dependency of one document borrowing from the other. However, it does not always work that way.[6]

For example, the prologue to John's gospel (John 1:1–18) has been compared to every type of source imaginable: Old Testament, Jewish wisdom literature, rabbinic writings, the Dead Sea Scrolls, Philo, Gnosticism, Mandaean literature, and much, much more. Many scholars have claimed that the real meaning of John's prologue is found in "X" or that "X" was even the source from which John took his ideas. Indeed, John 1:1–18 has been a parallelomaniacs playground.[7] Now there is no denying that literary parallels do matter for context and background, but they should assist in illuminating rather than overpowering the literary and rhetorical analyses of a given text. A whole scale reliance on *parallelizing* our sources to try to understand them is actually *paralyzing* for good historical investigation of texts.

Second, we must also remember that analogy does not mean genealogy. Just because there are verbal and conceptual similarities between Christian claims about Jesus and Greco-Roman claims about divine figures does not prove that Christians borrowed from pagan sources. For example, while scholars have often claimed that the gospel birth narratives are largely modeled on Greco-Roman accounts of the birth of heroes like Alexander the Great and Augustus, which Ehrman points to, closer precedents are probably found in Old Testament birth stories, like the story of Hannah and Samuel (1 Samuel 1–2) and Ahaz and Hezekiah (Isaiah 7–11). In the case of the similarities between the gospel accounts of Jesus and Philostratus' biography of Apollonius of Tyana, written at least a hundred years after the Gospels, it seems clear to me that Philostratus' biography has been written as a polemical parody of the Gospels, a type of refutation by imitation. Apollonius could be held up as a pagan antitype to Jesus Christ. If so, there were occasions when pagans modeled stories from Christian sources rather than vice-versa.

Third, a good account of Christian origins will give equal attention to both its similarities and its differences with other literature. On the one hand, the faith of the early church was not expressed in a vacuum. Christian discourse about Jesus, in proclamation, worship, and debate, was expressed in Jewish, Greek, and Roman idioms that had currency in their setting. The New Testament authors probably intended to make deliberate connections between their accounts and the literary forms and literary culture around them. Such connections were certainly perceived by subsequent Christian readers and by pagan critics alike.[8] I would also add that in order to understand how Christianity is different from Greco-Roman religions, we must first understand how they are similar, whether that pertains to beliefs about God, social structures, or ethics. We should expect no less because Christianity took root in the synagogue as much as the agora; it was lived in the real world and engaged with various philosophies and religions, so comparisons of its claims about God within the intellectual world of the time were inevitable.

On the other hand, we should not use the various similarities as a reason to skim over the hard job of understanding Christian claims about Jesus on their own terms, in their own context, and with a mind to determining their distinctive shape.[9] For instance, the worship of a crucified and risen Messiah was definitely unique and incredibly scandalous to all audiences, whether Jewish or Greek. To Jewish audiences, worshiping a crucified man was blasphemy; it was about as kosher as pork sausages wrapped in bacon served to Jews for a jihad fundraiser. To Greeks, worshiping a man recently raised from the dead was like doing obeisance to the first zombie you met in a zombie apocalypse. If Christian ideas about God were so snug and down within the ancient world, then why was Paul flogged by Jewish communities (2 Cor 11:24) and laughed out of the Athenian Areopagus by Greek philosophers (Acts 17:32)? Could it be that the Christian idea of God was startling, odd, and even offensive to Jews and pagans, who had trouble swallowing its claims about Jesus? Perhaps the reason why New Testament authors like Paul, Luke, and John spent so much time talking about Jesus and God is because they meant something very different by "God" than what their Jewish and pagan neighbors thought, and it took some effort to get the redefinition of God across.

For a case in point, Philo, the cosmopolitan Jewish philosopher, rejected the iconic worship of human figures by saying, "Sooner could God change into a man than a man into God."[10] From this it seems as if Philo is saying that if Jews can scarcely imagine God becoming a man, they have an even harder time imagining a man, like a Roman emperor, becoming God. In which case, Jewish beliefs about intermediary figures were not necessarily interchangeable with Greco-Roman beliefs about semidivine figures.

On top of that, it is surely interesting that a second-century pagan critic like Celsus—who was not averse to pointing out the similarities between pagan mythologies and the Gospels—could deny that gods or sons of the gods became human. He wrote: "O Jews and Christians, no God or Son of God either came or will come down [to earth]. But if you mean that angels did so, then what do you call them? Are they gods, or some other race of beings? Some other race of beings [doubtlessly], and in all probability daemons."[11] Celsus did not think that pagan mythologies provided a precedent for Christian claims about Jesus, and he really struggled to understand exactly what kind of divine visitation Christians thought happened in the coming of Christ.

In terms of uniqueness, it is fair to say that early Christian beliefs about Jesus were a revised form of Jewish monotheism. Christian devotion to Jesus was not a syncretistic experiment with Greco-Roman religious ideas that gradually broke away from Jewish monotheism. More likely it was a reconfiguration of Jewish monotheism, operating under its key premises, but spurred on by the impact of

Jesus on his followers and by religious experiences to express this monotheism in light of fresh convictions about God, Messiah, and Spirit. The first Christians held to the Jewish belief in one God, but this God was now known as God the Father, the Lord Jesus, and (eventually) the Holy Spirit.

Unsurprisingly in the early years of the church there emerged a clear binitarian devotion focused on God the Father and the Lord Jesus.[12] Note how Paul opens his earliest letter that we possess with the words: "To the church of the Thessalonians in God the Father and the Lord Jesus Christ: Grace and peace to you" (1 Thess 1:1). Or again, look at what he said to the Galatians in another letter opening: "Grace and peace to you from God our Father and the Lord Jesus Christ, who gave himself for our sins to rescue us from the present evil age, according to the will of our God and Father, to whom be glory for ever and ever. Amen" (Gal 1:3–5). God the Father and Lord Jesus go together like peanut butter and jelly, like Australia and kangaroos, like cheese and wine, or like baseball and beer! When the early Christians mentioned God, they had to mention Jesus as well, and whenever they mentioned Jesus, they felt constrained to mention God in the same breath. It's like God was Jesified and Jesus was Godified.[13] For this reason, a number of scholars have spoken about a "christological monotheism." The God of Israel is revealed in, through, and even as the Lord Jesus Christ. Of course, to say that monotheism has been revised raises some good questions about monotheism itself.

ANCIENT MONOTHEISMS

Ehrman seems to think that a strict and absolute monotheism was a later invention that took place in the fourth century as part of the Christianization of the Roman Empire.[14] He goes so far as to say that, apart from Jews, "everyone was a polytheist."[15] The problem is that this is just plain untrue. There was a long tradition of pagan monotheism well before the Christian era.[16] Celsus, a second-century critic of Christianity, was himself a pagan monotheist. It was possible in the ancient world to be a pluralistic monotheist by giving the one God different names. So in the *Epistle to Aristeas* 16 it is said that the Jewish God is known to the Gentiles as Zeus or Jove. The Jewish author Aristobulus said about philosophers who speak about Zeus that "their intention is to refer to God."[17] The pagan author Varro claimed the "God of the Jews to be the same as Jupiter."[18] Celsus could even say that it made no real difference whether one worships Zeus, Adonai, Sabaoth, or Amoun because it was all the same God.[19]

The cult of the Most High God, extant around Asia Minor and Greek cities near the Black Sea, provided an expression of monotheism that was ambiguous enough to accommodate Jews and pagans in a common worship.[20] Pagan monotheism may have even prepared for the spread of Judaism, the rise of Christianity, and the eventual conquest of Islam in the east. So to borrow a line from James Crossley, ancient religious belief wasn't all *Jason and the Argonauts* or *Clash of the Titans*.[21]

I am convinced by the study of several scholars that Jewish monotheism was, generally, strict.[22] There is one Creator God, who stands above all other reality, and this is the God who covenants with Israel. God's unique identity is bound up with his sacred name, YHWH, revealed to Israel. Monotheism entails monolatry, the worship of the one true God to exclusion of all others. These elements of one Creator, divine name, and exclusive worship make up the substance of Jewish monotheism. Such views permeate the sources in every era. The *Shema*, the famous prayer that all faithful Jews are meant to recite every day, goes, "Hear, O Israel: The LORD our God, the LORD is one" (Deut 6:4).

We see the same thing in a prayer from the second century BCE recalling Nehemiah's words at the resumption of sacrifices in the temple: "O Lord, Lord God, Creator of all things, you are awe-inspiring and strong and just and merciful, you alone are king and are kind, you alone are bountiful, you alone are just and almighty and eternal" (2 Macc 1:24–25). Even Philo, who could refer to Moses as "God and King of the whole nation" and call the Logos a "second God," still touted monotheistic principles: "Therefore, of first importance, let us inscribe in ourselves this first commandment as the holiest of all commandments, to think that there is but one God, the most high, and to honor him alone; and do not permit polytheistic doctrine to even touch the ears of any person who is accustomed to seek after the truth, with a clean and pure of heart."[23] Note the emphasis: God alone, God alone, God alone!

The Jewish people in the Roman era had an acute case of "mono," not mononucleosis from playing spin the bottle with dirty Gentile teenagers, but *monotheism* and *monolatry*. This exclusive devotion to one God isn't based on abstract philosophical speculation or a generalized belief about the world above. Instead, it is a clear, crisp, and sharp belief that Israel's God was the Creator of all, unique among all claimants to divinity, and Israel's God is and will be King over all.[24] Of course, that doesn't mean that every Jew was faithful to this belief. Some Jews made offerings at pagan shrines or even departed from the Jewish faith altogether and became pagan.[25] That said, all things being equal, Jews were generally devout monotheists, so much so that a pagan author like Tacitus could comment that "the Jews conceive of one god alone."[26]

Given this Jewish monotheistic context—giving honorific status to Jesus' name, identifying Christ as Creator, and making him a recipient of worship—was theologically adventurous, sociologically scandalous, and historically unprecedented as far as I can tell. This is clear from several lines of investigation. To proffer but a few off-the-cuff examples. In the Christ hymn of Philippians 2, which I take to be pre-Pauline, the words of YHWH about his sovereignty found in Isa 45:23 ("Before me every knee will bow; by me every tongue will swear") are nonchalantly applied to Jesus with these words: "at the name of Jesus every knee should bow, in heaven and on earth and under the earth" (Phil 2:10). In another Christ hymn, this time from Colossians, we are told that "in him all things were created: things in heaven and on earth, visible and invisible, whether thrones or powers or rulers or authorities; all things have been created through him and for him" (Col 1:16).

In addition, early patterns of devotion show Jesus worshiped in a way fitting for YHWH, seen in prayers offered to Jesus or in his name, invocation of his name as "Lord," baptism in his name, hymns and doxologies exalting his role as Creator and Savior, memorial meals in his honor, and prophetic inspiration deriving from him. According to Hurtado, "This concern to define and reverence Jesus with reference to the one God is what I mean by the term 'binitarian.' Here we see the powerful effect of Jewish monotheism, combining with a strong impetus to reverence Jesus in unprecedented ways, in the innovative and vigorous devotional pattern advocated and reflected in Paul's letters."[27]

ANCIENT MONOTHEISM AND INTERMEDIARY FIGURES

But how does this strict Jewish monotheism square with all these "intermediary figures" like angels who become human or humans who become angels? For ancient Jews, the heavens were full of angels, and there was ample room for the involvement of such figures from God's heavenly council in the operation of God's sovereignty over the world. Jews could imagine beings who took the divine name within them, were referred to by one or more of God's titles, and were so endowed with divine attributes that were often difficult to distinguish from God, functioning as personal extensions of his powers and sovereignty.[28] Yet rather than place devotion to Jesus under the aegis of a revised Jewish monotheism, i.e., "christological monotheism," Ehrman prefers to see Jesus' divinity as part of this phenomenon of powerful angels who take human form or else exalted human figures who become divine.

For the sake of brevity, let me focus on my favorite chief angel, Metatron. I like Metatron, mainly because his name sounds like "Megatron," the leader of the Decepticons, the evil robots who menace earth in the Transformer movies. Only yesterday I received my copy of the recently published *Old Testament Pseudepigrapha: More Noncanonical Scriptures*. I randomly opened to the middle of the book, found a document called *Sefer Zerubbabel*, and the first thing I read was this:

> Michael, who is (also) Metatron, answered me saying: "I am the angel who guided Abraham throughout all the land of Canaan. I blessed him in the name of the Lord. I am the one who redeemed Isaac and [wept] for him. I am the one who wrestled with Jacob at the crossing of the Jabbok. I am the one who guided Israel in the wilderness for forty years in the name of the Lord. I am the one who appeared to Joshua at Gilgal, and I am the one who rained down brimstone and fire on Sodom and Gomorrah. He places His name with me: Metatron in *gematria* is the equivalent of Shadday. As for you, Zerubbabel son of Shealtiel, whose name is Jeconiah, ask me and I will tell you what will happen at the End of Days.[29]

This quotation is from a medieval Jewish apocalypse (much later than the time of Christian beginnings), but it showcases the fascination with angelic figures like Metatron by Jewish authors. So who is

Metatron and what does he have to do with monotheism? Metatron is a chief angel in Jewish angelology known mainly in rabbinic and hekhalot literature about visions and ascents to heavenly palaces. His name means "The lesser YHWH," kind of like YHWH's own lieutenant-governor. He operates as a divine vice-regent and as a lesser manifestation of the divine name. In some literature, he is identified with the angel of the Lord, as in the *Sefer Zerubbabel* cited above, and elsewhere Enoch is absorbed into Metatron after his translation to heaven (*3 En.* 15.1–2).[30] According to *3 Enoch* (a document produced around the fourth or fifth century CE but with literary precursors), Metatron is the highest of archangels, who functions as God's personal secretary (*3 En.* 4.5; 10.3–6; 12.1–5). Metatron even has his own little throne where he holds court over celestial beings, and even angels fall prostrate before him (*3 En.* 4.9; 16.1–2). Metatron is identified with Enoch, the son of Jared (*3 En.* 4.3).

Yet lest we think that the Metatron tradition has shown that Jewish monotheism was not quite so strict, we must remember a few things. First, in *3 Enoch*, there is vigorous emphasis on God's sovereignty over the world and his spatial remoteness from the human race. As per much Jewish mystical literature, God resides in the seventh heaven, and he is inaccessible to humans from there. In fact, the angels complain to God why he bothers with humans like Adam and Enoch, good for nothing idolaters that they are; in response, God withdraws his glory from the face of the earth (*3 En.* 5.10–14). In this setting, figures like Metatron are not examples of heavenly beings with absolute divine power, but they are the only conduits by which visionaries and mystics may experience God, precisely because God is so distant and transcendent.

Second, Metatron's place in heaven is by appointment and by no means assured. Metatron is given his position by God to be a type of grand vizier over all things (*3 En.* 4.3; 6.3; 10.1–2), but this excludes authority over the eight angels charged with guarding the gates to the heavenly palaces (*3 En.* 10.3–4). Moreover, at one point a mystic named 'Aher (i.e., Elisha ben Abuya, according to other sources) sees Metatron in all of his enthroned splendor in the heavenly court, and 'Aher cries out, "There are indeed two powers in heaven." When 'Aher says this, a voice from God rebukes him, while another angel goes up to Metatron and strikes him with sixty lashes of fire and forces him off his throne, just so everyone knows who is really in charge (*3 En.* 16.1–5). So Metatron, for all his might and marvel, is still a created and subordinated being before God. Evidently exalted angels serve God, but they do not share his rule, nor do they receive his worship.

There is a reason why angels like Metatron or Michael could never level up and become the object of devotion equal to God. There was a strong Jewish prohibition about the worship of angels (e.g., Tob 12:16–22; *3 En.* 16.1–5), which carries over into the New Testament (Col. 2:18; Rev. 19:10; 22:9). Ehman infers from this: "We know that some Jews thought it was right to worship angels in no small part because a number of our surviving texts insist that it *not* be done"[31] Well, okay, maybe some Jews were a bit too enthusiastic in their devotion to angels (much like some teenage girls I've heard about in the American Bible Belt!). That said, the worship of angels was not necessarily the same as worship of God. In our ancient sources angels could be venerated or invoked in any number of ways: (1) by prayers and even by magical manipulation for assistance, protection, good health, and vengeance; (2) their heavenly worship could be seen as mysterious and worthy of mimicking; (3) angels could be objects of thanksgiving in relation to various functions or activities that they performed on God's behalf.[32] After a meticulous survey of the evidence about angel veneration, Loren Stuckenbruck concludes:

> Therefore, on the basis of the texts it would be hasty for one to speak of *the* veneration of angels in Early Judaism. The relevant sources do not allow us to infer a common practice, but rather seem to reflect *specific* contexts within which worship of angels, in a variety of forms, could find expression.... Angel veneration is not conceived as a substitute for the worship of God. Indeed, most often the venerative language is followed by an explanation which emphasizes the supremacy of God.[33]

That is interesting because in the book of Revelation we have clear prohibitions of angel worship (Rev 19:10; 22:9), but also lucid accounts of the heavenly worship of the "Lord God Almighty" (4:1–11) and "the Lamb" (5:1–14). In other words, Jesus receives the worship that is given to God but forbidden for angels. In Revelation, the worship given to Jesus is not angel worship but God worship!

In that biblical book we have the deliberate treatment of Jesus as an object of worship right alongside a deliberate retention of the Jewish definition of monotheism by exclusive worship of the one God.[34]

Let's look at one more example of these intermediary figures who are thought to be divine by Ehrman. A good candidate for examination is the "Son of Man" found in *1 Enoch*, a composite Palestinian document probably composed in the first century (and note that in one part of the document, though probably a later interpolation, the Son of Man is identified as Enoch [*1 En.* 70–71]). It should be of obvious relevance to us since "Son of Man" is a term of self-reference for Jesus in the Gospels and a title for Jesus in other parts of the New Testament. Ehrman surveys the relevant parts of *1 Enoch* and concludes about the Enochic Son of Man:

> He is a divine being who has always existed, who sits beside God on his throne, who will judge the wicked and the righteous at the end of time. He, in other words, is elevated to God's own status and functions as the divine being who carries out God's judgment on the earth. This is an exalted figure indeed, as exalted as one can possibly be without actually being the Lord God Almighty himself.[35]

Is Jesus "divine" in the same way that the Enochic Son of Man is divine?

The fact that Enoch's Son of Man is placed on God's throne, exercises judgment on God's behalf, and is worshiped by kings and rulers is troublesome to Bauckham, so much so that he concedes that the Enochic Son of Man is the "one exception which proves the rule" about the strict nature of Jewish monotheism.[36] I am not quite willing to fold on this. The fact that kings and nations worship him, even while on God's throne, is still merely the acknowledgment that he is God's appointed agent who will gather the elect and punish wicked kings and nations who have not acknowledged the one true God and his people.[37]

Keep in mind that angelic creatures, who were part of God's heavenly court, and biblical heroes like Enoch, who were thought to have ascended to heavenly glory, were not treated as rightful recipients of cultic worship in Jewish circles. Jewish devotion showed a concern to preserve God's uniqueness, and in their cultic worship they maintained an almost paranoid anxiety about exclusivity. The upshot is that Jewish practice was concerned with safeguarding monolatry, which suggests a genuinely robust commitment to a strict monotheism. In this case, devotion to Jesus Christ—not as a second god, not as an angel beside, but as an expression of faith in the *one* God—is strikingly unusual.[38]

The best way to understand these intermediary figures is by adopting the taxonomy proposed by Bauckham. These intermediary figures were not ambiguous semidivine beings that somehow straddled the boundary between God and creation. Some were aspects of God's own unique reality (Logos, Word, Wisdom), while most others were unambiguously creatures, exalted servants by all accounts, but still distinct from God's person, God's sovereignty, and God's worship (e.g., angels, exalted patriarchs, etc.).[39]

In sum, therefore, there was in Jewish thought accommodated beliefs and honorific titles given to various agents like chief angels such as Metatron and to exalted humans such as Enoch. However, a sharp line was drawn between the veneration of intermediary figures and the worship of the one God (so Hurtado), and this was based on the fact that such beings were not part of God's divine identity (so Bauckham). In this case, and contra Ehrman, the continuity between Jewish monotheism and New Testament Christology does not flow from intermediary figures, but from christological monotheism.

TOUCHED BY AN ANGEL CALLED "JESUS" ... NOT!

I grew up watching great American TV shows about angels like *Highway to Heaven* and *Touched by an Angel*. We all love angels. What's not to like? Big wings, divine superpowers, sometimes they look like Hollywood actor Nicholas Cage, and they can fly. As proof of our culture's angel fixation, while writing the first draft of this book, there are news feeds about alleged angel appearances at the funeral of Nelson Mandela in South Africa. On the topic of angels, I even used to go up to girls in bars and say, "Hey, are you alright? Did you hurt yourself when you fell?" To which the girl would typically reply, "What? Who fell?" Then smiling I'd add, "When you fell from heaven. Cause you have the face of an angel." Sometimes I'd get a giggle and a blush, but usually I was just told to take my routine elsewhere. But I did marry an angel. I'm convinced my wife Naomi is an angel for two reasons. First, she has a positively angelic glow when she smiles. Second, she said that if I ever forget her birthday again as I did in 2007, that she's gonna smite me the same way that the angel of the Lord smote the Assyrians (see 2Kgs 19:35). So I'm pro-angel to the max! But was Jesus an angel?

The idea that one becomes an angel upon death is called "angelomorphism," and in relation to Christ is known as "angelomorphic Christology." Ehrman rightly points to examples of Enoch and Moses as persons reckoned in some sources to have become an angel after their deaths, and he seizes on them as a potential scheme applicable to early depictions of Jesus.[40] There is some traction to this view in Christian sources. First, consider Acts 12, where Peter escapes from prison, goes to the house of Mary, the mother of John Mark, and knocks on the door. Rhoda hears Peter's voice, runs back, and tells the others that Peter is outside the premises. But they don't believe her that it is Peter, and they infer that "it must be his angel" (Acts 12:13–16). In other words, they think that Peter is already dead and the dude at the door must be his angelic doppelganger.

Second, among the church fathers, the strange "angel of the Lord" in the Old Testament (see, e.g., Gen 16:13; 21:17–18; 22:11–13; etc.) was regarded as an appearance of the preincarnate Christ (i.e., a "christophany"), a tradition that is as early as Justin Martyr in the mid-second century.[41]

Third, the descriptions of Jesus in Rev 1:13–16 and 14:14–16 do have angelomorphic qualities as Jesus is described in terms reminiscent of angels, like the one mentioned in Rev 10:1–3. So, is Jesus simply the human manifestation of the "angel of the Lord"? Did Jesus morph into an angel after his exaltation to heaven? I doubt it!

First, the identification of the "angel of the Lord" with the preincarnate Christ does make sense if one engages in a self-consciously retrospective and deliberately canonical and christological reading of the Old Testament.[42] Whether the appearances of the "angel of the Lord" was a precedent that early Christians drew on to explain the coming of Jesus is, however, quite another matter. While New Testament authors could regard Jesus as preexistent and present with the Israelites in their sacred history (see 1 Cor 10:4, 9; Jude 5), there is no indication that he was ever identified with the angel of the Lord, not at least until the time of Justin Martyr in the second century. The angel of the Lord remains an anomalous figure because he not only brings a message from God, but he speaks for God in the first person. So in one biblical episode we read: "The angel of the LORD went up from Gilgal to Bokim and said, 'I brought you up out of Egypt and led you into the land I swore to give to your ancestors'" (Judg 2:1).

Elsewhere the angel not only represents God but even embodies God's presence, which explains why the angel of the Lord who appeared to Moses in the burning bush said, "I am the God of your father, the God of Abraham, the God of Isaac and the God of Jacob," and was the one who revealed the divine name to Moses (Exod 3:2, 6, 14). Paradoxically the angel of the Lord both *is* YHWH and *is not* YHWH. He is the subject in mysterious divine encounters that attempted to speak of God's immanence with his people without forfeiting his transcendence. However, ambiguities of this order (don't get me wrong, there are other ambiguities to deal with) did not shape expressions of belief in Christ. The problem with the angel is whether or even how he is identifiable with YHWH's own presence and person. However, Christ's person was understood as being distinct from God the Father, and his mode of divine presence was couched in far more concrete language, like "form" of God, "glory" of God, "image" of God, and even "God enfleshed."

Second, on an alleged angelomorphic Christology, it has little currency as an explanatory framework for what the early Christians thought of Jesus. In regards to the presentation of Jesus' earthly life according to the Gospels of Matthew, Mark, and Luke, known as the Synoptic Gospels, Jesus remains distinct from the angels and even possesses a complete authority over them. Angels are said to serve him when he was in the wilderness (Matt 4:11; Mark 1:13), he has authority to call on the angels if he wanted to (Matt 4:6; Luke 4:10), and up to twelve legions of angels would come to his defense if he summoned them (Matt 26:53). The various sayings about the coming of the Son of Man describe the angels as his vanguard or attendants, and the Son of Man is never identified as one of them (see Matt 25:31; Mark 8:38; Luke 12:8). The angel of the Lord is active in predicting Jesus' birth and resurrection in such a way that it was unlikely that confusion of the two ever entered the Evangelists' minds (see Matt 1:20, 23; 2:13, 19; 28:2; Luke 1:11; 2:9).[43]

The New Testament authors are at pains to emphasize that Jesus has been exalted above all powers and authorities, presumably including all tiers of angels (see Phil 2:9–11; Col 1:16–17; 2:8–10, 20; Heb 1:5–9; 2:5–9; 1 Pet 3:22; Rev 5:11–14). The descent and ascent motif related to the Son's two stages of humiliation and exaltation results in Jesus having a status high above any of the angels (Phil 2:5–11; Heb 2:5–9, 16–18). In one of the Pastoral Epistles, Paul gives a ministerial charge to Timothy before a hierarchy of witnesses including "God and Christ Jesus and the elect angels" (1 Tim 5:21). Clearly, Jesus is never depicted as one of the angels; rather, he is always depicted as inherently superior to them in view of his unique relationship to God the Father and his unique relationship to believers.

Third, in Revelation, the risen Jesus is similar in many respects to glorious angels, the living creatures, and the elders. For example, the presentation of Jesus in Rev 1:13–16 is indeed similar to the description of the mighty angel in Rev 10:1–3. However, there is no reason to see the two as identical, and the Apocalypse more probably presents the divine figure of Jesus in Revelation 1 as temporarily taking up angelic form in order to underscore the heavenly character of his message.[44] The mighty angel in Revelation 10 is not Christ either, but deliberately is like Christ because John wants to emphasize that this angel reflects some of Christ's own glory and has come with Christ's own authority.[45]

At one point, Ehrman cites Hurtado saying that principal angel speculation provided Christians with a basic scheme for accommodating Christ next to God without compromising Jewish monotheism.[46] That is true, but Hurtado says in the same place that the principal angel is no ordinary angel as he is set apart in his various functions from the other angels; the analogy with principal angels proves only that Christ can act as a divine agent without lapsing into di-theism, and the angel analogy breaks down when it is remembered that God rather than angels is the worthy recipient of divine worship. For Hurtado, none of this does anything to prove that Christ was perceived in early Christian tradition to be or to have become an angel. Furthermore, Hurtado's own summary of his book says quite the opposite: "I have demonstrated in *One God, One Lord*, we have no analogous accommodation of a second figure along with God as recipient of such devotion in the Jewish tradition of the time, making

Revelation 1:13–16: Jesus	Revelation 10:1–3: The Mighty Angel
[13]... and among the lampstands was someone like a son of man, dressed in a robe reaching down to his feet and with a golden sash around his chest. [14]The hair on his head was white like wool, as white as snow, and his eyes were like blazing fire. [15]His feet were like bronze glowing in a furnace, and his voice was like the sound of rushing waters. [16]In his right hand he held seven stars, and coming out of his mouth was a sharp, double-edged sword. His face was like the sun shining in all its brilliance.	[1]Then I saw another mighty angel coming down from heaven. He was robed in a cloud, with a rainbow above his head; his face was like the sun, and his legs were like fiery pillars. [2]He was holding a little scroll, which lay open in his hand. He planted his right foot on the sea and his left foot on the land, [3]and he gave a loud shout like the roar of a lion. When he shouted, the voices of the seven thunders spoke.

it very difficult to fit this inclusion of Christ as recipient of devotion into any known devotional pattern attested among Jewish groups of the Roman period."[17]

CONCLUSION

Ehrman asks a legitimate question: In what *sense* was Jesus considered to be "god" by the first Christians? If an absolute monotheism did not exist in the first century, as Ehrman alleges, then could Jesus be divine in the same sense as a deified king or an angelic creature? Ehrman thinks so, but there are reasons to question this.

First, Ehrman's use of sources verges on parallelomania, and he overemphasizes the similarities between various intermediary figures and Christian conceptions of Christ as divine to the detriment of the serious differences. Early Christology was not so unique as to be unintelligible in its religious environs, but the story of Jesus and rituals of Jesus devotion entailed a thorough redefinition of what Christians meant by "God." The early church did not invent a strict monotheism; rather, they inherited it from Judaism. But they did create a christological monotheism, where the one God was now known through, in, and as the Lord Jesus Christ.

Second, in regards to monotheism itself, contra Ehrman, there were pagan monotheists, but Jewish monotheism was strict. The various intermediary figures known in ancient sources, whether angelic or human, do not make monotheism malleable, because such figures shared neither in God's exclusive worship nor in God's unique identity, whereas Jesus certainly did.

Third, while not discounting the relevance of angelomorphism to views of Jesus in the early church, it proves in the end to be a red herring rather than an explanatory paradigm for early beliefs about Jesus.

If the preceding analysis is correct, the early church did not simply rip off existing ideas of descending gods and ascending humans and not-so-subtly apply them to Jesus. Rather, it seems that what happened was that the among Jesus' earliest followers there was an immediate move to reconfigure Jewish monotheism, whereby the one God of Israel was now known and experienced as the Lord Jesus Christ and God the Father.

EXCURSUS 1

Kings, Angels, and Holy Men

FIGURE 1 Fresco of an angel on a rock in Osogovo Monastery, Macedonia.

Since Ehrman talks about the relevance of gods becoming human and humans becoming divine for early Christology, it is worth looking at a few examples to get an awareness of what these texts about intermediary figures actually say. The ancient world certainly knew of the divinization of kings and semidivine intermediary figures like angels. What follows is a sample of texts illustrating this phenomenon:

1. ISRAEL'S KING AS ONE WHO SITS AMONG THE GODS

Your throne, O God, will last for ever and ever;
    a scepter of justice will be the scepter of your kingdom.
You love righteousness and hate wickedness;
    therefore God, your God, has set you above your companions
    by anointing you with the oil of joy. (Ps 45:6–7)

Psalm 45 was originally a wedding psalm recited to celebrate the marriage of a Judean king to his new bride. The king is addressed as "God" (*Elohim* in Hebrew and *Theos* in Greek). The identification of the king as "God" is not meant to be taken literally, but it is an honorific title that was customarily used in the Ancient Near East for monarchs. The psalmist notes that the king still has his own God (i.e., "your God"), upon whom he is reliant for the reception of his reign. Since ruling and judging were principally prerogatives of God, the king had to be Godlike in the just execution of his regal responsibilities.

2. AUGUSTUS AS GOD AND LORD

… for the god and lord emperor. (P.Oxy 1143.4)

In three papyri from Egypt, the Roman Emperor Augustus (reigned from 31 BCE–14 CE) is given the title "Lord" and "God." At his accession, he was known as the "Son of the Divine Julius," named after his adopted father, Julius Caesar. Augustus was well acquainted with the eastern tradition of worshiping kings and queens as living manifestations of the gods, but remained mostly allergic to it. He permitted the erection of temples to the emperor and imperial family in provincial areas of Gaul, Italy, Greece, and Asia Minor, but expressly forbade such worship in Rome itself. Such prohibitions did not extend to popular media like papyri and ostraca that circulated in the provinces. It was only after his death that Augustus was officially granted celestial honors and declared to have become a god by apotheosis, that is, by ascending into the realm of the heavens. Subsequent emperors, especially Caligula, Nero, and Domitian, did not show such restraint, and they not only accepted divine honors, but in some cases they even demanded them of their subjects. Many scholars claim that the New Testament confession of Jesus Christ as "Lord" is meant as a deliberate challenge to the honorific status and divine power claimed by the Roman imperial apparatus. In other words, to confess that "Jesus is Lord" was to imply that "Caesar is not."[48]

3. MOSES ON GOD'S THRONE

Ezekiel the Tragedian also speaks about these things in the *Exagōgē*, including the dream seen by Moses and interpreted by his father-in-law. Moses himself speaks with his father-in-law in dialogue:

> On Sinai's peak I saw what seemed a throne
> so great in size it touched the clouds of heaven.
> Upon it sat a man of noble mien,
> becrowned, and with a scepter in one hand
> while with the other he did beckon me.
> I made approach and stood before the throne.
> He handed o'er the scepter and he bade
> me mount the throne, and gave to me the crown;
> then he himself withdrew from off the throne.
> I gazed upon the whole earth and round about;
> things under it, and high above the skies.
> Then at my feet a multitude of stars
> fell down, and I their number reckoned up.
> They passed by me like armed ranks of men.
> Then I in terror wakened from the dream.

And his father-in-law interprets the dream as follows:

> My friend, God gave you this as a sign for good.
> Would I might live to see these things transpire.
> For you shall cause a mighty throne to rise,
> and you yourself shall rule and govern men.
> As for beholding all the peopled earth,
> and things below and things above God's realm:
> things present, past, and future you shall see.[49]

In this intriguing story, Moses has a dream that he visits the throne room of heaven, and while there God basically vacates the throne and invites him to sit on it. Moses' father-in-law interprets the dream as meaning that Moses can expect to one day hold a position of kingly power over the peoples of the earth. Lest this seem too incredible, it is worth remembering that in the book of Exodus there is a curious passage where God tells Moses, "See, I have made you like God to Pharaoh" (Exod 7:1), which means that Moses will have absolute divine power over Pharaoh and the Egyptian gods. The Alexandrian Jewish author Philo could also depict Moses as both a king and as a Godlike figure (e.g., Philo, *Life of Moses* 1.55–62; *Worse* 160–62; *Sacrifices of Cain and Able* 9–10). The dream is obviously surreal and therefore not a real statement of Moses' divinity; instead, Moses represents the elevation of Israel to rule over the nations, a point found in other writings too (e.g., Dan 7:18, 22, 27; Rev 5:10; *4 Ezra* 6:55–59).

4. TIERS OF ANGELS

Angel Iao, may you give all success
and power and favour and assistance
to Asklepiakos with [the help of the]
first angels
and
middle angels
and final angels
throughout [his] life
and bodily protection,
Abrasax O Da[mnamene]us
forever. (NDIEC, 10:16–19)

The inscription is found on a gem stone and is datable to 150–250 CE. The inscription is basically a prayer by a man named Asklepiakos to the angel Iao for help from these lesser angels in blessing him with physical health and well-being. The petition exhibits an unprecedented description of a hierarchy of angels. It was probably angelic hierarchies such as this that Paul responded to when he wrote to the Colossians about avoiding the "worship of angels" (Col 2:18). For all the ancient speculation and devotion to angels, Jewish and Christian authors retained a strong prohibition against the worship of angels (see e.g., Rev 19:10; Tob 12:16–22; *3 En.* 16.1–5; *Asc. Isa.* 7:21; 8:5; *Apoc. Zeph.* 6.11–15.).

CHAPTER 3

Did Jesus Think He Was God?

Michael F. Bird

INTRODUCTION

I did not grow up in a religious home. As a kid, everything I knew about Christianity I learned from Ned Flanders from the TV show *The Simpsons*. But we had a chaplain at my public high school, a lovely guy named Graham, a local Baptist pastor. At our graduation ceremony Graham told us, "The most important question you will ever ask is who is Jesus? Is he a lunatic, a liar, or Lord?" I just rolled my eyes at the time, but for some reason the question stuck with me. Who is this Jesus anyway, and what is all the fuss about? Years later, while I was a paratrooper of all things, I came to the decision that Jesus was definitely Lord. But that's another story. Confessing that Jesus is Lord is one thing, but believing that Jesus believed himself to be the Lord is quite another. Whatever faults there are in Ehrman's study of Jesus, at least he's forcing us to ask some good and honest questions about faith, history, and Jesus. Who is Jesus, and who did he think he was?

It is worth noting that the question of "Who is Jesus?" began in the pre-Easter period, where followers and critics of Jesus alike were all confronted with the question as to who Jesus was and, more importantly, who *he* thought he was.[1] Indeed, the question continued to be asked steadily thereafter in the nascent church and even into the period of the church fathers. Christians spent the best part of four hundred years trying to find the best language, imagery, categories, and scriptural texts to answer Jesus' question to his disciples: "Who do you say that I am?" (Mark 8:29). When the dust finally settled, the church's final verdict was that Jesus was "God from God, Light from Light, begotten, not made, of one Being with the Father," as stated in the Nicene Creed.

What everyone wants to know, however, is to what extent Jesus shared that evaluation of himself. Did the disciples think that Jesus was their God? Did Jesus himself know he was God? Did Jesus ever explicitly say he was God?[2] Ehrman gives a negative answer on all fronts. According to him, Jesus "thought he was a prophet predicting the end of the current evil age and the future king of Israel in the age to come."[3] Jesus saw himself as the Messiah, but also looked forward to the "imminent arrival of the Son of Man, who would judge the earth and bring in God's good kingdom."[4] Although the gospel of John claims that Jesus is equal with God (John 8:58; 10:30; 14:9; 17:24), Ehrman contends that such claims are late and secondary, so that "the divine self-claims in John are not historical."[5] Ehrman reaches this conclusion: "What we can know with relative certainty about Jesus is that his public ministry and proclamation were not focused on his divinity; in fact, they were not about his divinity at all."[6]

In response to Ehrman, my objective is to show that Jesus identified himself as a divine agent with a unique authority and a unique relationship with Israel's God. In addition, he spoke as one who spoke for God in an immediate sense and believed himself to be embodying the very person of God in his mission to renew and restore Israel. While the early church may have said more than that, they certainly never said less. The point to note is that Jesus' presentation of himself to his followers was arguably the singular most important factor in shaping their subsequent devotion to him and the way that it developed. However, before we get down to what Jesus thought about himself—his "self-understanding" as it is often called—we need to say something about Ehrman's methodology for studying Jesus.

EHRMAN'S METHOD: ERRONEOUS MANUSCRIPTS, HISTORICAL CRITERIA, AND THE HISTORICAL JESUS

I have to confess that whenever I read Bart Ehrman saying anything about the historical Jesus, I always feel like tweeting "@BartEhrman

#epicfacepalm." Here's why. On the one hand, Ehrman has courted notoriety and fame for arguing that the New Testament manuscripts were corrupted and distorted to the point that we cannot realistically talk about recovering an original autograph. He has written:

> Not only do we not have the originals, we don't have the first copies of the originals. We don't even have copies of the copies of the originals, or copies of the copies of the copies of the originals. What we have are copies made later—much later.... And these copies all differ from one another, in many thousands of places ... these copies differ from one another in so many places that we don't even know how many differences there are.[7]

> If one wants to insist that God inspired the very words of scripture, what would be the point if we don't *have* the very words of scripture? In some places, as we will see, we simply cannot be sure that we have reconstructed the original text accurately. It's a bit hard to know what the words of the Bible mean if we don't even know what the words are![8]

> The fact that we have thousands of New Testament manuscripts does not in itself mean that we can rest assured that we know what the original text said. If we have very few early copies—in fact, scarcely any—how can we know that the text was not changed significantly before the New Testament began to be reproduced in such large quantities?[9]

At a Society of Biblical Literature panel discussion I've even heard Ehrman declare, "We can't talk about the 'Word of God' since we don't know what the original words even were."[10] So it would seem that the New Testament manuscript tradition is messed up and we have little prospect of recovering the original text.

Nevertheless, something strange happens. Ehrman is somehow still able in his voluminous writings to use this corrupted and contaminated textual tradition as his primary source to reconstruct the career of the historical Jesus. In fact, he's written an entire book about the historical Jesus![11] Not only that, but Ehrman is also able to uncover the real stories about Peter, Paul, and even Mary Magdalene.[12]

Absolutely amazing stuff, I have to say. Amazing, because what Ehrman says about the New Testament manuscripts makes his inquiry about Jesus methodologically impossible.[13] If the New Testament was so heavily corrupted, then how can you use it as your primary source to reconstruct Jesus' life? Well, to be honest, you can't, but for some reason Ehrman is not perturbed by this. Ehrman likes to play the part of the super-skeptic when it suits him, but on other occasions he seems to move seamlessly from his English Bible all the way back to Jesus of Galilee as if none of these critical issues existed. It's as if he says in one book that "the emperor has no clothes," and then in the next book he says, "I just love what the emperor was wearing at the Vanity Fair Oscars party; oh my, he looks gorgeous in Armani." Ehrman has been accused of a great many things by his critics, however, and quite obviously, methodological consistency will not be one of them.[14]

A further problem with Ehrman's method is his entire attitude toward historical Jesus studies. He thinks that we cannot take the Gospels at face value as historically reliable accounts of the things Jesus said and did. Ehrman makes some broad and sweeping comments about the sources behind the Gospels and the nature of the Gospels as faith-documents that should render us historically suspicious of their accounts of Jesus. He does not think that the Gospels are useless as historical sources, but because they are more interested in proclaiming Jesus than with giving a true history of Jesus, we have to sift through the Gospels with the aid of various criteria to separate the fictions from the facts.[15] A couple of comments are required here.

First, if the Gospels are not, in their basic outlines at least, somehow reliable, then we might as well stop wasting our time and go fishing. I like how Dale Allison puts it:

> Either they [the Gospels] tend to preserve pre-Easter memories or they do not. In the former case, we have some possibility of getting somewhere. But in the latter case, our questing for Jesus is probably pointless and we should consider surrendering to ignorance. If the tradition is seriously misleading in its broad features, then we can hardly make much of its details.[16]

Similar is Sean Freyne: "Either we accept that the early followers of Jesus had some interest in and memory of the historical figure of Jesus as they began to proclaim the good news about him, or we must abandon the process entirely."[17] Approaches like Ehrman's, which begin by casting doubt on the historical value of the Gospels for reconstructing the life of Jesus, but then proceed to formulate a hypothesis about the historical Jesus anyway, are essentially creating a vacuum and then filling it with scholarly fiction.[18]

Alternatively, I would advocate that the Gospels are generally reliable and coherent sources for studying the historical Jesus.[19] As long as the early church knew the "Lord Jesus" to be the same as "the crucified one," the historical Jesus was always going to be properly basic for the church's faith. The things Jesus said and did pre-Easter mattered for what the church believed and said about him post-Easter.

That is not to deny that the Gospels are documents designed for proclamation, theologically loaded, and written to create faith. The Gospels are, then, the interpretation and application of the memory of Jesus for readers in the Greco-Roman world.[20] A memory was carried by eyewitnesses and was put into the custody of corporate interest in the Jew from Nazareth. Thus, what the Gospels produce is not the transcript for CNN-style video footage of Jesus' career. A better analogy is that they offer a dramatic representation, much like a documentary drama, of Jesus' actions in the past and his voice for the present available through the corporate memory of Jesus. Consequently, the memory of Jesus deposited in the Gospels bequeaths to us both authenticity and artistry, fact and faith, history and hermeneutic. The objective of the Evangelists was not to write a life of Jesus to satisfy modernist demands for detail, nor was it to offer an image of Jesus that they pretty much made up to satisfy their own ideological bent. The Evangelists intended to narrate a story and evoke the significance of one called "Jesus," Israel's Messiah and the world's rightful Lord.[21]

Second, Ehrman is dependent on the use of several "criteria" to establish the authenticity of stories about Jesus in the Gospels. Generally speaking, criteria of authenticity are useful as a way of trying to figure out which traditions in the Gospels go back to Jesus. I've used them myself at times, but like others I've become increasingly aware of their limitations and become convinced that they do not offer a path to an objective history of Jesus. For a start, trying to sort out the authentic traditions from the inauthentic traditions is not really that easy, for the simple fact that the history of Jesus has been thoroughly welded together with the early church's proclamation of Jesus at every point. Trying to separate the history from theology in the Gospels is a bit like trying to separate blue from red in the color purple. What is more, many of the criteria have been critically examined and found to be inadequate as a way of establishing the historical or unhistorical nature of any given unit in the Gospels.[22] Dale Allison speaks with candor on this: "The older I become, the less I trust anyone's ability to answer this sort of question, to trace the history and origin of a particular saying.... It is not so easy to establish that any particular saying goes back to Jesus, and it is not so easy to establish that any particular saying does not go back to him."[23]

For case in point, let's consider Ehrman's use of the "criterion of dissimilarity," which on his account dictates that a given unit in the Gospels is historically authentic if "it is dissimilar to what the early Christians would have wanted to say about him."[24] This criterion is well-known and has received a devastating barrage of criticism to the point that I am, to be frank, at a loss as to why Ehrman continues to use it. It jumped the shark about the same time that the TV show Dawson's Creek did.[25] In extreme cases some scholars looked for a double dissimilarity, whereby a tradition is authentic when it is dissimilar to both Judaism and to the early church. Ehrman wisely uses it in its less extreme form and only applies it to dissimilarity from the early church.

But even then it verges on the ludicrous. Think about it. A story about Jesus or as a saying attributed to Jesus is only historical if it does not sound anything like what the church was saying about Jesus. What historian would say that the historical Plato is different from what the platonic school said about Plato? Who would say that reliable information about the Teacher of Righteousness who founded a community by shores of the Dead Sea can only to be found when material attributed to him in the Dead Sea Scrolls sound nothing like the Dead Sea Scrolls? Who thinks that the real John Wesley can only be retrieved by searching for un-Wesleyan things that Wesleyans said about John Wesley? The criterion of dissimilarity posits a huge rupture between a movement founder and his or her subsequent movement that is simply absurd. You end up with a Jesus who said, thought, and did nothing that his earliest followers believed that he said, thought, and did. Jesus becomes a free-floating iconoclast artificially insulated from the movement that took its name from him, claimed to follow his teachings, and memorialized his deeds and actions.

No wonder, then, that the criterion of dissimilarity has been near universally abandoned and replaced with something far more credible, like a criterion of historical plausibility. We can regard a unit in the Gospels as claiming a high degree of historical authenticity when a saying or event attributed to Jesus makes sense within Judaism (i.e., plausible context) and also represents a starting point for the early church (i.e., a plausible consequence).[26]

Rather than try to drain the theological dross from the historical silver in the Gospels through several fallible criteria, more recently scholars have been interested in the application of social memory research to the study of the historical Jesus.[27] In other words, how did the things Jesus said and did create a memory in his followers, a memory that was faithfully transmitted, yet also refracted according to the theological framework that the early church was developing. In which case, we cannot hope to penetrate the impregnable bedrock of the church's interpretation and proclamation of Jesus found in the Gospels and discover a deeper layer of historically accurate data laid beneath. At the end of the day the best way to read the Gospels responsibly and historically is to narrate the story of Jesus in a way that has realism and explanatory power—a story that makes Jesus fit plausibly into his Jewish context, that brings all of the sources together, that explains the shape and direction of the early church, and that accounts for why and how the Gospels are what they are. Allison again puts it well:

> As historians of the Jesus tradition we are storytellers. We can do no more than aspire to fashion a narrative that is more persuasive than competing narratives, one that satisfies our aesthetic and historical sensibilities because of its apparent ability to clarify more data in a more satisfactory fashion than its rivals.[28]

Ehrman's entire approach to historical Jesus studies does not commend itself as a good way of doing history.

JESUS, THE RESTORATION OF ISRAEL, AND THE RETURN OF YHWH TO ZION

Okay, back to our question: Did Jesus think he was God?

Well, to begin with, there is no reason to see Jesus as anything other than a good monotheist. Jesus proclaimed the kingdom of God (Mark 1:14–15), he prayed to God as Father (Mark 14:36; Matt 6:9–13/Luke 11:1–4; John 11:41–42), he affirmed the Jewish confession of God's oneness, the *Shema* (Deut 6:4; Mark 12:29–30), and he called for steadfast devotion to God (Matt 6:24/Luke 16:13). All this would seem to fit neatly into Ehrman's thesis that Jesus was a prophet and a messianic claimant, but not the Son of Man, and definitely did not think of himself as God's equal.

But then again, Jesus may have spoken of himself in far more elevated ways than Ehrman imagines. It is certainly not the case that Jesus proclaimed God's kingdom and later on the church proclaimed Jesus. For even within Jesus' kingdom message there was always an implicit self-reference. Not only is the kingdom coming, but Jesus is the one who inaugurates it through his mighty deeds, exorcisms, healings, and preaching. Jesus is remembered as saying: "But if it is by the finger of God that I cast out demons, then the kingdom of God has come upon you" (Luke 11:20; cf. Matt 12:28). Jesus is not simply the FedEx delivery boy announcing the kingdom; he is its harbinger and hero in the then and there!

But before we go any further, I need to clear the deck. I think it is necessary to explode a popular caricature where Jesus cruises around Galilee announcing, "Hi, I'm God. I'm going to die on the cross for your sins soon. But first of all I'm going to teach you how to be a good Christian and how to get to heaven. And after that I thought it would be fitting if you all worshiped me as the second member of the Trinity." This might seem a rather silly way to understand Jesus' identity, but it is a sketch of Jesus that many Bible-believing Christians have. When I contend that Jesus understood himself to be divine, this is definitely not what I am talking about. When I say that Jesus knew himself to be God, I mean that he was conscious that in him the God of Israel was finally returning to Zion (i.e., Jerusalem) to renew the covenant and to fulfill the promises God had made to the nation about a new exodus.

Let's have a look at a saying from the Gospels that Ehrman is rather fond of, namely, Matt 19:28 and Luke 22:28–30:

Matthew 19:28	Luke 22:28–30
Jesus said to them, "Truly I tell you, at the renewal of all things, when the Son of Man sits on his glorious throne, you who have followed me will also sit on twelve thrones, judging the twelve tribes of Israel.	You are those who have stood by me in my trials. And I confer on you a kingdom, just as my Father conferred one on me, so that you may eat and drink at my table in my kingdom and sit on thrones, judging the twelve tribes of Israel.

This short saying is important because it shows that Jesus regarded the object of his ministry as the reconstitution of Israel. When all things come together, the Son of Man will be enthroned, and the twelve apostles will be charged with leading a renewed Jewish people. The background to this saying is that ever since the Assyrian exile (ca. 722 BCE) and the Babylonian exile (ca. 587 BCE), the twelve tribes of Israel had long since been dispersed. A remnant had returned to Judea from Babylon (ca. 538 BCE), but the vast majority of Jews in Jesus' day lived dispersed across the Mediterranean and Middle East in major population centers like Babylon, Alexandria, and Rome. During the subsequent period, Israel's political fortunes were mixed and ranged from independence, to occupation, to autonomy under foreign powers. For the most part, however, Israel found itself as the battleground that great military powers in Africa, Asia, and Europe trampled over to extend their power. Even though the Babylonian captivity had technically ended, the next half millennium was hardly a golden age of Israel's political and spiritual fortunes. According to Jewish scholar Joseph Klausner, the actual fact was

> slavery to foreign governments, wars, tumults and torrents of blood. Instead of all nations being subject to Judah, Judah was subject to the nations. Instead of the "riches of the Gentiles," godless Rome exacted taxes and tribute.... Instead of the Gentiles "bowing down with their faces to the ground" and "licking the dust of their feet," comes a petty Roman official with unlimited power of Judea. Instead of Messiah the son of David, comes Herod the Edomite.[29]

However, the hope of Israel, going back to the prophets, was that one day God would restore the twelve tribes, bring them back together, forgive the sins that led to Israel's exile, defeat Israel's enemies, bring forth a new Davidic King, inaugurate a new covenant, and build a new temple. There would be great agricultural fecundity, and the nations would flock to Zion to worship Israel's God as well. Furthermore, another crucial element of that hope was that YHWH himself would return to Zion.[30]

It is no surprise, then, that in the first century various prophetic and protest movements in Judea looked for the coming of the kingdom of God and with it the coming of God.[31] According to John Meier, when such groups spoke about the "kingdom of God," they had in mind "not primarily a state or place but rather the entire dynamic event of God coming in power to rule his people Israel in the end time."[32] It meant a divine visitation with the accompanying effects of a new exodus, the forgiveness of Israel's sins, the renewal of the covenant, a new temple, and God's victory over evil.

On the coming of God as king, a passage that kindled the candle of many hopes was Isaiah 40–55, which has among its opening words:

> A voice of one calling:
> "In the wilderness prepare
>   the way for the LORD;
> make straight in the desert
>   a highway for our God." (Isa 40:3)

This verse was programmatic for both John the Baptist out in the Judean wilderness and the Qumran community on the shores of the Dead Sea, as both were quite literally out in the desert preparing for this future event of God's coming, either by way of prophetic warning to the masses (John the Baptist) or by separating from the impurity of the masses (Qumran).[33]

The wider context of Isaiah 40 is illuminating, for later in the same chapter we read more about YHWH's coming reign and YHWH's return to Zion:

> You who bring good news to Zion,
>   go up on a high mountain.
> You who bring good news to Jerusalem,
>   lift up your voice with a shout,

lift it up, do not be afraid;
    say to the towns of Judah,
    "Here is your God!"
See, the Sovereign LORD *comes with power,*
    and he rules with a mighty arm.
See, his reward is with him,
    and his recompense accompanies him.
He tends his flock like a shepherd:
    He gathers the lambs in his arms
and carries them close to his heart;
    he gently leads those that have young. (Isa 40:9–11, italics added)

And a little later in Isaiah we find something similar:

How beautiful on the mountains
    are the feet of those who bring good news,
who proclaim peace,
    who bring good tidings,
    who proclaim salvation, who say to Zion, "Your God reigns!"
Listen! Your watchmen lift up their voices;
    together they shout for joy.
When the LORD *returns to Zion,*
    they will see it with their own eyes.
Burst into songs of joy together,
    you ruins of Jerusalem,
for the LORD has comforted his people,
    he has redeemed Jerusalem.
The LORD *will lay bare his holy arm*
    in the sight of all the nations,
and all the ends of the earth will see
    the salvation of our God. (Isa 52:7–10, italics added)

The Isaianic announcement of YHWH's kingship means YHWH is going to bring the exile to an end in a new exodus, where YHWH will return to Zion and judge Israel's enemies, and then he will dwell with his people.

Such a motif is not restricted to Isaiah, but is found amply in other prophetic books. The themes of the end of exile, a new temple, a new covenant, and a new Davidic king are rehearsed with prophetic poise and power in the book of Ezekiel. At one point, God speaks to the exiles:

    " 'Therefore, you shepherds, hear the word of the LORD: As surely as I live, declares the Sovereign LORD, because my flock lacks a shepherd and so has been plundered and has become food for all the wild animals, and because my shepherds did not search for my flock but cared for themselves rather than for my flock, therefore, you shepherds, hear the word of the LORD: This is what the Sovereign LORD says: I am against the shepherds and will hold them accountable for my flock. I will remove them from tending the flock so that the shepherds can no longer feed themselves. *I will rescue my flock from their mouths, and it will no longer be food for them.*

"'For this is what the Sovereign LORD says: *I myself will search for my sheep and look after them. As a shepherd looks after his scattered flock when he is with them, so will I look after my sheep. I will rescue them from all the places where they were scattered on a day of clouds and darkness. I will bring them out from the nations and gather them from the countries, and I will bring them into their own land. I will pasture them on the mountains of Israel, in the ravines and in all the settlements in the land. I will tend them in a good pasture, and the mountain heights of Israel will be their grazing land. There they will lie down in good grazing land, and there they will feed in a rich pasture on the mountains of Israel. I myself will tend my sheep and have them lie down, declares the Sovereign LORD. I will search for the lost and bring back the strays. I will bind up the injured and strengthen the weak, but the sleek and the strong I will destroy. I will shepherd the flock with justice.'"* (Ezek 34:7–16, italics added)

According to Ezekiel, YHWH stands against the false shepherds, and he is coming, coming to regather and to shepherd the people. Yet, just a few verses later, we read something rather peculiar:

I will save my flock, and they will no longer be plundered. I will judge between one sheep and another. *I will place over them one shepherd, my servant David, and he will tend them; he will tend them and be their shepherd.* I the LORD will be their God, and my servant David will be prince among them. I the LORD have spoken. (Ezek 34:22–24, italics added)

This speech starts off by saying that YHWH is coming to shepherd his people, but then we are told that the one doing the actual shepherding will be "my servant David." Now obviously this does not mean that David is YHWH, but neither is David just a kind of subcontractor. What it does mean is that David will be to the people what YHWH has promised he will be to the exiles: a shepherd.

This narrative of Jewish restoration hopes formed not only the backdrop but the script for Jesus' own words and actions. When Jesus declared the coming of God's kingdom, he was talking about the coming of God as King. Jesus' selection of twelve followers was a way of symbolically showing that Israel's restoration was beginning at last with his own ragtag band of disciples (see Mark 3:13–16).[34] The various healings and exorcisms Jesus performed were meant to be tangible signs that the day of deliverance was at hand and God was at last becoming king (see Matt 11:1–6/Luke 7:20–23, which correlates exactly with 4Q521 2.1–21 in the Dead Sea Scrolls).

I concur with Ehrman that Jesus saw himself as the king of this coming kingdom, the Messiah,[35] but on the back of Jewish restoration eschatology I want to say more than that. Jesus believed that in his ministry and even in his person, YHWH was finally returning to Zion. In light of that premise, it is useful to read afresh a number of episodes from Jesus' career that illustrate that the lines between divine author and divine agent were becoming blurred. Several stories and sayings in the Synoptic Gospels point toward Jesus' unique role as a divine *agent* with an unprecedented *authority* and who undertakes divine *action*.

To begin with, the exchange that takes place between Jesus and the scribes in a healing story is a perfect illustration as to what Jesus was claiming about himself:

> A few days later, when Jesus again entered Capernaum, the people heard that he had come home. They gathered in such large numbers that there was no room left, not even outside the door, and he preached the word to them. Some men came, bringing to him a paralyzed man, carried by four of them. Since they could not get him to Jesus because of the crowd, they made an opening in the roof above Jesus by digging through it and then lowered the mat the man was lying on. When Jesus saw their faith, he said to the paralyzed man, "Son, your sins are forgiven."
>
> Now some teachers of the law were sitting there, thinking to themselves, "Why does this fellow talk like that? He's blaspheming! *Who can forgive sins but God alone?*"
>
> Immediately Jesus knew in his spirit that this was what they were thinking in their hearts, and he said to them, "Why are you thinking these things? Which is easier: to say to this paralyzed man, 'Your sins

are forgiven,' or to say, 'Get up, take your mat and walk?' But I want you to know that the Son of Man has authority on earth to forgive sins." So he said to the man, "I tell you, get up, take your mat and go home."

He got up, took his mat and walked out in full view of them all. This amazed everyone and they praised God, saying, "We have never seen anything like this!" (Mark 2:1–12, italics added)

In this episode, Jesus pronounces the forgiveness of sins on a paralytic man, which leads to a charge of blasphemy by the teachers of the law. Ordinarily there was nothing wrong with someone declaring a person's sins forgiven, as long as that someone was a priest and everyone was in the temple. But nobody says, "Hang on, you're not a priest!" or "Wait a minute, this isn't the temple!" Rather, the complaint is, "Who can forgive sins but God alone?" (Mark 2:7; see Isa 43:25). The offense that Jesus' words provoke is by his presumption to speak with a divine prerogative. Clearly Jesus' declaration of forgiveness in such a context was tantamount to assuming the authority to forgive on God's behalf. When Jesus explains why he is able to do so, declaring that "the Son of Man has authority on earth to forgive sins," he makes that claim explicit.[36]

Ehrman takes this story to mean that "Jesus may be claiming a priestly prerogative, but not a divine one."[37] I'm afraid not! Jesus was not acting like a rogue priest. He was not from the tribe of Levi anyway, and he wasn't anywhere near the temple. So by what authority could he pronounce the forgiveness of his sins? The scribes do not complain, "Who can forgive sins but a priest alone?" Nor does Jesus explain his action by saying, "I want you to know that I've recently purchased a Galilean franchise on the priesthood licensing me to forgive sins, preside at weddings, and officiate at bar mitzvahs." No, instead he says, "But I want you to know that the Son of Man has authority to forgive sins," which turns out to be a divine authority. He commands the paralytic man to stand, pick up his mat, and go home. Even more astounding, the man does so. A miraculous healing takes place. Jesus claims for himself an unmediated divine authority that, to those steeped in Jewish monotheism, looks absolutely blasphemous. Yet, somehow, the paralytic man is healed. The bite of Jesus' rhetoric is that he's proven right. *If* he can make a paralytic walk, *then* he has the authority to pronounce the forgiveness of sins.

In other places it is clear that Jesus expressed a sense of unmediated divine authority that led the authorities to query him about its origin (Mark 11:27–33), and public opinion was that he spoke with a unique authority that set him apart from the scribes (Mark 1:22, 27; Matt 8:9/Luke 7:8). Jesus reconfigured divine commandments based on his own authority (Matt 5:21, 27, 33, 38, 43), and in one instance he claimed authority to transcend the Sabbath since the Son of Man was "Lord of the Sabbath" (Mark 2:27–28). The renowned Jewish scholar Jacob Neusner, in an interview about his book *A Rabbi Talks with Jesus*, said that he found Jesus' approach to the law so unsettling that it made Neusner want to ask Jesus, "Who do you think you are — God?"[38]

Elsewhere Jesus identifies himself as the Son of God who is Lord to the Son of David, an agent of divine wisdom, the seat of the divine presence, and even an expression of divine power over evil. Jesus is remembered as referring to the Messiah as David's own Lord (Mark 12:35–37), to himself as an envoy of divine wisdom (Matt 11:19/Luke 7:35; Matt 11:28–30), one who is greater than the temple (Matt 12:6), and one who is stronger than the Satan (Mark 3:27; Matt 12:29/Luke 11:21–22). These are not claims to superhuman abilities, but claims to be the one who embodies God's reign, carries God's wisdom into the world, conveys God's presence in a manner greater than the temple, and is able to defeat God's adversary, Satan. Jesus is then identifiable with God's own activity in the world and his victory over evil. Heed this point well. None of this material is a cheap ripoff from Homer or Virgil ostentatiously read back into Jesus' life; rather, these ideas are all enmeshed in thoroughly Jewish ways of conceiving of God's presence in the world and God's purposes for the world.[39]

It is fascinating how Luke portrays Jesus as approaching Jerusalem, not as a religious tourist but as something far more grandiose. The whole sequence of Luke 19 is that Jesus' arrival is uncannily like … could possibly be … strangely resembles … YHWH's return to Zion. To be sure, Jesus comes as Israel's Messiah, but in that same coming is the manifestation of Israel's God.

First, Jesus' journey through Jericho became the occasion to engage in some scandalous activity seen in his willingness to dine in the house of the much-despised tax collector named Zacchaeus (Luke 19:1–10). Of course, reclining with such reprehensible scoundrels was one of the most characteristic parts of Jesus' career (see Mark 2:15–16; Matt 11:19/Luke 7:34; Luke 15:1). His practice of open table fellowship with sinners was a symbol of the openness of the kingdom and represented a radical challenge to presumptions of who is "in" or "out" with God. At the end of the story, once Zacchaeus's repentance has become public, Jesus explains why he does such things by saying: "The Son of Man came to seek and to save the lost" (Luke 19:10). Jesus does not talk like an ancient prophet and tell wayward sinners to seek out God while he may be found (see Amos 5:4; Zeph 2:3). Instead, Jesus is seeking out marginalized Israelites in a manner reminiscent of how God in his climactic return to Zion was believed to be coming to regather the lost flock of Israel (Jer 31:10; Ezek 34:8–10; Zech 9:16). It is not hard to hear the echoes of such texts here with the coming of YHWH to seek out and to shepherd his people as representing a fitting description for Jesus' own activity.

Second, the following parable of the talents in Luke 19:11–27 about a nobleman who goes abroad to receive his kingdom and then returns has long been read as a prediction of Jesus' second coming. Matthew's version of the parable (the parable of the pounds in Matt 25:14–30) certainly gives that impression by marrying the parable to some subsequent remarks about the Son of Man judging all the nations in 25:31–46. However, when Luke and Matthew share material from the sayings tradition (often called "Q"), the Lucan version is usually regarded as the more primitive version and most like any "original" telling by Jesus.[40]

On top of that, Luke's account of the parable is not dealing with what a generation of scholars once thought it was, the dreaded delay of the return of Jesus, trying to explain why Jesus' second advent is taking *sooo* long. Note this: the occasion for the parable is not the problem of the kingdom's postponement; quite the contrary, Luke explicitly tells us that the reason why Jesus uttered the parable was because his audience had a heightened expectation of the kingdom's imminence (Luke 19:11). Far from extinguishing such hopes for the kingdom's imminence, Jesus' parable actually excites them all the more as evidenced by the enthusiasm of his followers in the triumphal entry that soon follows (Luke 19:37–38).

On the parable of the talents itself, rather than think of it a morality tale for the faithful to be ready for the second coming that has been anachronistically projected back into Jesus' teaching syllabus, what if Jesus was not predicting his second coming, but simply retelling a well-known scriptural story about the return of YHWH to Zion? In doing so, he deliberately evoked hopes that God's saving justice was about to be dramatically revealed! In a nutshell, the notion of a king who returns after a short absence fits squarely within Jewish hopes for the return of YHWH to Zion.[41]

Third, in Luke's version of the triumphal entry, Jesus approaches Jerusalem weeping with grief upon the city, uttering an oracle of woe as much as an ode of lament: "They will dash you to the ground, you and the children within your walls. They will not leave one stone on another, because you did not recognize the time of God's coming to you" (Luke 19:44; cf. Matt 23:39). Jerusalem faces dire consequences, war with Rome, because they do not recognize that now is the time of deliverance, now is the day of God's visitation to his people. This language of "visitation" is also found in the Dead Sea Scrolls for the dramatic arrival of YHWH to deliver his judgment.[42] Tragically, the great day of YHWH's return has arrived, but it meets a mixed reception. If so, divine judgment may not be in Israel's favor, but might actually fall on Israel if they do not repent of their sins. All in all, Jesus returns to Jerusalem intending to enact, symbolize, and personify the climactic hope of YHWH returning to Zion. Israel's long-awaited return of the king was not the return of Aragorn to Gondor—apologies to LOTR fans—but God in Jesus of Nazareth coming to his people in a day of visitation.[43]

THE SAGA OF THE SON OF MAN

A final species of evidence we must consider is the Son of Man sayings. There is no area of discussion of Jesus more confusing and complicated as this body of material.[44] Ehrman's view is that Jesus, the good apocalyptic visionary he was, preached a message about the kingdom to be brought by the Son of Man. Yet this Son of Man was not Jesus himself but a heavenly or angelic figure. Ehrman goes so far as to say that in many of the sayings, there is no hint that Jesus is talking about himself when he mentions the Son of Man coming in judgment on the earth.[45] So did Jesus think that he was the Son of Man? I believe he did.

First, the phrase "Son of Man" in Hebrew (*ben adam*) can simply mean "human being." Think of Ps 8:4: "What is *man* [*enosh*] that you are mindful of him, or the *son of man* [*ben adam*] that you should care for him?" (NIV 1984). The verse contains synonymous parallelism so that "man" and "son of man" are identical terms for human beings, as our English translations make clear. In Ezekiel, the most frequent form of address by God for Ezekiel is "son of man," which appears to be the equivalent of something like "mere mortal" (see, e.g., Ezek 2:1, 3, 8).

The identification of "Son of Man" as signifying humanity in general has even left its imprint on the Synoptic tradition. Matthew arguably re-semitizes Mark's account of Jesus' healing of the paralytic man by underscoring the Semitic idiom at play:

> "But I want you to know that the *Son of Man* has authority on earth to forgive sins." So he said to the paralyzed man, "Get up, take your mat and go home." Then the man got up and went home. When the crowd saw this, they were filled with awe; and they praised God, who had given such authority to *man*. (Matt 9:6–8, italics added)

Matthew properly captures the meaning of the Semitic idiom by describing the crowd's elation at God giving such authority to a "man," because "Son of Man" in Hebrew and Aramaic means "man."[46]

Second, Daniel 7 was a crucial influence on Jewish and Christian messianism as it designated a human figure with royal and transcendent qualities who is enthroned beside God, and is even worshiped alongside God. In brief, Daniel 7 is a vision report about four terrifying beasts, which consecutively arise out of the sea to ravage the earth, including poor old Israel. But then the beasts are stripped of their power, and Daniel narrates:

> In my vision at night I looked, and there before me was *one like a son of man*, coming with the clouds of heaven. He approached the Ancient of Days and was led into his presence. He was given authority, glory and sovereign power; all nations and peoples of every language worshiped him. His dominion is an everlasting dominion that will not pass away, and his kingdom is one that will never be destroyed. (Dan 7:13–14, italics added)

The beasts symbolize the consecutive kingdoms of Babylon, Media, Persia, and Greece (Dan 7:17). The "one like a son of man" is a multivalent symbol for God's kingdom, God's king, and God's people. That is why the figure is closely connected with God's reign (7:13–14); he is the heavenly counterpart to the beasts, which are explicitly designated as kings (7:8, 11, 17, 23–24), and the dominion given to the human figure is the same as that given to the people of Israel (7:18, 27).

It is important to note that Daniel's "son of man" was given an explicit messianic interpretation in apocalyptic literature like *1 En. 37–71*, 4Q246 from the Qumran scrolls, obviously the Gospels, the book of Revelation, and the post-70 CE apocalypse *4 Ezra*. In the developing tradition, the Son of Man was also regarded as a heavenly and preexistent being. There is no doubt, then, that this story from Daniel influenced Jesus; on that, Ehrman and I are fully agreed.

Third, Jesus spoke Aramaic, and in Aramaic *bar enash* can have a generic meaning of "humanity," an indefinite sense of "a man" or "someone," or a definite connotation of "this man." Jesus seems to have used the Aramaic idiom as a form of self-reference, to designate himself as the person in question, or at least one within a particular class of people. In this case, Jesus probably employed *bar enash* in some instances as a form of self-reference. Consider the following:

> Jesus replied, "Foxes have dens and birds have nests, but the Son of Man has no place to lay his head." (Luke 9:58; cf. Matt 8:20)

> John the Baptist came neither eating bread nor drinking wine, and you say, "He has a demon." The Son of Man came eating and drinking, and you say, "Here is a glutton and a drunkard, a friend of tax collectors and sinners." (Luke 7:33–34; cf. Matt 11:18–19)

In these two sayings, both attributed to Q, we clearly have "Son of Man" used by Jesus as a form of self-reference, and it makes perfect sense in Aramaic as meaning something like "this man." Such sayings are probably authentic because, let's face it, who in the early church would invent the taunt of Jesus as a glutton and a drunkard, or celebrate Jesus' homelessness, so we are on good historical ground here. In light of this, I find it strange that the Aramaic background to the Son of Man sayings is never once mentioned by Ehrman.

As I said, the Son of Man material is complex because we have to deal with issues related to Aramaic idioms and how the "Son of Man" figure from Daniel 7 is interpreted in apocalyptic literature like *1 Enoch* and elsewhere. Here is what this means for Ehrman's case:

(1) If the Son of Man is a messianic figure in Jewish literature, and if Jesus thought he was the Messiah as even Ehrman admits, then what reason do we have for not thinking that Jesus referred to himself as the Son of Man? None as far as I can tell! The phrase "Son of Man" was a deliberately cryptic way of speaking about his messianic identity but still ambiguous enough to avoid creating a needless provocation to his royal aspirations.

Let me emphasize that understanding things this way avoids so many absurdities that Ehrman's view creates. For example, on Ehrman's account of Matt 19:28/Luke 22:30, the Son of Man (someone other than Jesus) sits on his glorious throne, with the twelve disciples judging Israel. But there's just one small problem in this interpretation: *Where the heck is Jesus?* The Son of Man gets a glorious throne, the disciples each get their own throne and preside over the twelve the tribes of Israel, but what does Jesus get for his efforts? A token piece of heavenly brisket? Front row seats at the Jewish comedy club in heaven? If Jesus believed himself to be, as Ehrman says, "the future ruler of Israel" and if "Jesus would be seated on the greatest throne of all, as the messiah of God," we should expect Jesus to be where the Son of Man is sitting![47] But if Jesus *is* the Son of Man in this saying, the absurdity is instantly removed.

(2) The phrase "Son of Man" is repeatedly a self-designation for Jesus across the Gospels. In fact, it meets Ehrman's own criteria for authenticity since it is in multiple sources like Mark, Q, John, and even the *Gospel of Thomas*. Not only that, but the title "Son of Man" was not even the church's preferred way of referring to Jesus. It occurs nowhere in Paul's letters, and it appears only four times in the entire New Testament outside of the Gospels (see Acts 7:56; Heb 2:6; Rev 1:13; 14:14). Moreover, in an early second-century document like the *Epistle of Barnabas*, there is a flat out denial that Jesus is the Son of Man.[48] Now that is what I call dissimilarity!

(3) In Aramaic, *bar enash* can be used in generic, indefinite, and definite ways, and when used definitely by Jesus, it either describes himself as an individual or at least as a leading individual among others. Jesus' usage of the phrase also has clear allusions to Dan 7:13 – 14 and the Son of Man figure therein described. The overwhelming testimony of the Jesus tradition is that Son of Man is an apocalyptically encoded way of Jesus self-describing his role as the one who embodies

God's authority on earth, achieves God's salvation by his death and resurrection, and shares God's glory in his enthronement. The "coming" of the Son of Man is often coterminous with the coming of God as King. Eugene Boring is surely right to conclude, "The Christological language of the Son of Man sayings is thoroughly theocentric."[49]

There is one particular saying that, I think, lets the cat out of the bag, and Jesus really outs himself not only as the Messiah, but as a Messiah enthroned with God.

> Again the high priest asked him, "Are you the Messiah, the Son of the Blessed One?"
>
> *"I am,"* said Jesus. *"And you will see the Son of Man sitting at the right hand of the Mighty One and coming on the clouds of heaven."*
>
> The high priest tore his clothes. "Why do we need any more witnesses?" he asked. "You have heard the blasphemy. What do you think?"
>
> They all condemned him as worthy of death. (Mark 14:61b–64, italics added)

The whole trial scene in the Gospels is a morass of textual, historical, and theological issues.[50] Suffice to say, it is plausible that at his trial Jesus was asked point blank by the high priest if the rumors were true; was he claiming to be the Messiah? The charge of blasphemy does not come from Jesus pronouncing the divine name, the Tetragrammaton "YHWH," when he says, "I am." More probably it comes from his conflation of Ps 110:1 and Dan 7:13 with the implication that he was going to be—or was already being—enthroned with God.[51]

Again the high priest asked him, "Are you the Messiah, the Son of the Blessed One?" "I am," said Jesus. "And you will see **the Son of Man** *sitting at the right hand* of the Mighty One and **coming on the clouds of heaven.**" (Mark 14:61–62)	In my vision at night I looked, and there before me was one like a **son of man, coming with the clouds of heaven.** (Dan 7:13)
	The LORD says to my lord: "*Sit at my right hand* until I make your enemies a footstool for your feet." (Ps 110:1)

The background to this saying and the explanation for why Jesus was thought to have committed blasphemy is something like a Jewish version of the TV show *Game of Thrones*. Does YHWH share his throne with anybody? In the previous chapter, we've already seen what happened in *3 En.* 16 when Elisha ben Abuya, who had a vision of Metatron on his throne, claimed that there were "two powers in heaven"; Elisha was summarily rebuked by God himself. Then there is the famous story of the great rabbi Akiba (died ca. 135 CE), who suggested that the plural of "thrones" in Dan 7:9 included "one for God, one for David." His proposal was apparently met with a charge of blasphemy, to which Akiba is said to have capitulated.[52] So, many Jews were fairly uncomfortable with the suggestion that Israel's Lord had a miniature throne buddy.

Yet Jesus was probably interpreting Psalm 110 and Dan 7:13–14 in a way similar to Akiba, and he sees them as referring to the Messiah's enthronement. More to the point, Jesus was clearly identifying himself with the enthroned messianic figure of Dan 7:13–14, an astounding claim to say the least, and we have no example of any person from the first century ever staking such a claim. We must remember that the whole point of Daniel 7 is that when God acted in history to deliver his people, the agent through whom he acted would be vindicated, honored, enthroned, and exalted in an unprecedented manner.[53] Jesus' claim is not that he's going to sit on his own little throne next to God; rather, he will sit at God's right hand on God's throne. If Jesus thinks that Dan 7:13–14 is about him, then he is placing himself within the orbit of divine sovereignty and claiming a place within the divine regency of God Almighty. If he's wrong, it isn't just bad theology; it is blasphemy and an affront to Jewish monotheism.

Ehrman seems to think that it was the resurrection that transformed Jesus from a failed prophet to a divine person (though only "divine" in a limited sense, like an angel or a king who becomes a god at death).[54] But that just won't do. Belief in the resurrection contributed to a Christology but did not create one from nothing. Belief in Jesus' resurrection would not mean he was the Messiah, the Son of Man, or an angel. The two witnesses in Revelation 11 rise from the dead and ascend to heaven without garnering further attention or veneration. Herod's view that John the Baptist had come back to life meant identifying him with Jesus, not with an angelic figure. In the *Testament of Job*, Job's children are killed when their house falls on them, and their bodies are taken to heaven; but no one thereafter begins to imagine that they are divine or angelic. If one of the bandits crucified with Jesus were thought to have come back to life, would anyone have seriously thought that he was the Son of Man, the Son of God, the angel of the Lord, or even God Almighty? I seriously doubt it!

The resurrection *alone* did not create a divine Christology. Easter faith did not turn Jesus into something other than what he was before. Jesus made extravagant claims about himself as to his authority, mission, and origin, and the resurrection was a divine affirmation that those claims were good. Viewed this way, the resurrection *magnified* rather than *manufactured* Jesus' claims to a divine status. Viewed this way, the resurrection *intensified* rather than *initiated* belief in Jesus' unique relationship with God. Viewed this way, the resurrection *transposed* rather than *triggered* recognition of Jesus as a divine figure. It would seem, as it does to Dale Allison, that "all the primary sources repeatedly purport that Jesus had astounding things to say about himself. One can dissociate him from an exalted self-conception only through multiple radical surgeries on our texts." Moreover, "we should hold a funeral for the view that Jesus entertained no exalted thoughts about himself."[55]

THE JOHANNINE TESTIMONY

Ehrman dismisses the gospel of John as a source about Jesus because the Johannine Jesus makes explicit claims to be equal with God that are not paralleled in the Synoptic Gospels and do not pass muster with any of the criteria of authenticity.[56] My gut response is that Ehrman's use of the criteria here amounts to trying to catch butterflies using a bazooka and a badminton net. On top of that, he basically indicts John for not being the same as the Synoptics.[57]

But, to be honest, the gospel of John does constitute something of a problem. Going from the Synoptics to John is like going from New York in peak hour traffic on Friday afternoon to a Rose Bowl parade on January 1. While many similarities exist between John and the Synoptics, John is clearly in a class of his own and is doing his own thing. That gospel has a unique texture, a distinctive feel, and a definite set of objectives.[58] My intuition is that John's gospel is indebted to the testimony of a Judean disciple of Jesus who established a church or cluster of churches in the vicinity of Ephesus. While it definitely has its own historical tradition and is a genuine source about Jesus, nonetheless this tradition has been well and truly interpreted through a pronounced theological lens. Many of its unique sayings about Jesus are probably based on a mixture of memory, metaphor, and midrash, a theological elaboration of words and impressions made by Jesus on his followers.

However, John and the Synoptics are not so different as to be like watching election night news reports by Fox News and CNN on split screens simultaneously. The four Gospels as a whole agree that Jesus is God's Son and that as the Son, he is the divine agent par excellence, and even part of the divine identity. John's claim that Jesus is "equal with God" (John 5:18) and "one with the Father" (10:18) is simply verbalizing what is already assumed by the Synoptics Gospels, namely, that Jesus has a unique filial relationship with Israel's God and Jesus possessed an authority equal to that of God.[59] For case in point, note the famous "Johannine Thunderbolt," a saying of Jesus appearing about the middle of Matthew and Luke, but which sounds strangely like the Fourth Gospel: "I praise you, Father, Lord of heaven and earth, because you have hidden these things from the wise and learned, and revealed them to little children. Yes, Father, for this is what you were pleased to do" (Matt 11:25–27/Luke 10:21–22).[60] The gospel of John expresses by way of several unique narratives and discourses that Jesus is the one-of-a-kind Son of God, whose very person is bound up with the God of Israel. It comprises a *magnification* rather than a *mutilation* of the claims of Jesus found in the Synoptic Gospels.

I think it is worth adding that John's ideas are not resourced in Greek philosophy, and they stand solidly within a Jewish conception of God's activity within the world. John actually tweets the incarnation, can you believe? I learned on Twitter the other day that John 1:14 in Greek is exactly 140 characters: "The Word became flesh and made his dwelling among us. We have seen his glory, the glory of the one and only Son, who came from the Father, full of grace and truth." John is saying that *just as* God's glory dwelt in the temple, *just as* God's wisdom dwelt in Torah, *so now* God's word dwells in human flesh. John's theology of incarnation did not emerge from an extended encounter with Hellenism; rather, incarnation is a Jewish doctrine if there ever were one.

The church's encounter with Hellenism in the following centuries has shown that rather than imagining God enfleshed, sharing in the muck and mire of human existence, what Hellenism actually pushed many toward—and some jumped at the chance—was docetism. Docetism is the view that Jesus was not really a physical human being, but more like a phantasm. On some accounts this phantom Jesus had little to do with Israel's God, but was imbued with some great ideas for spiritual self-discovery. In other words, a thoroughly Hellenized Christianity would not give us the incarnational theology of John, or Tertullian, or even Nicea; it was more likely to produce a cross between Caspar the Friendly Ghost and Dr. Phil the TV therapist!

Let's wrap things up. First, John's theology of divine sonship, while distinctive in some respects, is certainly compatible with the Synoptic Gospels and is drawn from a parallel and interlocking pool of tradition. Second, John's high Christology did not get high by inhaling the fumes of a Hellenistic philosophy that overpowered his historical sensibilities about Jesus. The gospel of John remains a thoroughly Jewish story, with its own historical contribution, and it makes an authentic interpretation of the life of Jesus as validated by the testimony of the "beloved disciple." The real historical question that folks like Ehrman need to answer is *why* there are so many parallels between the Synoptics and John and *how* did such an interpretation of Jesus as "equal with God" arise in the first place.

CONCLUSION

I believe that the topic we have engaged in this chapter is an important one. Somebody once said: "The Church cannot indefinitely continue to believe about Jesus what he did not know to be true about himself."[61] If Jesus did not think he was God, then it does not seem viable for the church to continue to profess faith in him as God. If Ehrman is right, if Jesus never claimed to be in any meaningful sense "divine," then the central claims of the Christian canon and creed are meaningless.

Ehrman claims that Jesus thought of himself as the Messiah, but not as God. He looked forward to the advent of a figure called the "Son of Man" to usher in the kingdom in the future, and material in the Gospels that explicitly identifies Jesus as divine was a later invention of the early church. I dispute these claims.

First, I began by noting some methodological problems with Ehrman's approach. Specifically, (1) Ehrman's skepticism about recovering the text of the New Testament cannot be reconciled with using the New Testament as a primary source in historical research; and (2) Ehrman's use of several alleged criteria to establish the historicity of materials is problematic and not a reliable index for determining the historical authenticity of the Gospels.

Second, Jesus' aims should be located within the context of Jewish restoration hopes for the future, and chief among those hopes was the return of YHWH to Zion. Jesus believed that in his own person this return was happening, God was becoming king, and the day of judgment and salvation was at hand. Jesus' belief on this point can be correlated with several actions and activities he undertook that suggest he not only spoke with an unmediated divine authority, but that he acted in such a way as to identify himself with God's own activity in the world.

Third, and contra Ehrman, Jesus most definitely did refer to himself as the Son of Man. The sayings about a future Son of Man still make the best sense if Jesus is speaking of himself as the principal subject (e.g., Matt 19:28/Luke 22:30). If Jesus spoke Aramaic, then *bar enash* was used by Jesus in a definite sense to refer to himself as the person spoken about. Furthermore, at Jesus' trial, he most likely spoke to the effect that he believed that he was the figure of Dan 7:13–14 and that he was rightfully enthroned beside God.

Fourth, the evidence of the gospel of John contributes much to our understanding of Jesus, albeit obliquely. The Johannine Evangelist interprets the Jesus tradition in a specific theological trajectory, but he shares with the other Evangelists a conception of Jesus as the Messiah and one-of-kind Son of God, in whom God is definitively revealed.

If I am right, if this argument has cogency and substance, I think the summation of Craig Evans is a perfectly apt way of putting it: "The New Testament's deification of Jesus Christ, as seen especially in the theologies of Paul and the fourth evangelist, has its roots in the words and activities of the historical Jesus."[62]

CHAPTER 4

Getting the Burial Traditions and Evidences Right

Craig A. Evans

INTRODUCTION

In chapters 4 and 5 Bart Ehrman rightly underscores the importance of the resurrection of Jesus for his followers' growing appreciation of their Master's divine identity. However, he also arrives at a number of negative conclusions that must be challenged. Among these is the idea that the burial of Jesus in a known tomb is a late fiction and that therefore there probably was no tomb discovered by his followers. Indeed, Ehrman believes it unlikely that Jesus was even buried. Another negative conclusion that must be challenged is the claim that the discovery of an empty tomb—assuming that such a discovery was actually made—would have played little or no role in awakening faith in Jesus' followers. I will address at length the first negative claim and will then offer a few brief comments regarding the second.

WAS THE BODY OF JESUS PLACED IN A TOMB?

Ehrman believes that the burial of Jesus in a tomb and the subsequent discovery of the tomb empty "are unlikely."[1] He thinks the story of the burial and discovery was a later development, perhaps originating in Christian circles where women were influential. He argues for this on the basis that no tomb is mentioned in the earliest creed and on the basis of history and archaeology. I begin with the first point, the nonmention of a tomb in the earliest creed.

The earliest creed to which Ehrman refers is Paul's summation of the "gospel" in his letter to the Christians of Corinth. The original creed, Ehrman thinks, may have looked something like this:[2]

>1a Christ died
>>2a For our sins
>>>3a In accordance with the Scriptures
>>>>4a And he was buried.
>1b Christ was raised
>>2b On the third day
>>>3b In accordance with the Scriptures
>>>>4b And he appeared to Cephas.

1 Cor 15:3b–5a

Why doesn't Paul speak of Jesus buried *in a tomb*? Moreover, why isn't Joseph of Arimathea, the man who buried Jesus mentioned by name? After all, the creed states that Jesus "was seen by Cephas [Peter]." (The RSV translates "appeared to Cephas," but the Greek literally reads "was seen by Cephas.") Ehrman makes much of the nonappearance of a name associated with the burial of Jesus.[3] He reasons that 4a ("And he was buried") should parallel more closely 4b (lit., "And he was seen by Cephas" [i.e., Peter]). If Jesus had really been buried by one Joseph of Arimathea, as the Gospels relate (Matt 27:57–60; Mark 15:42–46; Luke 23:50–56), then why doesn't 4a read, "And he was buried by Joseph"? Ehrman believes that the author of the creed "surely would have included" reference to Joseph, a respected member of the Jewish Council, had he known of such a tradition.[4]

The nonappearance of Joseph's name leads Ehrman to conclude that the "tradition that there was a specific, known person who buried Jesus appears to have been a later one."[5] He further notes that in Paul's speech in Acts nothing is said of Jesus being buried by Joseph.[6] All we hear is the vague "they took him down from the tree, and laid him in a tomb" (Acts 13:29).[7] Ehrman believes he has found a discrepancy, telling us that "here it is not a single member of the Sanhedrin who buries Jesus, but the council as a whole. This is a different tradition. There is no word of Joseph here, any more than there is in Paul's letters."[8] Ehrman also underscores the Roman practice of not allowing someone crucified to be buried, which casts further doubt on the story about Joseph of Arimathea.

All of this leads Ehrman to suspect that Jesus was probably not buried, or if he was, his disciples did not know where. Accordingly, the discovery of the empty tomb is probably a later fiction and therefore the empty tomb and missing body of Jesus did not really play any role in early Christianity's understanding of Jesus' resurrection and divinity.

There are several problems in the position Ehrman has taken here. His description of Roman policy relating to crucifixion and non-burial is unnuanced and incomplete, especially as it relates to policy and practice in Israel in the time of Jesus. His arguments relating to Joseph of Arimathea do not take into account Jewish law and custom. He has also failed to take into account the archaeological evidence. We will now address these topics.

What was Rome's Policy regarding the Burial of the Crucified?

It is often stated that people crucified in the Roman Empire were not buried but were left hanging on the cross to rot and be picked apart by animals and birds. There are some gruesome references to this in ancient writings. Horace (ca. 25 BCE) speaks of "hanging on a cross to feed crows" (*Epistles* 1.16.48). Suetonius (ca. 110 CE) reports that an angry Octavian (ca. 42 BCE) assured a man about to be executed (probably by crucifixion) who had expressed concern about this burial, "The birds will soon settle the question" (*Augustus* 13.2). Juvenal (ca. 125 CE) gives expression to gallows humor when he says, "The vulture hurries from dead cattle and dogs and crosses to bring some of the carrion to her offspring" (*Satires* 14.77–78). A third-century text describes the crucifixion victim as "evil food for birds of prey and grim picking for dogs" (*Apotelesmatica* 4.200). On a second-century epitaph the deceased declares that his murderer, a slave, was "crucified alive for the wild beasts and birds" (Amyzon, cave I). Many other texts spare readers such gruesome details, but do mention the denial of proper burial (e.g., Livy 29.9.10; 29.18.14).[9]

With evidence such as this in mind, Ehrman argues that the body of Jesus was probably not taken down from the cross and buried, especially in light of the fact that it was by Roman authority that Jesus was put to death. He states: "It was not Jews who killed Jesus, and so they had no say about when he would be taken down from the cross. Moreover, the Romans who did crucify him had no concern to obey Jewish law and virtually no interest in Jewish sensitivities."[10] Later Ehrman adds that "what *normally* happened to a criminal's body is that it was left to decompose and serve as food for scavenging animals."[11]

In fact, we are not sure how "normal" leaving the corpse on the cross, unburied, was in the Roman Empire. That it often happened is not in dispute. But the evidence is more variegated than Ehrman and others have assumed. An interesting passage that bears on this question is found in Philo (ca. 20 BCE–50 CE), in his account of the malfeasance and demise of Flaccus, the governor of Egypt. Ehrman cites and discusses this passage, in which mention is made of mercy shown victims of crucifixion. Here is part of the quotation:

> I have known cases when on the eve of a holiday of this kind, people who have been crucified have been taken down and their bodies delivered to their kinsfolk, because it was thought well to give them burial and allow them the ordinary rites. For it was meet that the dead also should have the advantage of some kind treatment upon the birthday of the emperor and also that the sanctity of the festival should be maintained. (*Flaccus* 83)

Philo is building his case against Flaccus, the Roman governor of Egypt appointed in 32 CE. Philo claims that although the governor served well enough in his first five years in office, things changed when Emperor Tiberius was succeeded by Caligula in 37 CE. Thereafter Flaccus not only did nothing to curb pagan hostilities toward the Jewish population of Alexandria, but he actually encouraged it. Philo complains of the insults visited on the recently appointed Agrippa I when he visited Alexandria: the desecration of synagogues, the looting of Jewish homes, and the flogging and crucifixion of some of the Jewish councilors—on the day of the emperor's birthday no less. The fact that these poor men were crucified and then denied burial on a day when normally mercy is shown (and the anti-Semitic Alexandrians knew full well how important burial was to Jews) only underscores the brutality and callousness of the governor's behavior.

Ehrman thinks this passage offers no support for the New Testament Gospels' report that Pilate permitted the body of Jesus to be taken down from the cross and be properly buried. He thinks it is the "exception that proves the rule," that is, that the bodies of crucifixion victims were not normally buried, "because it goes *against* established practice."[12] Ehrman further notes "the cases when on the eve of a holiday of this kind" involved families of influence, and that the "holiday of this kind" was a Roman holiday (e.g., the birthday of an emperor), not a Jewish holiday (such as Passover). Accordingly, Ehrman thinks Philo's passage lends no support to the New Testament Gospels' narrative of Jesus' burial. Had Jesus been crucified in Alexandria, Ehrman's point would be well taken. But Jesus was crucified in Jerusalem, in the land of Israel, where very different political and religious factors were in play. I will return to this point shortly.

What is important in the *Flaccus* passage for the matter at hand is that this sorry incident demonstrates that it was in fact Roman practice, under various circumstances, to permit bodies of the crucified to be taken down and be buried. If there was no such Roman practice, this part of Philo's complaint loses all force. Indeed, the Romans not only permitted the bodies of the executed, including the crucified, to be buried; they even pardoned those in prison and sometimes even pardoned those awaiting or faced with the threat of execution, whether by crucifixion or other means.

The Roman practice of granting clemency is attested in a variety of sources. We find in a text dating to about 85 CE, the words of Septimius Vegetus, governor of Egypt, addressed to one accused of a serious crime: "You were worthy of scourging ... but I give you to the crowds."[13] Pliny the Younger, governor of Bithynia in Asia Minor in the early second century, speaks of those imprisoned being released. Under what circumstances and under whose authority was his only concern (*Epistles* 10.31). An inscription from Ephesus relates the decision of the proconsul of Asia to release prisoners because of the outcries of the people of the city.[14] Livy (5.13.8) speaks of special dispensations whereby chains were removed from the limbs of prisoners.

What these examples show is that on some occasions Roman officials, serving in various capacities and at various ranks, sometimes showed mercy to the condemned. This mercy at times extended to those who had been crucified. Clemency sometimes was occasioned by a holiday, whether Roman or a local non-Roman holiday, or simply out of political expediency, whatever the motivation. We actually have evidence that Roman justice not only allowed for the executed to be buried, but it even encouraged it in some instances. We find in the summary of Roman law (known as the *Digesta*) the following recommendations:

> The bodies of those who are condemned to death should not be refused their relatives; and the Divine Augustus, in the Tenth Book of his *Life*, said that this rule had been observed. At present, the bodies of those who have been punished are only buried when this has been requested and permission granted; and sometimes it is not permitted, especially where persons have been convicted of high treason. Even the bodies of those who have been sentenced to be burned can be claimed, in order that their bones and ashes, after having been collected, may be buried. (48.24.1)

> The bodies of persons who have been punished should be given to whoever requests them for the purpose of burial. (48.24.3)

This summation of Roman law makes it clear that bodies were sometimes released to family and friends. (The whole of *Digesta* book 48 is concerned with criminal prosecution and punishment.) Indeed, the *Digesta* argues that the bodies of the executed "*should* be given to whoever requests them for the purpose of burial" (emphasis added). In light of what we read here and in light of what we find in other sources, it is simply erroneous to assert that the Romans did not permit the burial of the executed, including the crucified. Bodies were in fact released to those who requested them.

Josephus himself makes this request of Titus, son of Vespasian, and Titus granted it (*Life* 420–21). Of course, Roman authorities often did not permit burial, request or no request, especially in cases of "high treason," as the *Digesta* states. Nonburial was part of the horror—and the deterrent—of crucifixion. But crucifixion, especially during peacetime, just outside the walls of Jerusalem was another matter. Given Jewish sensitivities and customs, burial would have been expected, even demanded.

We do have evidence that relates to Roman acts of clemency in Israel itself. When Governor Albinus (procurator of Israel, 62–64 CE) prepared to leave office, he released all prisoners incarcerated for offenses other than murder (Josephus, *Antiquities* 20.215). The Mishnah (a compendium of rabbinic interpretations of the laws of Moses) says that "they may slaughter (the Passover lamb) for one ... whom they have promised to bring out of prison" on the Passover (*m. Pesaḥim* 8:6).[15] Who the "they" are is not made clear (Jewish authorities? Roman authorities?), but it is interesting that the promised release from prison is for the express purpose of taking part in Passover. In her book on Pontius Pilate, Helen Bond comments: "Pilate, and possibly other governors, may have occasionally released lesser criminals as a gesture of Roman goodwill, especially during such a potentially volatile festival as the Passover."[16]

Peacetime administration in Palestine appears to have respected Jewish burial sensitivities. Indeed, both Philo and Josephus claim that Roman administration in fact did acquiesce to Jewish customs. In his appeal to Caesar, Philo draws attention to the Jews who "appealed to Pilate to redress the infringement of their traditions caused by the shields and *not to disturb the customs which throughout all the preceding ages had been safeguarded without disturbance by kings and by emperors*" (*Embassy to Gaius* 300, emphasis added). In saying "without disturbance by kings and by emperors," Philo is speaking of *foreign*—not *Jewish*—kings. In his day "emperor" would refer to the Roman emperor. The whole force of his argument is that it had been customary of Roman authority to respect the customs of the Jewish people. This should come as no surprise, for the relationship between Rome and Israel started out on a friendly footing in the second century BCE, when Rome supported the Hasmoneans in their bid to free themselves from the Seleucid kingdom. The alliance between Rome and Israel was further strengthened in the time of Herod the Great and continued, though in weakened and less stable form, under his sons and successors.

A generation later, Josephus asserts the same thing. The Romans, he says, do not require "their subjects to violate their national laws" (*Against Apion* 2.73). The Jewish historian and apologist adds that the Roman procurators who succeeded Agrippa I "by abstaining from all interference with the customs of the country kept the nation at peace" (*Jewish War* 2.220), customs that included never leaving a "corpse unburied" (*Against Apion* 2.211). Had Roman governors—in Israel, especially in the vicinity of Jerusalem itself—regularly crucified Jews and left their bodies hanging on crosses, it is unlikely they would have "kept the nation at peace."

One of the incidents involving Pilate that Ehrman mentions supports the point I am making. I refer to the incident in which Pilate attempted to place Roman standards, bearing images of the emperor, in Jerusalem (Josephus, *Antiquities* 18.55–59). Josephus explains that Jewish law forbids the making of images (Exod 20:4) and that for this reason previous Roman governors *never attempted* to bring such images into the holy city. (What would have made these images especially offensive in Jewish eyes is that the Roman emperor was considered divine, a "son of god." Such images then would constitute a clear violation of the command not to make images of God or of other deities.) That the previous Roman governors never attempted to bring images into the city shows that Roman authority did indeed respect Jewish law and custom in Israel (and often outside Israel as well).

Pilate either did not understand Jewish law and custom and so acted in ignorance, or he did, thinking he could force on his Jewish subjects his allegiance to the emperor. In either case, he quickly learned how loyal the Jews were to their law and wisely backed down.[17] I find it hard to believe that later, acting in concert with the ruling priests in the execution of Jesus, on the eve of Passover, just outside the walls of Jerusalem, he would have defied Jewish law and sensitivities by not permitting the bodies of Jesus and the other two men to be taken down and buried prior to nightfall. (The ruling priests were ultimately responsible for the purity of Jerusalem, and they and the Sanhedrin were responsible for the proper burial of executed persons — more on this below.) Had Pilate and other Roman governors of Israel in the 6–66 CE period of time regularly crucified people (whether Jewish or Gentile) and left their bodies hanging on the cross unburied, thus defiling the land, there would have been riots, if not uprisings.[18]

Josephus applies this point specifically to crucifixion when he says, in reference to the rebels who had seized control of Jerusalem in 66 CE and killed some of the hated ruling priests: "They actually went so far in their impiety as to cast out their dead bodies without burial, although the Jews are so careful about burial rites [*peri tas taphas*], that *even malefactors who have been sentenced to crucifix-*

ion are taken down and buried before sunset" (*Jewish War* 4.317, italics added). Those "sentenced to crucifixion" in the time of Josephus were people crucified *by the Romans* (and not by Jewish rulers, such as the Hasmoneans). And although crucified by the Romans, these unfortunates were "taken down and buried before sunset."

The reference to being "buried before sunset" alludes to the law of the execution and burial of criminals in Deut 21:22–23: "And if a man has committed a crime punishable by death and he is put to death, and you hang him on a tree, his body shall not remain all night upon the tree, but you shall bury him the same day, for a hanged man is accursed by God; you shall not defile your land which the LORD your God gives you for an inheritance." This is, of course, an old Mosaic law. Was it observed in the time of Jesus?

After crucifixion came to be practiced in Israel (probably first by the Persians, then later by the Greeks, Hasmoneans, and Romans), Deuteronomy 21 was paraphrased in a new way, as we see in the Temple Scroll found at Qumran:

> If a man is a traitor against his people and gives them up to a foreign nation, so doing evil to his people, you are to hang him on a tree until dead. On the testimony of two or three witnesses he will be put to death, and they themselves shall hang him on the tree. If a man is convicted of a capital crime and flees to the nations, cursing his people and the children of Israel, you are to hang him, also, upon a tree until dead. But you must not let their bodies remain on the tree overnight; you shall most certainly bury them that very day. Indeed, anyone hung on a tree is accursed of God and men, but you are not to defile the land that I am about to give you as an inheritance. (11Q19 64:7–13a)[19]

Deuteronomy's order of "put to death," then "hang on tree," is reversed in the Temple Scroll, where it is "hang on tree," then "until dead" (twice, first in lines 8 and again in 10–11). Most interpreters believe the Temple Scroll's reversal of Deuteronomy's sequence reflects the practice of crucifixion, to which the people of Israel had become accustomed when the Temple Scroll was written (first century BCE). What is interesting is that the Temple Scroll, like Deuteronomy, commands Israel to bury the executed "that very day." Their bodies were not to "remain on the tree overnight" (line 11). Failure to take the body down and bury it is to defile the land (line 12). This is the key point. The concern, above all, is to avoid defiling the land. In the passage quoted earlier, Josephus confirms that the law of Deuteronomy 21, even during the first century CE, when Rome governed Israel, was still very much in force.

Every source we have indicates that this was the practice in Israel, especially in the vicinity of Jerusalem, in peacetime. War was another matter, of course. When Titus besieged Jerusalem from 69 to 70 CE, thousands of Jews were crucified and very few of them were buried. The whole point was to terrorize the resistance and bring the rebellion to an end (as recounted by Josephus, *Jewish War* 5.289, 449). This was the true "exception that proves the rule": Roman authority in Israel normally did permit burial of executed criminals, including those executed by crucifixion (as Josephus implies), but they did not during the rebellion of 66–70 CE.

There is another important point that needs to be made. The process that led to the execution of Jesus, and perhaps also the two men crucified with him, was *initiated by the Jewish Council*. According to law and custom, when the Jewish Council (or Sanhedrin) condemned someone to death, by whatever means, it fell to the council to have that person buried. The executed were to be buried properly, but not in places of honor, such as the family tomb. This is clearly taught in the earliest writings of the rabbis: "They did not bury (the executed criminal) in the burying-place of his fathers. But two burying-places were kept in readiness *by the Sanhedrin*, one for them that were beheaded or strangled, and one for them that were stoned or burnt" (*m. Sanhedrin* 6:5, italics added). "Neither a corpse nor the bones of a corpse may be transferred from a wretched place to an honored place, nor, needless to say, from an honored placed to a wretched place; but if to the family tomb, even from an honored place to a wretched place, it is permitted" (*Semaḥot* 13.7).

Not only was the body of a criminal not to be buried in a place of honor, no public mourning for executed criminals was permitted: "they used not to make [open] lamentation ... for mourning has place in the heart alone" (*m. Sanhedrin* 6:6). None of this law would make any sense if executed criminals were not in fact buried. There would have been no need to set aside tombs for executed criminals. There would simply be no remains to transfer from a "wretched place" to an "honored place."

The Jewish Council was responsible to oversee the proper burial of the executed because their bodies were normally not surrendered to family and friends. The burial of the executed in "wretched places," that is, in tombs set aside for criminals, was part of the punishment. No public mourning and lamentation were permitted. The remains of the executed could not be transferred from these dishonorable tombs for one year. After one year (see *b. Qiddušin* 31b), the remains could be taken by family members to the family tomb or to some other place of honor.

The Jewish Council, in concert with the aristocratic priesthood (some of whom were members of the council), was charged with protecting the purity of the sanctuary, the temple precincts, Jerusalem, and the land. This sensitivity is clearly witnessed in texts and artifacts from the first century and earlier. One thinks of the inscriptions that warn Gentiles not to get too close to the sanctuary; if they do, they will be executed (*OGIS* no. 598; *CIJ* no. 1400; Philo, *Embassy to Gaius* 212; Josephus, *Jewish War* 5.193–94; *Antiquities* 12.145; cf. Num 1:51 "if anyone else comes near [the tabernacle], he shall be put to death"). According to Acts, Paul was nearly beaten to death when he was accused of defiling the sanctuary by bringing Gentiles into the restricted area (Acts 21:27–32).

One thinks also of some of the Qumran scrolls, which reflect priestly concerns for purity. According to one scroll, the reason God drove out the Canaanites, to make room for Israel, was because the Promised Land under the care of Gentiles had become "doubly filthy through impurity" (4Q381 frag. 69, lines 1–3). With Israel now in the land, the land "will be pure" (ibid., line 6). Another scroll, concerned with the bloody aftermath of the destruction of the Kittim (i.e., the Romans), charges Israel's high priest to oversee the cleansing of Israel from the "guilty blood of the corpses" of the Romans slain in the final great battle (4Q285 frag. 7, lines 5b–6 = 11Q14 frag. 1, col. i, lines 14–15). Similar ideas are expressed in early rabbinic tradition, where we hear that "the land of Israel is clean" (*m. Miqwa'ot* 8:1) and that "he who walks in the land of the gentiles in the hills or in rocks is unclean" (*m. 'Ohaloth* 18:6). (These concerns with maintaining the purity of Jerusalem and the land, as well as the obligation to bury those condemned to death by the Jewish Council, are relevant for understanding the role played by Joseph of Arimathea, which will be considered shortly.)

In the time of the Roman governors (6–66 CE) the Jewish Council lacked the authority to execute anyone. To do so, they had to present their case before the Roman authority. This is mentioned in the gospel of John, where the Jewish authorities acknowledge: "It is not lawful for us to put any man to death" (John 18:31). This is no fiction. Josephus provides important support. The first Roman governor sent to Judea in 6 CE, to replace the deposed ethnarch Archelaus, was "entrusted by Augustus with full powers, including the infliction of capital punishment" (Josephus, *Jewish War* 2.117). That these full powers, including capital punishment, remained in the hands of the Roman governor *alone* in the decades leading up to the Jewish revolt is witnessed in the murder of James the brother of Jesus and its aftermath. Josephus describes the incident, which took place in 62 CE shortly after the death of the Roman governor Festus. The account begins with reference to the audacity of the younger Annas, the son of Annas the high priest (Luke 3:2; John 18:13, 24; Acts 4:6).

> The younger Annas, who, as we have said, had been appointed to the high priesthood, was rash in his temper and unusually daring. He followed the school of the Sadducees, who are indeed more heartless than any of the other Jews, as I have already explained, when they sit in judgment. Possessed of such a character, Annas thought that he had a favorable opportunity because Festus was dead and Albinus was still on the way. And so he convened the judges of the Sanhedrin and brought before them a man named James, the brother of Jesus who was called the Christ, and certain others. He accused them of having transgressed the law and delivered them up to be stoned. Those of the inhabitants of the city who were considered the most fair-minded and who were strict in observance of the law were offended at this. They therefore secretly sent to the King Agrippa urging him, for Annas had not even been correct in his first step, to order him to desist from any further such actions. Certain of them even went to meet Albinus, who was on his way from Alexandria, and informed him that Annas had no authority to convene the Sanhedrin without his consent. Convinced by these words, Albinus angrily wrote to Annas threatening to take vengeance upon him. King Agrippa, because of Annas' action, deposed him from the high priesthood which he had held for three months and replaced him with Jesus the son of Damnaeus. (*Antiquities* 20.199–203)[20]

Josephus makes it clear that Annas the younger committed two breaches of policy and law: he convened the Sanhedrin, which was a breach of policy, and he executed James and "certain others" (probably also Christians), which was a breach of law, for only the Roman governor possessed the power of capital punishment, something Roman authority took very seriously.[21] Josephus notes that the "fair-minded" of Jerusalem urged King Agrippa to order Annas "to desist from any further such actions." Reference to "any further such actions" may imply that Annas was planning a major pogrom against the Christian movement.

In any event, when Albinus, the newly appointed governor, was informed of what had happened, he was angry and threatened to punish Annas. No doubt wishing to reestablish his own credibility in the eyes of Rome, the Jewish puppet king, Agrippa II, deposed Annas and replaced him with a member of a rival priestly family.

The evidence shows that the Jewish priestly aristocracy and the Jewish Council (or Sanhedrin) could condemn someone to death but could not carry out capital punishment (unless there was a serious infraction within the temple precincts themselves). Only the Roman authority held capital authority.

The Archaeological Evidence

We actually possess archaeological evidence from the time of Jesus that confirms the claims we find in Philo, Josephus, the New Testament, and early rabbinic literature, to the effect that executed persons, including victims of crucifixion, were probably buried.

The discovery in 1968 of an ossuary (ossuary no. 4 in Tomb I, at Giv'at ha-Mivtar) of a Jewish man named Yehohanan, who had obviously been crucified, provides archaeological evidence and insight into how Jesus himself may have been crucified. The ossuary and its contents date to the late 20s CE, that is during the administration of Pilate, the very Roman governor who condemned Jesus to the cross. The remains of an iron spike (11.5 cm in length) are plainly seen still encrusted in the right heel bone (or calcaneum; see fig. 2). Those who took down the body of Yehohanan apparently were unable to remove the spike, with the result that a piece of wood (from an oak tree) remained affixed to the spike. Later, the skeletal remains of the

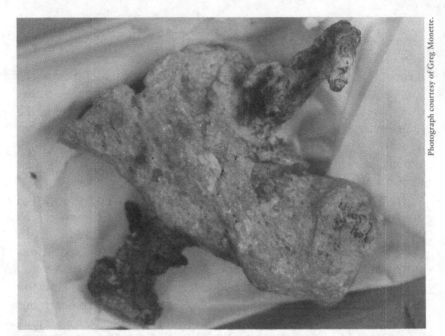

Photograph courtesy of Greg Monette.

FIGURE 2 Striking a knot in the wood, or perhaps the end of another nail, the sharp end of the nail became fish-hooked, making it impossible to extract. Yehohanan was buried with the nail still in his heel.

body—spike, fragment of wood, and all—were placed in the ossuary. Forensic examination of the rest of the skeletal remains supports the view that Yehohanan was crucified with arms apart, hung from a horizontal beam or tree branch. However, there is no evidence that his arms, or wrists, were nailed to this cross beam.

Yehohanan's leg bones were broken, but there is disagreement over how and when they were broken (i.e., while still on the cross, or after being taken down). Some think that the breaks in the lower leg bones of Yehohanan, including the cut to the talus bone of the foot, are due to *crurifragium*, the breaking of a victim's bones to hasten his death. Others do not think the talus suffered such an injury. Indeed, the talus under question may actually belong to one of the other two individuals, whose skeletal remains had been placed in the ossuary. Accordingly, the conclusion that Yehohanan's leg bones were broken before death and decarnation is disputed. Because of the age and degraded condition of the skeletal materials, a measure of uncertainty remains.

If Yehohanan's legs were broken before death, we then know not only that he was taken down and buried (as indicated by the discovery of his remains in an ossuary), we also know that his death was intentionally hastened. The most likely and most compelling reason for hastening death in this manner was so that his corpse could be taken down from the cross and placed in a tomb before nightfall, as commanded in the law of Moses (Deut 21:22–23) and as Jewish custom required. The Romans had no reason of their own to expedite death by crucifixion, but they permitted it for reasons discussed above.

In Giv'at Ha-Mivtar's Tomb D were the remains of a man (aged 50), who had been decapitated. Two strokes were required to take off the man's head, which was the norm in antiquity.[22] Although he had been executed (possibly for murdering a relative interred in Tomb C), he was buried properly, first (we may assume) in a place of dishonor, and then later in an ossuary in his family tomb.

Perhaps the most dramatic recent development is the reassessment of the nails, skeletal materials, and inscription from the so-called Abba Cave in Jerusalem, also in the neighborhood of Giv'at Ha-Mivtar. The cave was discovered in 1970 and on the inside wall was found a remarkable inscription, in Palaeo-Hebrew script (i.e., Hebrew written in very old forms of letters), that identifies the occupant of an ornate ossuary as one "Mattathias son of Judah." In 1974 J. M. Grintz published a brief study in which he concluded that the inscription referred to none other than Antigonus son Aristobulus II, whose Hebrew name was Mattathias son of Judah, the last Hasmonean ruler, the man defeated by Herod the Great in 37 BCE.[23] Grintz's interpretation was supported by Nicu Haas later that year. Haas described the skeletal remains as belonging to a tall man in his mid-twenties, which would have been the age of Antigonus son of Aristobulus II at the time of his death. A recent study by Yoel Elitzur has confirmed the views of Grintz and Haas.[24] In all likelihood, the ossuary and skeletal remains of the last Hasmonean prince have been discovered.

What makes this case interesting is that Mattathias/Antigonus had suffered both crucifixion and beheading. According to Josephus, Marcus Antonius *beheaded* Antigonus in Antioch (Josephus,

Antiquities 15.8–9; cf. Plutarch, *Life of Antony* 36.4). Dio Cassius seemingly contradicts Josephus when he specifically refers to *crucifixion*, but his full statement can be harmonized with what Josephus says. The Roman historian says: "Antony bound Antigonus to a cross and flogged him—a punishment no other king had suffered at the hands of the Romans—and afterwards he slew him" (*History* 22.6). The slaying "afterwards" probably refers to beheading, which is what Josephus relates.

This is what Haas thought had happened to the man whose skeleton remains were recovered from the Abba Cave. He had been nailed to a cross (and three nails, still bearing traces of human calcium, were recovered from the ossuary)[25] and then (after passing out?) was beheaded, either with a sword or very sharp axe.

How many other skeletons have been recovered of persons executed by crucifixion, beheading, or strangulation is hard to say. If the neck bones are fairly well preserved (and they often are not), signs of decapitation are pretty clear (as in the case of Mattathias/Antigonus and the man in Giv'at Ha-Mivtar Tomb D). Signs of strangulation would be almost impossible to detect, while signs of crucifixion are also difficult to detect because the bones that would show these signs (i.e., hands, wrists, feet, ankles) are bones that rarely survive intact. Indeed, had the iron nail, with its fish-hooked sharp end that made extraction impossible, not remained imbedded in Yehohanan's right heel, I doubt anyone would have thought that the poor man had been crucified.[26] Of all the human skeletons that have been recovered from tombs in and around Jerusalem (and other locations in Israel), we simply do not know how many had been executed, by whatever means.[27]

But there are indications that suggest that many executed persons, including victims of crucifixion, were given proper burial. I refer to the discovery of dozens, perhaps more than one hundred, nails that have been recovered from tombs and ossuaries, some of which bear traces of human calcium. These nails, especially those with traces of calcium, were used in crucifixion and, strangely, were viewed as talismans.[28] The presence of calcium, sometimes encircling the nail, indicates its use in crucifixion and suggests that the corpse, still pierced by the nails, was buried and sometime later (when the calcium had adhered to the nail) the nails were recovered and put to new use (see **fig. 3**).[29]

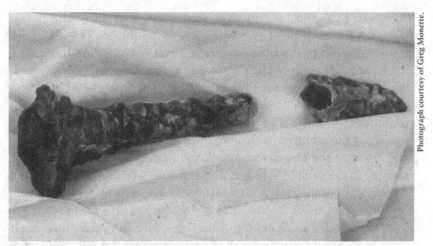

Photograph courtesy of Greg Monette.

FIGURE 3 Nails found in or near the Caiaphas Ossuary are thought to have been used in crucifixion. Many of these nails were probably buried with the remains of the executed. After the passage of time, human calcium and bone became attached and remained attached even after the nails were recovered and put to secondary usage.

What about Joseph of Arimathea—Did He Bury Jesus?

The Jewish people buried their dead, then later gathered the bones and placed them in containers called ossuaries or a vault set aside for this purpose. The practice of gathering the bones of the deceased is called ossilegium, or secondary burial (cf. *y. Mo'ed Qaṭan* 1.5: "At first they would bury them in ditches, and when the flesh had decayed, they would gather the bones and bury them in ossuaries").

Burial took place the day of death or, if death occurred at the end of the day or during the night, burial took place the following day. Knowing this lends a great deal of pathos to some otherwise familiar gospel stories (see Matt 9:23; Luke 7:12). Following death, the body was washed and wrapped. We can find this custom mentioned in several episodes in the Gospels and elsewhere. We see it in the story of Lazarus, who was bound and wrapped with cloths (John 11:44). The body of Jesus was wrapped in a clean linen shroud (Matt 27:59; Luke 23:53; John 19:40). The body of Ananias was wrapped and buried (Acts 5:6); so also Dorcas, who "fell sick and died; and when they had washed her, they laid her in an upper room" (Acts 9:37).

Moreover, the corpse was usually perfumed (Josephus, *Antiquities* 15.61; for spices, see *Antiquities* 17.196–99; John 19:39–40).

The day of burial was the first of seven days of mourning (*Semaḥot* 12.1). This is clearly stated by first-century Jewish historian Josephus, in reference to the death, burial, and funeral of Herod the Great (d. 4 BCE): "Now Archelaus [Herod's oldest surviving son] continued to mourn for seven days out of respect for his father—the custom of the country prescribes this number of days—and then, after feasting the crowds and making an end of the mourning, he went up to the temple" (Josephus, *Antiquities* 17.200). The custom of seven days of mourning arose from Scripture itself: Joseph "made a mourning for his father seven days" (Gen 50:10); and, in reference to the remains of King Saul and his sons, Israelite men "took their bones and buried them under the tamarisk tree in Jabesh, and fasted seven days" (1 Sam 31:13).

One year after death it was customary to gather the bones and place them in a bone niche or in an ossuary. This is readily observed in the archaeological excavations of Jewish tombs in the time of Jesus. It is also attested in later rabbinic literature: "When the flesh had wasted away they gathered together the bones and buried them in their own place" (*m. Sanhedrin* 6:6); "My son, bury me at first in a niche. In the course of time, collect my bones and put them in an ossuary but do not gather them with your own hands" (*Semaḥot* 12.9; cf. *Semaḥot* 3.2). As already noted, the custom of the interval of twelve months from primary burial to secondary burial is also attested in rabbinic literature (cf. *b. Qiddušin* 31b).

I have already discussed how burial practices for the executed were at some points different. For them there could be no public lamentation. They could not be buried in their family tomb or any place of honor. For them awaited tombs reserved for criminals. In these "wretched places" their corpses had to remain for one year. When the flesh had wasted away, their bones could be collected and taken to the family tomb. According to Jewish law, it was the responsibility of the council to bury the executed (at least in Jerusalem; the traditions elsewhere in Israel may have been different).

It is against this legal and cultural backdrop that the story of Joseph of Arimathea should be understood. Because the Jewish

Council (or Sanhedrin) delivered Jesus to the Roman authorities for execution, it was incumbent upon it to arrange for proper burial (as in *m. Sanhedrin* 6:5, cited above). This task fell to Joseph of Arimathea, a member of the council. The gospel narratives are completely in step with Jewish practice, which Roman authorities during peacetime respected. Joseph may have volunteered for this assignment, perhaps because he felt pity for the family of Jesus or because he sympathized with some of Jesus' aims. He may have volunteered to show this mercy as a way of registering his disapproval of Caiaphas and supporters.[30] His request (Mark 15:43; Greek: *aitein*) for the body of Jesus reflects the language used in petitioning officials in Roman late antiquity (see P.Pintaudi 52 [29 CE], where one is directed to approach an official and make a request [*aitein*]; and O.Did. 344 [ca. 80 CE], where an officer promises to make a request [*aitein*] on behalf of a lower-ranking solider).

Pilate's response to Joseph's request, in which he inquires into Jesus' condition (Mark 15:44), reflects the practice of Roman officials (see P.Oxy. 475 [182 CE]: "take a public physician and view the dead body that has been shown and having delivered it up for burial make a report in writing"; P.Oxy. 51 [173 CE], in which an official orders the inspection of a corpse).

In short, there is nothing irregular about the Gospels' report that a member of the Sanhedrin requested permission to take down the body of Jesus and give it proper burial, in keeping with Jewish burial practices as they related to the executed. It is entirely in keeping with all that we know from the literature and from archaeology. This is why Jodi Magness, a Jewish archaeologist who serves on the faculty of the University of North Carolina at Chapel Hill, is able to say that the "Gospel accounts of Jesus' burial are largely consistent with the archaeological evidence. Although archaeology does not prove there was a follower of Jesus named Joseph of Arimathea or that Pontius Pilate granted his request for Jesus' body, *the Gospel accounts describing Jesus' removal from the cross and burial are consistent with archaeological evidence and with Jewish law.*"[31] When all of the relevant evidence is considered, we should conclude that it is probable that the body of Jesus, in keeping with Jewish customs of his time, was given proper burial.

THE ROLE OF THE EMPTY TOMB AND THE BELIEF THAT JESUS HAD BEEN RESURRECTED

Ehrman makes light of the tradition that women observed where Jesus was buried and were the first to find the tomb empty.[32] But if the gospel stories were filled with as much fiction as Ehrman thinks, one must wonder why the Evangelists did not alter the stories and give more prominence to men. However prominent and influential women may have been in early Christian leadership (and the appeal to Junia the apostle in Rom 16:7 is appropriate), the male Evangelists would surely have been aware that having women as first discoverers of the empty tomb would make it easier for skeptics—Jewish and Gentile alike—to raise doubts. This in fact happened, as we see in the mocking challenges offered by pagan skeptics like Celsus and Porphyry. The second century *Gospel of Peter*, which claims that hostile Jewish leaders and Romans, along with the male disciples themselves, witnessed the resurrection, was composed to answer that criticism.[33]

The closest followers of Jesus may have run away (understandably fearing that they too could be subject to arrest), as the Gospels tell us, but other followers and family members would have been available to visit the tomb of Jesus and show their respects (quietly and privately, as Jewish law and custom permitted). After all, there is no evidence that the authorities rounded up Jesus' followers and imprisoned them in the immediate aftermath of Jesus' arrest and execution. In my view the tradition of the women as first discoverers of the empty is a strong piece of evidence in favor of the historicity of the empty tomb, if not the reality of the resurrection also.

At this time I want to return to Ehrman's point about Paul's non-mention of the empty tomb in the creed that he quotes in 1 Corinthians 15. He believes the nonmention of Josephus of Arimathea, the man who buried Jesus, and the nonmention of a tomb constitute evidence that there probably was no tomb in the earliest stories and traditions.

I find this reasoning wholly unpersuasive. By their very nature creeds are terse and minimalistic. To read "and he was buried *in a tomb*" would have struck all as redundant. To be "buried" *is to be placed in a tomb*. Of course, as Jews, Jesus' earliest followers would have been well versed in Jewish burial practices. They would have known that the executed were taken down and placed in certain tombs reserved for executed criminals. The creed, especially in Jewish thinking, really doesn't have to allude to burial at all. Just to say that "Christ died" is to imply burial. But the creed mentions "was buried" in order to have a counterpart to "was raised." Paul himself in his letter to the Christians of Rome seizes on this contrast in order to make a theological point: "We were buried . . . as Christ was raised" (Rom 6:4).

The creed's statement, "he was buried," flies in the face of the speculation that the body of Jesus was not given proper burial, that his body had been left hanging on the cross to rot and be eaten by birds and animals. It is hard to see how such an ancient creed (and its antiquity is conceded by Ehrman) could have taken shape in a Jewish context and include a matter-of-fact reference to burial, if in fact Jesus had not been buried.

I find it strange to think that the absence of the name of Joseph of Arimathea in the creed of 1 Corinthians 15 is evidence that no one named Joseph had buried Jesus. Being *buried by Joseph* is hardly the equivalent to being *seen by Cephas* (i.e., Peter). Who saw the risen Jesus was important, both to the creed and to the point that Paul is making in 1 Corinthians. Who buried Jesus was not. There are many other things that Paul and the creed do not mention, such as Jesus' death in *Jerusalem*, at the time of *Passover*, at the request of the *Jewish Council*, and at the hands of *Pontius Pilate* (though Pilate will finally make it into the Apostle's Creed, sometime in the third century). The failure to mention these details does not mean they did not happen or were not involved.

But what about Ehrman's argument that for the followers of Jesus to believe that their Master had been resurrected there really was no need for an empty tomb? Theoretically Ehrman could be correct. After all, if the appearances of Jesus to his followers were so vivid, that he could actually be touched, that he was not transparent or ghostlike, I suppose his followers might well conclude—even if the body of Jesus remained in a tomb—that Jesus had truly been resurrected.

But I do have my doubts. Jews of late antiquity who believed in resurrection spoke of the body being raised up. The scriptural basis for this expectation centered on Ezekiel's vision of the bones regaining flesh and life (Ezekiel 37) and, especially, Isa 26:19 and Dan 12:2. The first reads, "[Your] dead shall live, their bodies shall rise. O dwellers in the dust, awake and sing for joy!" What is translated "bodies" in the Hebrew could also be translated "corpses." The Old Greek version of this verse reads, "The dead will rise, and those in the tombs will be raised up. . . ." The Greek translator clearly understands the dead of Isaiah's passage to refer to corpses "in tombs." The Isaiah passage is echoed in Dan 12:2, "And many of those who sleep in the dust of the earth shall awake, some to everlasting life. . . ." These verses inspired the Maccabean martyrs, who suffered at the hands of the Seleucid king Antiochus IV (see 2 Maccabees 7). These martyrs not only spoke of being "raised up," but expected to have their limbs and bodies restored (2 Macc 7:10–11). For them resurrection involved the body and not simply a spirit.

As best as we can determine, the expectation of a bodily resurrection was the belief of the Pharisees, a religious-political sect that sometimes was antagonistic toward Jesus and later toward his following. Saul of Tarsus, who after his conversion became the well-known apostle Paul, missionary to the Gentiles, was a Pharisee. It was the resurrection of Jesus that attracted some of these Pharisees to the Jesus movement (see Acts 15:5) and led some, who were members of the Jewish Council, to defend Paul when he stood before them (Acts 23:6–9).

I find it difficult to explain Paul's proclamation of Jesus as *resurrected*, had the followers of Jesus spoken only of a spiritual resurrection and had the body of Jesus remained dead and decomposing in a tomb. After all, the Jewish people had their traditions of ghosts, spirits, and visions, which did not lead to the conviction that people had been *resurrected*. There was something about the appearances of the risen Jesus that convinced his followers, including the indifferent (such as brothers James and Jude) and the hostile (such as Saul of Tarsus), that they had encountered the resurrected Jesus and not simply the ghost of Jesus. But I doubt that they would have spoken of *resurrection* if Jesus' corpse was still in the tomb.

Another important point to make is that the whereabouts of the place where Jesus' corpse was interred would have been known. No matter what people said about seeing the risen Jesus, the place of burial would have remained important. Had his corpse remained in the tomb, that would have been known and its eventual retrieval for burial in an honorable place (whether the family tomb in Galilee or perhaps a tomb near Jerusalem) would have been planned.

I conclude that the burial of the body of Jesus in a known tomb, according to Jewish law and custom, is highly probable. I think it is also probable that the tomb in which family and friends knew the body of Jesus had been placed was known to be empty. I think it is also probable that the first to discover this tomb were women, among whom Mary Magdalene was the most prominent. These conclusions make the most sense of the evidence. It was the knowledge of the tomb and the discovery that it was empty, in addition to the appearances of Jesus, that led the followers of Jesus to speak in terms of resurrection and not in other terms.

CHAPTER 5

What Did the First Christians Think about Jesus?

Simon J. Gathercole

INTRODUCTION

The beginning is obviously an important part of any story. How the earliest disciples thought about Jesus at the beginning of the church is a key question for anyone, like Bart Ehrman, who wants to tell a convincing story about the views of Christians in the ancient world. As the title of Ehrman's book—*How Jesus Became God*—implies, he sees a story of a transformation: a kind of "ugly duckling" or *Sound of Music* tale. In this story, someone who is a normal human being, and one even rejected by many and executed as a political danger, eventually becomes—to quote the Nicene Creed—"God from God, Light from Light" and "of one being with the Father."

That transformation, on Ehrman's view, is not by any means instantaneous, but an evolution that took place over centuries. Ehrman's account of the journey begins even before the historical Jesus and proceeds to the Council of Chalcedon in 451 CE. Even so, the most important elements in the story happen early on. It is the resurrection appearances that are the key turning point in the story, for it is at the resurrection that Jesus becomes elevated to the right hand of God. These visions of the risen Jesus—in which some of the earliest disciples really *thought* they saw Jesus—Ehrman acknowledges as historical fact, whatever one thinks of the historical truth of the resurrection of Jesus itself. These visions triggered the great changes in how Jesus was understood, and the principal changes took place in what scholars call the "tunnel period" of around twenty years between the historical Jesus and the first Christian writings (i.e., ca. 30–50 CE).

When the disciples considered that Jesus had really been raised from the dead, their view of who he was changed drastically. As a result of their visions, they came to believe, according to Ehrman's *How Jesus Became God*, that Jesus had been adopted as God's Son and had—in some sense at least—become divine. In the course of that "tunnel period," Jesus gradually came to be seen as even more significant. He subsequently came to be regarded as having become God's Son even earlier. Some saw this "adoption" as taking place at his baptism; others took this back still further, to his very birth and even conception. Ehrman goes on to express the view that in Paul's writings, Jesus is seen as an angel-like being—"pre-existent," that is, existing even before becoming human.

The key technical terms in Ehrman's account for our chapter here are "exaltation Christology" and "adoptionist Christology." It is with the perception of Jesus' *exaltation*, or elevation, to the right hand of God that Christology begins. According to *How Jesus Became God*, the view of Jesus held by the earliest believers was that after Jesus' death, God elevated him to a position of supreme authority ("Christology" simply means *what one thinks or says about Christ.*) Not only that, but God had "adopted" Jesus as his Son, even if he did not have the same kind of divine nature as his newfound Father. Nevertheless, he could be worshiped by the earliest Christians, and because they were Jews, he was worshiped not as a separate deity, but alongside God the Father.

In this chapter I propose to deal with three main areas, touched on in a number of places in *How Jesus Became God*, but especially in chapter 6: "The Beginning of Christology: Christ as Exalted to Heaven." We will work backward chronologically, looking first of all at the "Christologies" of Matthew, Mark, and Luke, all written in the second half of the first century. Then, in the second part of this chapter, we will move back in time into the shady territory of the "tunnel period." Finally, we will give a different account of what took place at Jesus' exaltation. Overall, we will see in the course of this chapter that the evidence does not enable us to plot a gradual development in the early Christians' view of Jesus.

JESUS ACCORDING TO MATTHEW, MARK, AND LUKE

I need to begin by reordering this list of Gospels, because—as almost every biblical scholar acknowledges—Mark's gospel was written first. There is a bit more controversy about which came next, Matthew or Luke, but my impression is that most scholars probably favor the order Mark–Matthew–Luke (especially those who think that Luke used Matthew's gospel—conversely, hardly anyone thinks that Matthew used Luke). In fact, I need to change it again, because I am going to work backward in time from Matthew and Luke to Mark. Following that, in the second part of this chapter, I will deal with the "tunnel period" before the Gospels.

Becoming Son of God at Birth? The Christologies in Matthew and Luke

Ehrman's views of the Christologies of Matthew and Luke overlap to a large extent. He does not see either as containing a "preexistent" Jesus, that is, a Jesus portrayed as having a back story in heaven. Rather, *How Jesus Became God* defines Jesus in these two gospels as coming into existence as God's Son at his conception or birth. In Luke, the Holy Spirit comes upon Mary and therefore the holy child will be called the Son of God.[1] Ehrman sees Matthew as not quite so explicit about the process whereby Jesus is conceived, but still this gospel views Jesus as Son of God from the moment of conception. As a result, Jesus is—in a loose or weak sense, at least—divine from the beginning of his earthly existence. Ehrman is at pains to emphasize, however, that Matthew and Luke certainly cannot be regarded as agreeing with the definition of Jesus in the creeds:

> I should stress that these virginal conception narratives of Matthew and Luke are by no stretch of the imagination embracing the view that later became the orthodox teaching of Christianity. According to this later view, Christ was a preexistent divine being who "became

incarnate [i.e., 'human'] through the Virgin Mary." But not according to Matthew and Luke. If you read their accounts closely, you will see that they have nothing to do with the idea that Christ existed before he was conceived. In these two Gospels, Jesus comes into existence at the moment of his conception. He did not exist before.[2]

I cannot resist responding to this paragraph, because I once wrote a whole book arguing the opposite view, specifically on the topic of the preexistence of Christ in the gospels of Matthew, Mark, and Luke.[3] Among a few other points, I focused attention especially on the "I have come" sayings of Jesus, of which there are a number in Matthew and Luke (as well as in Mark). Jesus on various occasions sums up his mission in phrases such as the following:

It is not the healthy who need a doctor, but those who are sick. *I have not come to call the righteous, but sinners.* (Mark 2:17/Matt 9:13/ Luke 5:32; Luke adds *"to repentance"*)[4]

Do not think that I have come to abolish the Law or the prophets. I have not come to abolish them, but to fulfill them. (Matt 5:17)

I have come to cast fire onto the earth, and how I wish it were already kindled. (Luke 12:49)

Do not think that I have come to bring peace on the earth; I have not come to bring peace but a sword/division. (Matt 10:34/Luke 12:51)

For I have come to divide man against father and daughter against mother, and daughter in law against mother-in-law. (Matt 10:35)

For even *the Son of Man came not to be served, but to serve, and to give his life* as a ransom for many. (Mark 10:45/Matt 20:28)

For *the Son of Man came to seek and to save what was lost.* (Luke 19:10).

I would suggest that the natural sense of these sayings is that they imply that Jesus has come from somewhere to accomplish his mission. (Jesus is not talking in each case about how he has arrived in a particular town, having "come," for example, from Nazareth to Capernaum.) When one examines these sayings of Jesus, the closest matches with them in the Old Testament and Jewish tradition are statements that angels make about their earthly missions (within the

Old Testament, see, e.g., Dan 9:22–23; 10:14; 11:2). I found twenty-four examples in the Old Testament and Jewish tradition of angels saying, "I have come in order to ..." as a way of summing up their earthly missions.[5] A prophet or a messiah in the Old Testament or Jewish tradition never sums up his life's work this way.

I am not for a moment suggesting that Jesus is viewed as an angel in the Gospels, but rather that he is seen as having come *from* somewhere to carry out his life's work, namely, from heaven. Ehrman insists that if you read Matthew and Luke carefully, "you will see that they have nothing to do with the idea that Christ existed before he was conceived."[6] But I think if you read Matthew and Luke carefully in the light of their Jewish background, you can see that they have everything to do with Christ existing before he was conceived, before he "came" to embark on his earthly mission.

Becoming Son of God at Baptism? The Christology in Mark's Gospel

The description in *How Jesus Became God* of Mark's gospel overlaps with the pictures of Matthew and Luke in that Ehrman does not see Jesus as a preexistent being in Mark. (The points made about preexistence just now, however, apply to Mark too, because Jesus' "I have come" statements are scattered across Matthew, Mark, and Luke.) According to Ehrman, Mark's "orthodox" credentials are even weaker, however, because—in contrast to Matthew and Luke—Mark's Jesus is not born of a virgin either. He is still regarded as the Son of God, but in Mark Jesus attained to that position later than he did in Matthew and Luke, namely, at his baptism. Ehrman's view here is based on the words of the voice from heaven at Jesus' baptism: "You are my Son, whom I love; with you I am well pleased" (Mark 1:11).

Commenting on this verse, Ehrman asserts: "This voice does not appear to be stating a preexisting fact. It appears to be making a declaration. It is at this time that Jesus becomes the Son of God for Mark's Gospel."[7] I chose the word "asserts" deliberately here, because that is about all it is. Ehrman goes on to say, perhaps by way of explanation, that after the baptism Jesus does all kinds of remarkable deeds, but this does nothing to show that Jesus became Son of God for the first time at his baptism. What is striking is that a voice from heaven comes later on in Mark's gospel and says something similar. At the transfiguration, God says of Jesus: "This is my Son, whom I love. Listen to him!" (Mark 9:1). Presumably God is not adopting Jesus again. But it is hard to see how the voice at the baptism could refer to God's adoption of Jesus and the similar-sounding voice at the transfiguration could mean something different.

Jesus as Divine in Matthew, Mark, and Luke?

Perhaps surprisingly, Ehrman would answer this question: Yes! At the same time, however, it is important to recognize what he means: in Matthew, Mark, and Luke, Jesus occupies a certain position in the divine hierarchy or pyramid, but he is certainly not at the top. He is *divine*, but not in the sense that he shares in the identity of the one God of Israel. Briefly in this section I aim, first, to set out some of the ways in which Jesus in these three gospels demonstrates or implies his divine identity. Then, second, I will discuss briefly (more detail can be found in the chapters in this volume by Mike Bird and Chris Tilling) why this divine identity cannot be seen as a lower-grade divine identity, because of the absolute distinction between God and creation presupposed in the religious environment of the earliest disciples.

There are a number of points at which Jesus in Matthew, Mark, and Luke does look like he has the privileges of YHWH, God himself. I have described this evidence in more detail elsewhere, and so I will only give a brief sketch here.[8] Strikingly, Jesus says and does things that not only overlap with what God in the Old Testament says and does. Jesus says and does things that are privileges *uniquely* of the God of Israel. When Jesus speaks and acts this way, responses—unsurprisingly—include worship on the one hand and accusations of blasphemy on the other.

One of the most remarkable statements is Jesus' authority to forgive sins, seen once in Matthew and Mark and twice in Luke (Mark 2:1–10 and parallels; also Luke 7:49). It is difficult to see this as merely something Jesus can do as a god low down in the divine pecking order because it is something—as the scribes in Mark 2 recognize—that is a prerogative uniquely of the one true God. This was something that no angel, prophet, or even nondivine Messiah, or any other figure, had the authority to do.[9]

One of the best known facts about Jesus is that he chose twelve disciples, and scholars usually take this as Jesus forming the nucleus of a renewed people of God, with the twelve disciples representing the twelve tribes of Israel (Mark 3:13; Luke 6:13).[10] This looks, therefore, as if Jesus is occupying the position of God in the Old Testament, and this is echoed in the fact that Jesus has the power of electing people to be saved elsewhere in the Gospels. This appears in the famous saying in Matthew and Luke, where Jesus states: "No one knows the Son except the Father, and no one knows the Father except the Son and *those to whom the Son chooses to reveal him*" (Matt 11:27/Luke 10:22): Jesus chooses who can know the Father. The people of God in Mark can even be called "his [i.e., Jesus'] elect" (Mark 13:27/Matt 24:31): the people of God belong to Jesus. In the same verse, one of my coauthors in this book, Craig Evans, has drawn attention to what an extraordinary thing it is that Jesus refers to angels belonging to him as well (see also Matt 13:41; 25:31).[11]

Other features of Matthew, Mark, and Luke, such as the sea miracles, Jesus' sending of prophets, his exercise of supernatural knowledge, his belonging in the divine triad Father-Son-Spirit (Matt 28:19), all imply that Jesus shares in the identity of the one true God of Israel.

This identity is reflected in the responses to Jesus in Matthew, Mark, and Luke. We have already mentioned the accusations of the scribes: "Why is he speaking in this way? He is blaspheming! Who can forgive sins but God alone?" (Mark 2:7). This accusation resurfaces at the end of Mark's gospel, when Jesus claims to share the authority of God in heaven. The high priest states: "What further witnesses do we need? You have heard the blasphemy!" (14:63–64).

On the more positive side, there are various kinds of reverence offered to Jesus in Matthew, Mark, and Luke. Some of these exceed the bounds of esteem for a mere human being, and as we will soon see, such reverence cannot be regarded simply as worship of a second-tier god. This is especially apparent in Luke, because he considers it inappropriate to give reverential prostration to mere human beings. (Other authors may well use the term more liberally than Luke.) The Greek word for this reverential prostration is *proskynēsis*, a kind of technical term. This was the reverence that in 327 BCE, Alexander the Great imposed on his fellow Greeks as an obligation; some of them refused, denying him what amounted to formal worship as a god.[12] Luke narrates a scene in Acts that is almost a mirror image of that, in which Cornelius bowed down to (*prosekynēsen*) Peter, after which Peter said: "Stand up, for I too am a man" (Acts 10:25–26). So when the disciples offer *proskynēsis* to Jesus at the end of Luke's gospel, it is clearly worship due uniquely to God that is in view (Luke 24:52).

We can explore further this question of what kind of divine identity the events in Matthew, Mark, and Luke imply about Jesus. Ehrman repeatedly emphasizes the need to ask not just whether Jesus is seen as divine or not, but also in what sense he is divine. Chapter 1 of his book rightly emphasizes that deity in the wider Roman Empire was a rather flexible affair, and that in a few cases (although I think chapter 2 of *How Jesus Became God* exaggerates), some Jewish texts can have a degree of flexibility too. Matthew, Mark, and Luke, however, imply that the Jewish milieu, which Jesus inhabited, was one in which there was a strict God/creation divide. The scribes in Mark 2, for example, do not think that Jesus' forgiveness of sins was an interesting experiment in the degree to which a human being might participate in the divine realm, but accused Jesus of blasphemy, as one crossing the creator/creature boundary and encroaching upon divine privileges; the same is true, as we have seen, in Mark 14.

New Testament authors frequently appeal to this boundary as important. Revelation emphasizes it, as is seen in the places where John, dazzled by the glory of the angels he encounters, bows down to them. They promptly rebuke him, because they are merely fellow servants of the true God, who alone is worthy of worship (Rev 19:10; 22:8–9). Hebrews 1 also draws a clear line between angels on the one hand, and God and Jesus on the other. A further point of importance is that in four separate places in the New Testament, we find almost formulaic statements that through Jesus all things were created (John 1:3; 1 Cor 8:6; Col 1:16; Heb 1:2). There is a clear line between Creator and creature, and Jesus stands on the Creator's side of that line.

But there is a prime witness who needs to be called at this point— Paul. Not so much Paul the apostle, but Saul the Pharisee. It is notable that in Paul's writings there is an absolutely rigid and inflexible boundary between God the Creator and the created cosmos, a divide that is fundamental to his theology. At various points Paul contrasts God and creation and emphasizes that "from him and through him and for him are all things" (Rom 11:36). But the key statement comes in his condemnation of idolatry in Romans 1. What is fundamentally wrong with idolatry? The answer is that it is worship of the creation rather than its Creator: "they exchanged the truth about God for a lie, and worshiped and served created things rather than the Creator— who is forever praised" (Rom 1:25).

Why is Paul such a key witness? The answer is that he was active as a Pharisee just around the time of Jesus' ministry and its immediate aftermath, at the beginning of the "tunnel period" when Ehrman sees so much crucial development. Scholars generally agree, I think rightly, that the basic Creator/creation distinction was not a radically new thought for Paul at his conversion. His ideas about idolatry and its basis expressed in Rom 1:25 are almost certainly views he held earlier. Such a view reflects the milieu in which Jesus and the earliest disciples after the first Easter were active. We see this expressed in the response of the scribes and the high priest to Jesus in Mark's gospel, as well as in the view of Saul of Tarsus.

The implications of this are significant for how we regard the divine identity of Jesus. It implies that when Jesus in Matthew, Mark, and Luke says and does things that in the Old Testament are divine prerogatives, it can only be because he shares in the identity of the God of Israel.

Summary

Ehrman's argument that the Jesus of Matthew, Mark, and Luke is a Jesus fundamentally different from the later preexistent, divine Jesus of the creeds is a flawed one. For one thing, preexistence is more deeply rooted in the Gospels than Ehrman recognizes (although, to be fair, most other commentators on the Gospels also underestimate its significance). More importantly, a divine identity is attributed to Jesus in the Gospels, and not merely a divine identity of a low-level kind. The Gospels—as do Acts 10, Romans 1, Hebrews 1, and Revelation— reflect a Jewish milieu where a strict division between God and human beings, between Creator and creation, was much more in evidence than a continuum between the divine and human spheres.

THE "TUNNEL PERIOD": JESUS ACCORDING TO PRELITERARY FORMULAE

Even so, Matthew, Mark, and Luke might not, it could be argued, get us back to the earliest Christians mentioned in the title of this chapter. By general consensus, they belong to the second half of the first century. And in Ehrman's view, none of the Gospels in the New Testament reflects the views of the very first disciples.[13] Be that as it may, Ehrman seeks to go further back in time in order to discover the most primitive views of the earliest Christians.

How, one might ask, can one do this when no literature exists from between 30–50 CE, the period at the beginning? Ehrman's answer—and that of many other biblical scholars—is that within the final texts of the New Testament writings as they stand, one can detect traces of these earlier views. Ehrman calls these "preliterary traditions"—*traditions*, because they have been handed down, and *preliterary* because they were handed down *in oral form*, before the Christians became bookish.

In *How Jesus Became God*, we find the argument that these preliterary traditions reveal a view of Jesus that is more primitive than the views of Matthew, Mark, and Luke. Jesus did not become the Son of God at conception or birth, as put forward by Matthew and Luke. Jesus did not even become Son of God at the baptism, as maintained, on Ehrman's line, by Mark. One must look later on in Jesus' *curriculum vitae*. These preliterary traditions, according to Ehrman, take the line that Jesus was adopted by God at his resurrection.

Romans 1:3–4

Ehrman's first example of a preliterary formula about Jesus comes at the beginning of Romans:

> ... regarding his Son, who as to his earthly life was a descendant of David, and who through the Spirit of holiness was appointed the Son of God in power by his resurrection from the dead: Jesus Christ our Lord. (Rom 1:3–4)

103

Ehrman identifies, following a great many other scholars, a primitive Christian creed here, consisting of two elements: (a) Jesus' descent from David in fleshly, human terms, followed by (b) Jesus' descent (in the sense of sonship) from God in spiritual, superhuman terms—a descent that was conferred upon him by adoption at the resurrection.

There are two separate considerations here. The first (1) is the question of whether this is a "pre-Pauline" creed or not, and the second (2) is the matter of how one can identify the original wording of this creed. Ehrman concludes that Paul merely added to the primitive wording of the creed the phrase "in power" (after "Son of God") in Rom 1:4. The whole process is, of course, conjectural, but that is not necessarily fatal to the entire enterprise. To conclude (1) is a reasonable enough conjecture: the statement satisfies some of the criteria commonly invoked in these discussions—such as tightly paralleled structure and uncommon language (e.g., the phrase "Spirit of holiness" is unparalleled in Paul). There is a good sporting chance that this might be an early Christian creed.

Ehrman goes further and (3) identifies this formula as perhaps one of the earliest even of the preliterary formula because it seems to have an Aramaic background. It is "arguably the oldest fragment of a creed in all of Paul's letters."[14] Ehrman concludes that this goes back to an original creed in Aramaic, the language of Jesus and his first disciples. This is because the phrase "Spirit of holiness" in Rom 1:4 is an unusual Greek phrase, but one that may reflect the pattern of Aramaic or Hebrew phraseology (what scholars call a "Semitism" in Greek).

We have conjecture upon conjecture upon conjecture here. We can take them in reverse order. In (3) we are on unsteady ground. Even if the phrase "Spirit of holiness" may have the ring of a "Semitism," this is not sufficient evidence to say that the creed goes back to an Aramaic original. As has been widely recognized in scholarship for a century or so, Semitisms are much more complicated than that.[15]

It is in (2) that the speculative nature of the argument is most evident and the circularity most vicious. (I mean that the argument is a vicious circle, not that Bart Ehrman is being vicious!) One of the criteria, which Ehrman and other scholars use, is that one may be able to identify preliterary formulae that have been incorporated by a later author if that formula expresses an idea that is either inconsistent with, or at least unparalleled in, the author's other writings.

So in this case, one of the indicators that Rom 1:3–4 is not originally Pauline is evident from the presence of "ideas that are not found anywhere else in Paul," and that "this earlier tradition has a different view of Christ than the one that Paul explicates elsewhere in his surviving writings."[16]

There are two apparent theological oddities in the formula. The first is that "Jesus's earthly messiahship as a descendant of King David is stressed,"[17] and it is true enough to say that this is not *stressed* elsewhere in the undisputed letters of Paul (though note 2 Tim 2:8). However, it is not accurate to say that this Davidic messiahship is "a view not otherwise mentioned in the writings of Paul."[18] Fast-forward to the end of Romans, and we see Jesus invoked in the words of Isaiah as "the root of Jesse" (Rom 15:12, citing Isa 11:10)—a phrase that is a standard way of alluding to a Davidic Messiah.[19]

The second oddity is that, on Ehrman's view, the formula expresses the idea that Jesus was adopted as God's Son at the resurrection. This, of course, would not tally with Paul's thought elsewhere. This is evident for Ehrman not least from the fact that Paul has to modify it slightly: "Paul himself probably added the phrase 'in power' to the creed, so that now Jesus is made the Son of God 'in power' at the resurrection."[20] This, according to Ehrman, conforms the formula to Paul's own theology. It should be obvious why this can be styled a vicious circle. The following syllogism is at work in this reasoning (not just in Ehrman, but in other scholars as well):

The creedal formula propounds an adoptionist Christology.

"Son of God *in power*" undermines the adoptionist thought.

Therefore "*in power*" is Paul's addition.

So Paul incorporates an "adoptionist" fragment in Romans 1. But hang on—Rom 1:3–4 is not adoptionist. But we can make it adoptionist if we remove "in power." This reveals, I think, why the idea that "in power" ought to be seen as a Pauline addition to something older is an unwarranted prejudice. Dunn adds a further argument for why the idea that "in power" was inserted by Paul should be abandoned.[21]

I do not wish to abandon the idea (1) that Rom 1:3–4 might be a pre-Pauline formula. But if we do "adopt" such a view, we need constantly to remember that there is a considerable degree of speculation involved, which should give us pause before we *build on* that speculation. Ehrman, however, does build on it, stating (2) that there are clear criteria according to which one can distinguish within such creedal formulae which parts are original and which parts are additions by Paul. But this is a process fraught with difficulty. The key point is that one might well make the occasional speculation about this question, but *to grant one's speculations the force of probability such that one can then proceed to use them as foundations for other arguments* is— not to put too fine a point on it—indefensibly bad method.

At the time of writing this article (in January 2014), I am also reading Simon Singh's marvelous book *Fermat's Last Theorem*. In the 1600s, the French civil servant Pierre de Fermat stated that he had proven a great number of mathematical theorems (in his spare time!), but without setting out the actual proofs. Near the end of the twentieth century, all of these had been shown by others really to hold— other mathematicians had supplied proofs. One remained—hence Fermat's *last* theorem—which was finally solved by Andrew Wiles in 1995. During the course of Simon Singh's book, he comments on how disastrous it would have been for mathematicians to assume Fermat's last theorem to be true if it were not. Since theorems are fundamental building blocks in mathematics, had Fermat's theorem been assumed, any subsequent theorems built on it would turn out to be false if Fermat's theorem were false. Singh comments: "Any logic which relies on a conjecture is itself a conjecture."[22] The same applies to building on conjecture in the study of the New Testament, in this case, the study of Romans 1.[23]

Acts 13:32–33

Ehrman's next example is also an adoptionist fragment allegedly incorporated by an author who takes a different view—Luke. Luke does not think that Jesus was adopted as Son of God at the resurrection, as is evident from his account of Jesus' birth: as we have seen, for Luke, Jesus is "Son of the Most High" and "Son of God" (Luke 1:32, 35), as well as "Christ" and "Lord" (2:11), from the beginning. As a result, it might appear surprising to read Paul in Acts—the sequel to Luke's gospel—declaring:

> We tell you the good news: What God promised our ancestors he has fulfilled for us, their children, by raising up Jesus. As it is written in the second Psalm: "You are my son; today I have become your father." (Acts 13:32–33)

Ehrman clearly sees it as surprising:

> I am not sure there is another statement about the resurrection in the entire New Testament that is quite so astounding.... In this pre-Lukan tradition, Jesus was made the Son of God at the resurrection. This is a view Luke inherited from his tradition, and it is one that coincides closely with what we already saw in Romans 1:3–4. It appears to be the earliest form of Christian belief: that God exalted Jesus to be his Son by raising him from the dead.[24]

I fear I am not so astounded. When one looks at the way in which the New Testament books use the Old Testament, those New Testament authors often quote it in a way that is not assuming simply that the Old Testament text is a straightforward theological or historical account of what is now the case. Consider, for example, one of the first citations of the Old Testament in the opening pages of the New:

> When Herod realized that he had been outwitted by the Magi, he was furious, and he gave orders to kill all the boys in Bethlehem and its vicinity who were two years old and under, in accordance with the time he had learned from the Magi. Then what was said through the prophet Jeremiah was fulfilled: "A voice is heard in Ramah, weeping and great mourning, Rachel weeping for her children and refusing to be comforted, because they are no more." (Matt 2:16–18)

Here, Herod's slaughter of the infants is said to be a fulfillment of a report of a lament in Jeremiah 31. There are points at which Matthew and Jeremiah differ here: (1) Herod has ordered the slaughter of infants in *Bethlehem*, not Ramah, and (2) the matriarch Rachel is weeping, not the first-century BCE mothers of Herod's victims. But it would be flat-footed to say that the quotation of the psalm is inappropriate. Ramah is near Bethlehem, and Jacob's wife Rachel is one of the mothers—sometimes *the* mother[25]—of Israel as a whole. Overall, the oracle in Jeremiah is cited in Matthew because of its *suggestive similarities* with the circumstances surrounding Jesus' birth, rather than because it is a straightforward prediction of the slaughter of the innocents. Indeed, the oracle in the Old Testament is already metaphorical, because Rachel was already long-dead at the time of Jeremiah.

The same applies in Acts. In Acts 1, it is to make a point graphically that Peter applies the words of Psalm 69 to Judas: "May his place be deserted; let there be no one to dwell in it" (Acts 1:20, citing Ps 69:25). Peter does not necessarily want Judas's entire extended family to be wiped out. In Acts 2, in Peter's next speech, he cites Joel, announcing that with the arrival of the Spirit at Pentecost, various prophesied end-time events have come to fulfillment, such as the statement that "the sun will be turned to darkness and the moon to blood" (Acts 2:20, citing Joel 2:31). But there has—as far as we are told in Acts 2—been no extraordinary celestial transformation of the moon to make it look like one of the moons of Tatooine in *Star Wars*. Peter quotes these words—which, as in the Jeremiah/Matthew case just mentioned, were already metaphorical to start with—to make the point graphically that those present are experiencing an amazing act of God with cosmos-changing consequences.

We could go on. Still in Acts 2, Peter cites Ps 110:1: "The Lord said to my Lord, 'Sit at my right hand until I make your enemies your footstool.'" This is despite the fact that, of course, God does not really have a right hand, and he does not really intend to construct for Jesus a footrest out of the remains of his victims, like the Incan lord Pachacuti reputed to have made flutes out of the arm bones of those he conquered. Again, neither is the earth really God's footstool in the reference to Isa 66:1 in Stephen's speech (Acts 7:49).

So when we come to the citation of Psalm 2 in Acts 13, we should not necessarily be so astounded:

> We tell you the good news: What God promised our ancestors he has fulfilled for us, their children, by raising up Jesus. As it is written in the second Psalm: "You are my son; today I have become your father." (Acts 13:32–33)

Ehrman's interpretation is that this psalm quotation should be read as a quite literal statement, in which each component has a straightforward reference: *You are my son*—God declares that Jesus is his son. This is grounded in: *today*—the day of resurrection; *I have become your father*—I now adopt you.[26]

However, having gone through some of the ways in which the speeches in Acts use the Old Testament in the run-up to this case in Acts 13, we can see that the statement does not need to be understood so woodenly. The experience of David reflected in the Psalms—applied so widely to Jesus in the early chapters of Acts—is again seen as prefiguring the experience of Jesus. This is because of the suggestive similarity of (1) how David's miserable suffering was reversed by God, who exalted him to the throne of Israel, and (2) how Jesus' miserable suffering was reversed by God, who exalted him to his very own throne.

Acts 2:36

One of the places where a number of scholars have seen a primitive adoptionist formula is in the climax of Peter's Pentecost sermon:

> Therefore let all Israel be assured of this: God has made this Jesus, whom you crucified, both Lord and Messiah.

Strictly speaking, this statement cannot be taken as adoptionistic in the normal sense. Romans 1:3–4 and Acts 13:32–33 are concerned with *sonship*, which is the point of adoption. Here in Acts 2 we are dealing instead with Jesus being "Lord" and "Messiah"/"Christ." Again, Ehrman acknowledges the obvious fact that Luke does not himself think that Jesus became Lord and Christ at the resurrection. The same two terms appear in the well known Christmas reading: "Today in the town of David a Savior has been born to you; he is the Messiah, the Lord" (Luke 2:11). On Luke's own view, Jesus is already Messiah *and* Lord when he is less than a day old.

Ehrman's view of this passage is that it encapsulates the earliest Christian views of Jesus: it is at the resurrection of Jesus that God appoints him both Messiah and Lord. Jesus had taught his disciples privately that he was to be Messiah in God's kingdom when that kingdom came; now that he has been exalted to heaven, he has evidently now taken on that office of Messiah. More than that, he was also "Lord" in the sense that he was "ruling as Lord of the earth."[27]

The picture is made more complicated, though, when we look at the context at the end of Peter's speech. In the run-up to Acts 2:36 we see Peter making the following statements:

2:31 – David foresaw the resurrection of the Christ.

2:32 – Now God has raised up this Jesus, and of that you are witnesses.

2:33 – He has been exalted to the right hand.
– He has received the promised Spirit.
– He has poured out this Spirit.

2:34 – 35 – David heard God say to Jesus:
– "Sit at my right hand until I put all your enemies under your feet" (Ps 110:1)

2:36 – Therefore, let it be known that God made Jesus both Lord and Messiah.

Rather than extracting Acts 2:36 from Peter's speech and trying to understand it as a free-floating formula, we should try to understand it in its context. The build-up to this final statement explains what it means. Jesus sits at the right hand of God, which he was not doing in the course of his ministry. It also means that he received the promised Spirit and gave that Spirit to the church, taking on a new role in salvation history, in relation to a new entity (the church), which has not previously existed. He stands—or rather sits—in a new position vis-à-vis the world, because the world in its hostility to God is passing away, such that all Jesus' enemies will soon be vanquished, according to the words of Psalm 110. So there both is and is not change. This is something we can now, in closing this chapter, explore further.

AN ALTERNATIVE VIEW OF JESUS' EXALTATION

It will help to make sense of Acts 2:36 and the other passages discussed earlier if we look at how various New Testament books draw the contrast between Jesus' earthly mission and his position as exalted Lord at the right hand of God after his resurrection. Why do so many passages sound like they could be interpreted in an adoptionistic direction?

To some skeptical readers, it might seem that "conservatives" are engaged in a kind of special pleading when they attempt to explain away some of these passages. The objection might go: even if one might be able to find ways to wriggle out of an adoptionist under-standing of "God *made* Jesus Lord and Christ" in Acts, or Jesus being "appointed" Son of God in power in Romans, does that not seem to be what they are saying? And aren't there so many of these statements that some of them at least must be letting the adoptionist cat out of the bag?

The reason for this charge (or, conversely, an anxiety among some conservatives that it really is the case) is that there are exaltation pas-sages in the New Testament that do assign real roles that Jesus takes on at his exaltation. His activity in the course of his earthly ministry is different from his activity when seated at the right hand of God in glory. This needs to be carefully and precisely described.

Jesus' Earthly Mission

It is commonly emphasized across the New Testament that Jesus' earthly mission is one of suffering in order to bring salvation. Jesus states that even he does not know the day or the hour of the Son of Man's coming to judge the earth (Mark 13:32/Matt 24:36). Why does Jesus not know? Presumably the Evangelists, who generally thought that Jesus had all kinds of supernatural knowledge, assumed that this particular fact had not been vouchsafed to Jesus because his role on earth was not to exercise that judgment—i.e., the knowledge was not necessary to his earthly mission. Jesus came not to overwhelm the world with his heavenly glory, but as a suffering rescuer. The "ransom" saying in Mark and Matthew expresses this fact: "For the Son of Man came not be served but to serve and to give his life as a ransom for many" (Mark 10:45; cf. Matt 20:28). This is part of a wider pattern in Mark's gospel, in which the Son of Man (whom I take to be Jesus himself) announces his authority (Mark 2:10, 28), then declares that he is going to relinquish that power in death (8:31; 9:31; 10:45), but proclaims that he will finally reveal it to all at the end (13:26; 14:62).

John's Gospel also makes this point in different places:

> For God did not send his Son into the world to condemn the world, but to save the world through him. (John 3;17)

> For I did not come to judge the world, but to save the world. (John 12:47b)

111

We see the same picture here, then, as in Mark and Matthew, namely, that Jesus' earthly mission was limited to his work of salvation. The "Philippians hymn" in Phil 2:6–11—like the Gospels—also emphasizes the humility of Jesus' earthly mission, stressing that he humbled himself to death, even death on a cross (2:8). Hebrews also draws attention to the "crying and tears" that characterized "the days of his flesh" (Heb 5:7). This all stands in stark contrast to Jesus' exalted position.

Jesus' Exalted Position

Earliest Christian writings had a conception of Jesus' postresurrection characteristics and activities that were, understandably, very different from what he was seen as accomplishing in his earthly ministry. Some of these characteristics and activities can be briefly mentioned.

(1) *Glorious transcendent existence.* In the course of his earthly ministry, Jesus is assumed to be subject to bodily pain and human suffering, as is especially evident in the crucifixion. After the resurrection, Jesus is seen by all the New Testament writers who touch on the subject as transformed into a new state, albeit one that is still material and physical. Jesus, while still physical/material, nevertheless transcends the constraints that usually accompany such a nature. Mark says little on this subject. Matthew's Jesus has escaped from the tomb even *before* the stone is rolled away (unlike the scene in the *Gospel of Peter*). In Luke, Jesus' nature is such that his identity can be concealed from his two fellow travelers; this risen Jesus has "flesh and bones" and can eat (Luke 24:39, 42–43), but can also disappear and reappear (24:31, 36).

The picture in John is similar: he rises, again is apparently unrecognizable before being revealed (John 20:15–16), and appears from nowhere on several occasions (20:19, 26; 21:1). In John, one of Jesus' final prayers before his death is: "Father, glorify me in your presence with the glory I had with you before the world began" (John 17:5). Paul talks of Jesus' possession in the present of a "glorious body" (Phil 3:21). The constraints and weaknesses of his preresurrection physique have been left behind.

(2) *Giving the Spirit.* All four Gospel writers contrast John's baptism with water and Jesus' baptism with the Holy Spirit (Matt 3:11;

Mark 1:8; Luke 3:16; John 1:33; cf. Acts 1:5). John elaborates on this further with the statements in the Farewell Discourse about Jesus—with the Father—sending the Spirit, or "Paraclete" (John 14:26; 15:26; 16:7). Luke more extensively describes it, saying that the risen Jesus foretold the coming of the Spirit before his ascension (24:49), before Jesus again announces the Spirit's coming (Acts 1:8). Peter's speech agrees with the ambiguity in John's gospel about the cosending of the Spirit by the Father and Son: "Exalted to the right hand of God, he has received from the Father the promised Holy Spirit and has poured out what you now see and hear" (Acts 2:33).[28] This role as giver of the Spirit is a position he had not occupied before.

(3) *Lordship over the church.* Closely related to Jesus' action as giver of the Spirit is that the church has come into existence, of which he is Creator and Lord. This has a key place in the post-Easter period in various New Testament books. Matthew's Jesus states that he is building his church (Matt 16:18). He is now—as Paul puts it—head of the "body of Christ" (1 Cor. 12–14; Col 1:18, 24). The church is "in God the Father and in the Lord Jesus Christ" (1 Thess 1:1; cf. 2 Thess 1:1). Similarly, when speaking to Paul before his conversion in Acts, Jesus asks, "Why do you persecute *me*?" Jesus' identification with the church is strong. Christ "feeds and cares for" the church in Ephesians (Eph 5:29), because of the unity of Christ and the church, which is a "profound mystery" (5:32).

(4) *Cosmic rule and judgment.* To be sure, Jesus is portrayed in the Gospels as having extraordinary authority—to repeat examples noted already, he has authority on earth to forgive sins and authority over the Sabbath (Mark 2:10, 28). Matthew and Luke record a saying in which Jesus states that all things have been committed to him by his Father (Matt 11:27/Luke 10:22). Nevertheless, there is a clear sense in different authors that in his risen and exalted state, he exercises that authority in a way that he did not before. At the Great Commission, Jesus declares that "all authority in heaven and on earth" has been given to him (Matt 28:18); how exactly this differs from 11:27 is unclear, but it seems to reflect an intensification of his authority. In contrast to the saving work of his earthly ministry, Jesus also takes on the role of final judge.

Moving to John, it is probably proleptically—i.e., implying that it is in process, or about to happen—that Jesus states near the time of his death that he has "overcome the world" (John 16:33), with the "prince of this world" being cast out and condemned (12:31; 14:30–31; 16:11). The risen Jesus is not just Lord of the church, but, as both Acts and Romans put it, "Lord of all" (Acts 10:36; Rom 10:12). "Christ died and returned to life so that he might be the Lord of both the dead and the living" (Rom 14:9). This is the context of his future role as judge.

This is only a sketch of various results of the resurrection: (1) the constraints and weaknesses of Jesus' preresurrection physique have been left behind; (2) he has acceded to the position in which he is giver of the Spirit; (3) he has become Lord of the church, with that church having come into existence; and (4) his exercise of cosmic dominion has come into effect in a new way and will come to a climax in his return as judge.

So What Happened at Jesus' Exaltation?

How much do these four results of the resurrection mean a *change* in Jesus' nature or status or position? As far as (1) is concerned, in being freed from physical weakness, suffering, and death, he is really returning to his preexistent condition rather than being elevated to a brand new physical state. Jesus' role as (2) giver of the Spirit is an interesting case, because it marks a new point in salvation history. There is no sense here that Jesus' identity or nature has changed; he merely engages in a new activity, namely, giving the Spirit. Crucially, the Father is involved in this activity as well, and there is of course no sense that the Father "changes" his nature or identity in sending the Spirit. Similarly, in "becoming" (3) Lord of the church, Jesus has a new relationship, but this is simply because the church had not been in existence before.

Here it is necessary to invoke the category well-known where I live: the "Cambridge change." I originally thought that this had come to have its meaning of "apparent, but unreal change" because of the near immutability of the institution at which I work, but apparently the name was given because the idea was developed by John McTaggart and Bertrand Russell while they were working in Cambridge. The concept of a "Cambridge change" takes account of the fact that some types of change are real and metaphysical, but there are also changes that are changes of relation. Mortensen gives as an example that a boy can change from being "non-brother" to "brother" simply by virtue of his mother giving birth to a second son.[29] It would be interesting for students of New Testament Christology to engage more fully with philosophical understandings of change and apply them to questions of how Jesus may or may not be "different" after the resurrection. Jesus "becoming" Lord of the church seems a good example of a Cambridge change.

Finally, (4) Jesus' new cosmic lordship is a change of a sort, but it is again the result of new conditions of salvation history that have meant a change *in the cosmos* more than in Jesus. The powers, hostile to God, that held sway in the cosmos have been vanquished, or—putting it less strongly—at least sentence has been pronounced on them and their days are numbered. As a result, in this sense Jesus' authority has been extended. But again, as in the case of the giving of the Spirit, one could say much the same about God (the Father): when people pray "thy kingdom come, thy will be done," they pray not for God to change, but for the world to change.

Psalm 110:1 promises not that Jesus will climb over his enemies, but that God will place them under his feet. In this sense, the "change" in Jesus is the same as the "change" in God: eventually all things will be under his full control. Every knee "in heaven, on earth, and under the earth" will bow to Jesus, to the glory of God the Father (Phil 2:10–11). His authority—in parallel with the kingdom of God the *Father*—becomes more far-reaching. As an aside on Ehrman's view of Phil 2:9 that Jesus finally ascends to a position above where he had been before, God does not "hyperexalt" Jesus above his original, preexistent condition;[30] the point is that God superexalts him from the depths of the cross above everything below the earth, and on the earth, and even in heaven.[31] As a result, he takes on a further role that is radically different from his earthly mission—that of final judgment (Mark 8:38; Luke 12:8–9; John 5:26–27).

This is what it means that Jesus at the resurrection becomes Son of God *in power*, and Lord and Christ in a new sense. He is "Son of God in power," in stark contrast to his physical condition in his earthly ministry, which culminated in his death, "even death on a cross" (Phil 2:8). This "power," and his messiahship and lordship, also extend over the new sphere of the church, which had not existed before. Jesus is "Lord" in a new way, because he acts in a new way through the Spirit in the plan of God. His power, messiahship, and lordship extend further—in parallel to God's kingdom in the Lord's Prayer—now that Jesus has defeated death on the cross, and he has also set in train the utter defeat of those hostile powers. At the end, Jesus will judge from "the judgment seat of Christ" (2 Cor 5:10), and will also judge as "Lord" (2 Tim 4:8; Jude 14–15).

CONCLUSION

Having gone on so long already, I will keep this conclusion brief and merely summarize. The first part treated the view of Jesus in Matthew, Mark, and Luke, where we saw that Jesus is not viewed in Mark as adopted at the baptism. Similarly, these three gospels see Jesus as having preexisted and as divine in the strong sense of that word. The second part of this essay moves from the second half of the first century to the first half, or more specifically to the "tunnel period" of—roughly—30–50 CE. The fragments from Romans and Acts reputed to give evidence of an earlier, more primitive Christology of exaltation and adoption do not really do so. Nevertheless, as we saw in the third and final section, it is important to give a description of the character of Jesus' exaltation that takes seriously the verbs "made" and "appointed" in Acts 2:36 and Rom 1:4. These need to be understood as new roles that Jesus takes on, and an extension or intensification of his authority (in parallel with the extension or intensification of God's reign) in relation to a changed and still-changing cosmos, but not as indicating a change in his nature or his identity in relation to God.

CHAPTER 6

Problems with Ehrman's Interpretative Categories

Chris Tilling

INTRODUCTION

Imagine trying to explain the game of chess to someone who has never even heard of it. You could begin by describing how the pieces move, that players take turns to move, that the idea is to capture the opponent's king, and so on. You would be giving them a good framework for understanding the game and a way to interpret what chess players are actually doing.

But let's say that you decided to have a bit of fun with your non-chess-playing friend. Instead of offering this helpful introduction, you explain that the game is all about racism: do you want to fight as White or Black? The queen is the most powerful piece because Russian Marxist feminists wanted a powerful woman center stage, and so sat down and invented the game last century. The bishops don't move in a straight line because these Marxists wanted to show that religion is always off center, bending from the truth, the opium of the masses. After a few minutes of this, we run out of time and don't get round to summarizing the important stuff. The result: we have offered a poor way to understand what chess players actually do in playing the game. We have provided poor "interpretative categories" for grasping the game of chess.

In this chapter, I will argue that this is precisely what Ehrman has done with Christology. He has offered us poor interpretative lenses or categories for understanding the nature and development of early Christology. But although I have a number of critical things to say about Ehrman's arguments in *How Jesus Became God*, a number of positive things can and should be noted. I do this as I certainly do not want my essays to sound like apologetic Christian vitriol! I have had the privilege of meeting Bart Ehrman only once, and to me he seemed a true gentleman. That he no longer professes faith does not mean that he has nothing to teach Christians. Indeed, I have often found that I learn the most from reading those with whom I most vigorously disagree, as they approach the material with a different pair of interpretive eyes. In this vein, I must commend Ehrman for at least the following:

- He has pointed out the christological significance of at least one passage, namely, Gal 4:14, not often analyzed by scholars engaging in New Testament Christology. He is also entirely justified in maintaining that the *Similitudes of Enoch* should factor in attempts to understand early Christology.[1]
- I particularly appreciate that Ehrman wasn't seduced by an exhaustive analysis of the so-called "christological titles" ("Lord," "Son of God," etc.), even if such studies have their place.
- Ehrman is a clear writer and helpfully explains misleading or technical concepts for the beginner, such as "cult."[2] He is the American "Tom Wright" when it comes to clear prose. (Yes, I just made that comparison).
- Ehrman's book is extremely ambitious and wide-ranging, while still managing to organize a coherent argument.
- He is absolutely right that a key question to answer is: "In what *sense* did Christians think of Jesus as God?"[3]
- I also appreciate his exegetical honesty when rejecting an Adamic reading of Philippians 2:6–9. Here, at least, we agree!

More could be said, no doubt, but I did want to begin on a positive note before delivering what I think are some heavy blows to Ehrman's argument. As I have already intimated, in this chapter I will focus on some of Ehrman's highly problematic interpretive categories and moves, that is, key language that he uses to structure his arguments and judgments. In other words, here we deal with some of Ehrman's strategic decisions, focused on certain words, that he pushes through his entire book and that function as powerful tools of selection and evaluation. In particular, this will mean scrutinizing the crucial distinction between what he calls "exaltation Christologies" on the one hand, and "incarnational Christology" on the other. It will mean criticizing his use of the word "divine," his understanding of "Jewish monotheism," and more. These criticisms may make more sense when we trace what happens when Ehrman engages actual New Testament texts (see my next chapter). But it's a chicken-and-egg situation, so I'm going to jump straight in!

EHRMAN'S TWO CHRISTOLOGIES

Key to Ehrman's entire project is the distinction he draws between "exaltation Christologies" and "incarnational Christology." The earliest Christology, he tells us, understood Christ as a human like any other. He was later exalted at his baptism or resurrection to become Son of God, a divine being of some sort. As time passed, Christians gradually came to understand Jesus as "a divine being—a god—[who] comes from heaven to take on human flesh temporarily."[4] This incarnational Christology began early in the church, perhaps earlier than 50 CE, Ehrman speculates. In the letters of the apostle Paul one can see a transition between these two types of Christologies taking place. Only later were the earliest "exaltation Christologies ... deemed inadequate and, eventually, 'heretical.'"[5]

Although Ehrman does not always seem to be convinced by his own chronological distinction, at least understood simplistically,[6] he still contends "that the earliest exaltation Christologies very quickly morphed into an incarnational Christology."[7] There is for Ehrman, therefore, development within the New Testament, from the humble Christology of Jesus himself, through exaltation to incarnational Christologies. Only later still were these left behind for an understanding of Jesus akin to modern orthodox Christian confessions.[8]

What should we make of all of this? Although further problems with these claims will become evident as my argument progresses, I begin by pointing out that Ehrman's distinction does not explain the New Testament data. Even he doesn't find the New Testament texts themselves obeying the rules. Not just in Paul do exaltation and incarnational Christologies sit cheerfully together. The same is found in Hebrews and John, as Ehrman admits.[9] In other words, the distinction between two sorts of Christologies, which are then chronologically arranged, is artificial (I refer also to Chuck Hill's similar criticism in chapter 9). Nevertheless, he still allows this model to function as a historical plumb line, with interpretative power for making key decisions. For example, he suggests that there are "clear historical reasons" for thinking that the earliest Christians did not believe Jesus was equal with God. Why? The answer he immediately supplies: because of this distinction between exaltation and incarnation Christologies![10]

So Ehrman seems at points to recognize the problems associated with a rigid chronological distinction between two Christologies, and every now and then he backs away from it. But in doing so he makes understanding Christology in terms of *time* absolutely central. So when he turns to analyze material in John's gospel, where he would now expect only an incarnational Christology, he explains the presence of an exaltation Christology as follows:

> To be sure, Jesus comes to be "exalted" here.... But the exaltation is not to a higher state than the one he previously possessed, as in Paul. *For John, he was already both "God" and "with God" in his preincarnate state as a divine being.*[11]

Hence, in order to deal with the way the New Testament texts fudge his categories, he hangs on to his key "two Christologies" interpretative grid in the following way. He orders the Christologies according to the relation between Jesus' personal existence and time (i.e., whether they suggest his preexistence or not). But there are a number of unavoidable problems here. First, although Ehrman would not be the first to try to structure a New Testament christological study in terms of preexistence (to what extent or whether Jesus was understood to have existed before his own birth),[12] it remains the case that the vast majority of New Testament christological language is simply not focused on preexistence. It is not a major concern of the New Testament witnesses, and so one wonders to what extent his interpretative grid is going to be useful in explaining that data. Imagine trying to explain to an alien what a phonebook is. But instead of describing what the numbers are, what they are for, and why humans would need them listed, you spend all of your time speaking about the phonebook's typesetter and publishing house. That would be silly as you would leave out what is important and focus on that which is peripheral. Ehrman makes this same mistake.

This is not to deny that New Testament authors believed in the preexistence of Christ; they clearly did (and Paul did as well, as even Ehrman acknowledges)![13] Rather, and second, New Testament statements about Christ's relation to time seem logically derivative. Christ's preexistence is not a first principle that should be used to organize entire swathes of the New Testament. To go back to our phonebook analogy, we might be able to derive an equation, based on the telephone numbers, that could predict how many possible numbers could be listed. But the phonebook itself is primarily interested in simply listing the numbers so that people can dial and contact other people. Primary is the listing of numbers. Derivative is a theory about how many possible numbers there could be.

Likewise, the language of the New Testament depends on something more fundamental, namely, the way in which Christ shares the "transcendent uniqueness" of the one God of Israel (more on this below). To the extent that Christ does share this, it is logically derivative that he is also preexistent (and so some New Testament authors mention it in passing). In other words, Ehrman is getting the cart before the horse by forcing his analysis through this particular interpretive framework. He is not allowing the phenomenon of New Testament christological language to shape his presentation sufficiently, and so his entire project is misshaped.[14] The extent to which this is so will become clear a little later when we examine how all of this actually affects Ehrman's treatment of key New Testament texts. In sum, this means that he has to ignore a huge amount of important New Testament data, and then force the rest into his artificial grid.

GALATIANS 4:14 AS THE INTERPRETIVE KEY?

But this is just the beginning of a landslide of interpretative difficulties. Mention must now also be made of his use of Gal 4:14 in terms of his interpretive project ("you welcomed me as if I were an angel of God, as if I were Christ Jesus himself"). Later, we will see that Ehrman misunderstands Paul's Christology by claiming that Jesus is, for Paul, an angel that became human. But to do this he needs to make two questionable moves. (1) He uncritically adopts a disputed understanding of Gal 4:14. Gordon Fee and Darrell Hannah (no, not Daryl Hannah of the movies *Blade Runner* and *Splash*. I got excited for a moment too), neither of which Ehrman engages, reject this reading for good reason.[15]

(2) But more importantly for my present purpose, Ehrman, in a highly dubious move, uses his disputed reading of Gal 4:14 as the *interpretive key* for Paul's entire Christology! With this verse at the centre we are told:

> ... virtually everything Paul says about Christ throughout his letters makes perfect sense. As the Angel of the Lord, Christ is a preexistent being who is divine; he can be called God; and he is God's manifestation on earth in human flesh.[16]

But this interpretive approach toward Paul's Christology certainly does not allow Paul's own texts to set the agenda. Whole swathes of Pauline material cannot be explained (as we will see in my next chapter). Nor does Ehrman attempt to show why his claim would stand against potential objections. Once again, his interpretive—heuristic—categories seem highly problematic.

So not only is Ehrman's centrally important distinction between two types of Christologies awry, so too is his interpretive key for understanding Paul's Christology. And this leads to an additional two even more significant problems with Ehrman's project at the level of interpretive categories: his use of the word "divine" and his grasp of Jewish monotheism.

EHRMAN'S USE OF THE WORD "DIVINE"

Any project that claims to explore New Testament Christology, and particularly the relation between Jesus and God, must, naturally, make sure that it has a good grasp of the nature of Jewish faith in the one God. In light of this, one can then make judgments about how Jesus fits into any of it. It is to Ehrman's credit that he at least discusses Jewish monotheism, but that is where the praise must end.

We noted above that central to his project is the claim that the earliest Christologies were not incarnational, but about the exaltation of a simple man (not a god). Only later, after a lengthy developmental process, does it make it to orthodox Christian teaching. Yet Ehrman realizes that astonishing things are said about Jesus in the New Testament, and yes, in the earliest layers of the New Testament. So he finds a way to explain all of this without suggesting that the earliest layers approach anything like orthodox Christian teaching. His interpretive strategy at this point is largely rhetorical, but is structured as follows.

The term *divine* is used as a catch-all term deployed rhetorically to support his concrete position regarding the nature of first-century AD Jewish monotheism. In other words, the word "divine," for Ehrman, is a rather vacuous or nebulous receptacle. Under this label, he places the majority of New Testament christological language, God, angels, demons, and all manner of spiritual beings. This, then, is taken as evidence for an "inclusive" monotheism. In this section I will explain what I think has gone wrong with Ehrman's use of the word "divine." In the next section I will show how this supports his problematic understanding of monotheism. Both of these issues lead to interpretive confusion.

In analyzing divine humans in ancient Greece and Rome, Ehrman argues that the ancients did not consider there to be a sharp and hard division between the divine and the human realms.[17] Of course, some may object at this point, as Mike Bird does in chapter 2, but I have no major objections myself. Let's face it, stories of gods becoming human, and vice versa, have inspired a genre of literature from Homer to Rick Riordan's Percy Jackson novels (which are rather good, actually. Yes, I just wrote that). Three main problems start when Ehrman not only uses the word "divine" in unhealthily flexible ways in relation to Second Temple *Judaism*, but when he also incorporates "God" within this category. Behold the following:

- "Jews also believed that divinities could become human and humans could become divine."[18]
- "Jews also thought there were divine humans."[19]
- "God was the ultimate source of all that was divine. But there were lower divinities as well."[20]

- "There are other figures—apart from God himself—who are sometimes described as divine in ancient Jewish sources."[21]
- Then there is a whole section on "humans who become divine" in Judaism.[22]

The first key problem is that "divine" is too broad a category in these citations to facilitate helpful analysis. It could be replaced with other words, such as "spiritual" or "heavenly," without strain on his rhetoric. In other words, he has not sufficiently defined a term that, for him, is central in his interpretive project. In his introduction he states that "the key Christological question of them all [is]: How is it that the followers of Jesus came to understand him as divine in *any* sense of the term?"[23] But it matters a great deal what one means by divine for the question to mean much. Indeed, this claim stands in tension with the more helpful one he poses later: "In what *sense* did Christians think of Jesus as God?"[24]

Second, what compounds the already troublesome situation is that he then slides the word "God" into this nebulously deployed term. His language is like using a meat cleaver when a razor blade is called for. So he writes:

- "Just as within pagan circles the emperor was thought to be both the son of god and, in some sense, himself god, so too in ancient Judaism the king of Israel was considered both Son of God and—astonishingly enough—even God."[25]
- "There are passages in which the king of Israel is referred to as divine, as God."[26]

Third, in commentating on the way Ps 45:6–7 speaks of the human king as God, he adds: "There is not a question of identity or absolute parity here—the King, sitting at God's right hand—is not God Almighty himself.... The king is being portrayed as a divine being."[27] Again he writes: "The king is in some sense God. Not equal with God Almighty, obviously ... but God nonetheless."[28] In examining Philippians 2, we are told that the Christ is portrayed as "a divine being, an angel"; he is not "God Almighty," by which he means "not the Father himself."[29] Also in John: "I need to be clear: Jesus is not God the Father in this Gospel."[30]

So the christological import of Ehrman's three interpretative moves in terms of the word "divine" becomes clear. God and angels and demons and Jesus were all seen as divine in some sense. So exalted things could be said about Jesus; they mean he was "divine" or "God." But, and this is crucial, Jesus is not thereby "God" in the sense "God Almighty." He is merely "divine." So by deploying this word, he has created an interpretive space crucial to his argument.

The problems are legion (and whoever claimed that Jesus was God the Father in John or Paul?!),[31] and not just that Ehrman makes "divine" into a veritable contortionist among words.

(1) The rationale of these moves is not made explicit in Ehrman's argumentation. The effect is a rhetorical rug under which key issues are swept. Ehrman simply dodges such central question as these: What is it that distinguishes "God Almighty," the title that Ehrman appears, again without discussion, to reserve for Israel's one God as opposed to all other "divine" beings? On what grounds does he claim that such and such a divine being is "obviously" not "God Almighty"?

(2) This way of categorizing matters runs roughshod over the New Testament data itself, demonstrably fudging rather than clarifying matters, as we will see in the next chapter.

(3) Ehrman places tremendous interpretive pressure on language he does not discuss, namely, "God" and "Almighty." The latter word, "Almighty" (*pantokratōr*), only appears in two New Testament books (outside Revelation [9x], it is found in only one verse [2 Cor 6:18], and that one is an Old Testament quotation!). This fact alone should give us pause for thought before accepting too readily the key distinction Ehrman places on this word. Also, his use of the title "God" (*Theos*) is employed more for shock effect. In languages influenced by the Judaeo-Christian tradition, we write "God" (with a capital "G") as a way of distinguishing the one God from all other divinities and "gods." So it may indeed seem shocking that Moses or an Israelite king (or Melchizedek, for that matter, in 11QMelchizedek—something Ehrman doesn't mention) can be called "god." But Paul, in the New Testament, can call *Satan* "the god" (*ho theos*) in 2 Corinthians 4:4.[32] Hence translators simply help modern readers distinguish what is going on by using a capital "G" or lower case "g." There is no cover up or conspiracy theory here; the church has not needed to suppress the truth of what is actually in the Bible. So Ehrman argues

that "obviously" angels are not "God Almighty." But although Jesus is "God," he is also not "God Almighty." His argument proceeds due to the use of language that lacks definition or precision. He has succeeded in confusing matters.

(4) Ehrman doesn't discuss this central and interpretively weighty terminology in anything like a systematic way. Nor does he engage with the vast majority of those biblical scholars who have sought to employ careful distinctions and nuanced language when speaking of the divinity of the one God of Israel and Jesus.[33] For example, the German scholar Johannes Woyke realizes the complex issues involved in distinguishing and speaking of divinities, gods, and God in Paul's letters. For this reason he works with distinctions between monotheism, polytheism, monarchy, polyarchy, monolatry and polylatry, all of which can be further parsed in terms of other matters.[34] None of these key issues seem of interest to Ehrman.

(5) That said, Ehrman does at least distinguish between henotheism on the one hand, and monotheism on the other, but his definitions are anachronistic (a chronological inconsistency, as in the sentence, "The Apostle Peter gave Paul a call on his telephone"), as I will explain below. As a consequence, his distinctions are misleading, especially as he insists that beings other than God were also worshiped.[35] To explain this, it is now necessary to show how his use of the words "divine," "God," and "Almighty" rhetorically support a problematic understanding of "monotheism" in such a way that leads to confusion. His entire interpretive apparatus is creaking under the weight of ill-defined and inconsistent terminology that does little to illuminate.

EHRMAN'S MONOTHEISM

Mike Bird has already addressed this issue in chapter 2, and he argued that Ehrman engages in illegitimate parallelomania. Bird, with the majority of scholars, also makes a case for what he calls "christological monotheism." I will look at this important issue from the perspective of Ehrman's interpretive project, especially given what we've already said about his use of the word "divine."

The first thing to notice is that Ehrman endorses what could be called the problematic "inclusive monotheism" construct. Arguably the most up-to-date and scholarly representation of this position is offered by William Horbury (who is oddly not mentioned by Ehrman). Horbury argues:

> The interpretation of Judaism as a rigorous monotheism, "exclusive" in the sense that the existence of other divine beings is denied, does less than justice to the importance of mystical and messianic tendencies in the Herodian age—for these were often bound up with an "inclusive" monotheism, whereby the supreme deity was envisaged above but in association with other spirits and powers.[36]

That Ehrman's position is similar can be seen from the following:

> It is absolutely the case that by the time of Jesus and his followers most Jews were almost certainly monotheists. But even as they believed that there was only one God Almighty, it was widely held that there were other divine beings—angels, cherubim, seraphim, principalities, powers, hypostases. Moreover, there was some sense of continuity—not only discontinuity—between the divine and human realms.[37]

One should notice is how the term "divine" functions, for Ehrman, within this essentially inclusive monotheism. So the critique offered now in this section goes hand in hand with my comments about his use of terminology above.

Three things should be said in response. First, since Ehrman doesn't add anything new to this debate, I will simply repeat Bauckham's (arguably) devastating response to Horbury's version, one that is anyway far better documented than Ehrman's. Incidentally, I find it *astonishing* that Ehrman has not referred to Bauckham's important work at all in his book. Bauckham is the most creative and brilliant scholar working in early Christology, and Ehrman hasn't shown any evidence of having read him! But back to the task: Bauckham rightly points out that Horbury's definition of exclusive monotheism is *anachronistic*. In it, Horbury equates "other divine beings" with "other spirits and powers" (as does Ehrman). Bauckham continues (and it is worth citing him at length):

> If it [is] supposed that "rigorous" or "exclusive" monotheism must deny the existence of any supernatural or heavenly beings besides God, then it is clear that such monotheism never existed until the modern period. Traditional monotheism in the Jewish, Christian and Islamic traditions has always accepted the existence of vast numbers of supernatural beings: angels who serve and worship God, demons

who oppose God within an overall sovereignty of God over all. But such beings have been considered creatures, created by and subject to God, no more a qualification of monotheism than the existence of earthly creatures is.[38]

All Ehrman has done is deploy this problematic notion of monotheism in the garb of an imprecise wordplay with the terms "divine," "God," and so on. The game has worked to put all exalted language about Jesus in the New Testament in the "divine" box, all the while separating Jesus from "God Almighty." But the effect is a misleading rhetorical trick, not a position that sheds light on the data.

Second, one must remember that the majority of English and German biblical scholars, therefore, do not seriously court "inclusive monotheism." Rather, they promote versions similar to what Bird has called "christological monotheism" in chapter 2. For more names associated with this, arguably correct, view, see this footnote.[39] Why, then, did Ehrman think he could simply avoid engaging the concerns of the majority and their criticisms of his adopted version of monotheism? Imagine a conservative Bible scholar made a move—fundamental to his entire argument—that simply presupposed, without acknowledging scholarly counterarguments, the disputed Pauline authorship of the Pastoral Epistles. He would be ignored! Ehrman is not making a sympathetic reading of his book any easier with these problems.

Third, as scholars in this field know full well, central to first-century Jewish faith in God is the *Shema*, a set of Pentateuchal texts likely repeated twice daily in prayer by most Jews.[40] It is the closest thing Second Temple Judaism had to a creed, and it remains central to the monotheistic convictions of Jews and Christians alike. It begins:

Hear, O Israel: The LORD our God, the LORD is one. Love the LORD your God with all your heart and with all your soul and with all your strength" (Deut 6:4–5).[41]

I find it shocking that although Ehrman has a chapter on the nature of Jewish monotheism and others that look at faith in God in the New Testament, he does not mention the *Shema* even once! This is like talking about British politics during the Second World War, and forgetting to ever mention Winston Churchill! Rather, together with the majority of scholars, this leads to the assertion of a more than less "strict" monotheism (see, for starters, Mark 12:29–33; Rom 3:30; 11:36; 16:27; 1 Cor 8:4–6; Gal 3:20; Eph 4:6; Jas 2:19), which draws a sharp line between God and everything else, but nevertheless could still incorporate Christ "on the divine side of the line."[42] To do this one is served by reading these ancient Jewish texts inductively, as Larry Hurtado argued long ago,[43] and resisting the temptation to import later (anachronistic) definitions of monotheism back on to them.[44]

Two implications flow from this. (1) It means that the ontological separation between God and everything else is not a later church invention, as Ehrman asserts it is.[45] Bauckham rightly notes:

> The essential element in what I have called Jewish monotheism, the element that makes it a kind of monotheism, is not the denial of the existence of other "gods," but an understanding of the uniqueness of YHWH that puts him in a class of his own, a wholly different class from any other heavenly or supernatural beings, even if they are called "gods." I call this YHWH's transcendent uniqueness.[46]

God, for first-century Jews, contra Ehrman, is simply not "the highest member of a class of beings to which he belongs."[47] So, (2) the second implication is that the key question comes into sharp relief: On what basis or in what ways was God's transcendent uniqueness understood in the first century? As we saw above, this central matter is ignored by Ehrman because of his terminological confusion. We will explore answers to this question in my next chapter. But it should be observed before we move on that Ehrman notes the importance of "worship" for identifying God in his unique divinity. However, he suggests that although Jewish monotheism did forbid the worship of beings other than God, the very fact that it was forbidden means that some Jews *did* worship other figures. "Fair enough," I am tempted to say. But in a reckless move, Ehrman then takes this conclusion to be the interpretive key for the entirety of New Testament Christology![48]

All of this is a far cry from careful scholarship. It is an unsophisticated and inadequately researched presentation of the nature of monotheism, a fact that is something of a "wrecking ball" for Ehrman's entire argument. His understanding of monotheism, facilitated by a fudged notion of "divine," is the interpretive basis for everything he has to say about the relationship between God and Jesus in the New Testament. Ehrman's position is not only problematic, he also doesn't engage with those key and well-known scholars who have published books that contradict the views he has adopted.

OTHER INTERPRETATIVE MISSTEPS

Simon Gathercole and Mike Bird have already touched on matters relating to pre-Pauline traditions in their chapters, but I did want to flag up another interpretive misstep by pointing out how Ehrman's argument unfolds. Having (1) decided that there are two Christologies and that (2) these are chronologically arranged with exaltation Christologies coming first, Ehrman proceeds to offer evidence for this thesis from what he deems to be "our oldest surviving Christian sources."[49] He admits that our "earliest surviving [Christian] writing is probably 1 Thessalonians,"[50] but he does not make *any* significant use of this letter. Instead, in addition to examining "the speeches in Acts," he turns to the potentially speculative task of detecting pre-Pauline fragments in Paul's letters. This includes a look at Rom 1:3–4 and, in defense of a transitional Christology between "exaltation" and "incarnation" sorts, Phil 2:6–11. Much is arguably at fault here, and the litany of errors will be detailed in other chapters, including my next one.

But first, a methodological problem deserves mention. He claims that Rom 1:3–4 is a well-known early church creed that "encapsulated so accurately the common faith Paul shared with the Christians in Rome." However, he immediately adds: "As it turns out, Paul's own views were somewhat different and more sophisticated" than the adoptionist/exaltation Christology of Rom 1:3–4.[51] The problem I wish to show with this is threefold.

(1) Ehrman has been selective in his analysis of what counts as pre-Pauline. He has only focused on texts that would seem to support his chronological construal. He ignores passages that could be troublesome for his own thesis. What about the christological significance of, for example, 2 Cor 12:1–2? There Paul speaks of visions and revelations "given to me by the Lord Jesus,"[52] with one such vision dated to "fourteen years ago."[53] Ehrman doesn't even mention it. What about the significance of the language Paul uses to describe his conversion or calling? Indeed, many have made an argu-

ment for a fully divine Christology in Paul on the basis of just this issue.[54] Important here would be an analysis of the christologically rich 2 Cor 4:6, which Ehrman also does not mention. Also important would be an analysis of material in Phil 3:4–8, which speaks very much against Ehrman's proposal, as would the early christological implications of Gal 1:11–12; 2:19–20; 1 Cor 1:17; 3:5; 2 Cor 10:8; 13:10. I would not wish to propose that the earliest Christology was univocal, which is counterintuitive to say the least. It seems to me likely that different understandings of Jesus coexisted at the earliest period. The problem is that Ehrman does not reference any of these texts even once, and they arguably pose great problems for his thesis!

(2) The implication in all of this for Ehrman's interpretive strategy is significant. He has postulated a chronological scheme, relating to two different Christologies. This alone is problematic, as we saw above. But he then compounds the problem by ignoring evidence that his proposal would struggle to accommodate. It seems he wants to make the evidence fit his scheme, and his interpretative strategy here involves a carpet and a sweeping motion![55]

(3) Ehrman's overconfidence in his (selective) reconstruction also lacks historiographical self-awareness. Recent biblical scholarship, conversant with up-to-date historiographical theory, questions the idea that one can reconstruct the "what actually happened/what was actually believed" *behind* the sources in the way Ehrman attempts. It smacks of old-fashioned positivistic historiography. That is, to claim that "Paul's own views were somewhat different and more sophisticated" than Rom 1:3–4 will struggle to look most modern historiography and social memory theory in the eye with confidence. He even speaks of the Philippians' Christ poem as written by an "anonymous writer."[56] Ehrman has not sufficiently explained why it is that Paul appeals to *this* tradition in particular, and why the language remains as it is in Romans.[57]

In my next chapter, I will spend a bit more time on Christology in 1 Thessalonians to disrupt Ehrman's project at another level. But enough has been said about his interpretive devices at this point. Instead, I now continue examining a few final problems involving Ehrman's general interpretive posture.

So, second, Ehrman's rhetoric can be a little misleading. For example, he writes that "I am no longer a believer. Instead, I am a historian of early Christianity."[58] But some of us will respond that one can be a believer and a historian at the same time! Perhaps (I hope) he would agree, but his rhetoric is potentially misleading. This is especially so because he goes on to say that, as a historian, he is "no longer obsessed with the theological question of how God became a man."[59] But if the texts he is claiming to understand speak of such theological matters, he would do well to consider them seriously too.

This has immediate ramifications, for on the next page he claims that the idea a "particular human was a god—or that a god had become a human" was "not unique to Christians."[60] But to suggest that the incarnation of the one God of Israel in a Jewish peasant is "not unique" shows that his aversion to theological matters has not served his analysis well. It is also the reason for his rather rash rhetorical question: "Christians were calling Jesus God directly on the heels of the Romans calling the emperor God. Could this be a historical accident?"[61] Only if one wrongly equates both uses of "God" in this sentence in the way he does, an act arguably symptomatic of his theological aversion, will this strange question look sensible.

For this reason, too, he erroneously thinks that Christianity is an example of the "two-powers heresy" of Segal fame (no, not Steven Segal but Alan Segal; sorry to disappoint any ninja-obsessed readers),[62] and that the declaration of Caesar Augustus as "divine" neatly reflects material in Philippians 2 concerning Christ.[63] And he *does* himself engage in some theologizing when he postulates that a fully divine Christology provoked Christians toward anti-Semitism,[64] a point that Chuck Hill will discuss in chapter 8. One wishes Ehrman had read a little more theology at this point and pondered the Christology of German Christians. These theologians resisted the lower Christologies of German liberalism and managed, partly *because of* a high Christology, to find the space to construct a critique of anti-Semitism.[65]

Third, Ehrman's use of the work of experts in the field of early Christology needs to once again be noted. I have already expressed my disappointment that he shows no evidence of having read the important work of Richard Bauckham. But he also misrepresents Larry Hurtado. Ehrman states that Hurtado supports his view regarding divine agents (such as the principal angel) because this "provided the earliest Christians with the basic scheme for accommodating the resurrected Christ next to God without having to depart from their monotheistic tradition." "In other words," Ehrman summarizes, "to make Jesus divine, one simply needs to think of him as an angel in human form."[66] But this goes well beyond anything Hurtado wishes to argue. Whether one agrees with Hurtado's particular emphasis on agency categories or not,[67] Ehrman's summary of Hurtado's case is misleading. Finally, I should note that Ehrman uncritically makes use of the problematic arguments proffered in *King and Messiah as Son of God*.[68]

CONCLUSION

So what have we discovered about the language Ehrman uses to structure his arguments and proposals, i.e., his interpretive categories? This is an important question as Ehrman drives these key interpretive judgments throughout his book's argument as powerful tools of selection and evaluation. His postulated "two Christologies" are problems when seen in light of the New Testament data itself, and his chronological arrangement is artificial. His treatment of Gal 4:14 is problematic, and his use of the words "divine," "God," and "Almighty," sitting as they do alongside a misconstrual of Jewish monotheism, leads to profound interpretative confusion. In addition to these factors, we had reason to question his handling of so-called pre-Pauline traditions, his misleading rhetoric, and his use (or lack) of key experts in the field of early Christology. Like our less than helpful chess player described above, Ehrman has not provided the reader with a helpful framework for understanding key matters relating to Christology, monotheism, and much more besides. Just as the non-chess-playing friend won't be able to play chess properly after a speech about Marxist feminism and racism, so too Ehrman's readers will struggle to negotiate the terrain of early Christology.

CHAPTER 7

Misreading Paul's Christology: Problems with Ehrman's Exegesis

Chris Tilling

INTRODUCTION

In the news recently was a story about Amazon tribes in Brazil that have never before been contacted. They live their lives as nomadic hunter gatherers and have no idea about the so-called "developed" or "civilized" worlds. The report included an astonishing video of these uncontacted indigenous peoples shooting arrows at the film maker's plane as it flew overhead. I have often wondered what it would be like to meet such tribes. How would I describe to them what that plane was, for example? I could tell them that it was a flying monster made out of stone, but though they may understand me, it wouldn't be true. But Ehrman's analysis of Paul makes a similar mistake. He fails to explain what is really going on in Paul's letters. He says Paul's Christology is one thing, when it is actually something else.

What does Ehrman say about Paul, then? He makes a case that the earliest Christologies were of the "exaltation" type, that is, that the human being Jesus was seen to be exalted to "divine" status. Next, Ehrman argues that Christ came to be understood as "a divine being—a god—[who] comes from heaven to take on human flesh temporarily."[1] In Paul, he argues, there is a transition between the earlier "exaltation" Christologies to the later "incarnation" sort.

To make this claim, Ehrman first reiterates that Christology started "low," with the human being Jesus. But later in John, there is a clear "incarnational" view. As the earliest evidence does not see Jesus as "God during his lifetime," eventually he was understood to be something more. When this happened, Jesus was seen as "an angel or an angel-like being," as "a superhuman divine being who existed before his birth."[2] This, we are told, is "the incarnation Christology of several New Testament authors."[3] So Paul "understood Christ to be an angel who became human."[4] Only *later* authors went *even further* and maintained that Jesus was not merely an angel ... but was a superior being: he was God himself come to earth."[5]

Much of Ehrman's chapter 7 then involves an analysis of Paul's Christology. A smaller section looks at John's gospel and a few paragraphs are devoted to Colossians and Hebrews. This leads to his conclusion that "exaltation Christologies eventually gave way to incarnation Christologies, with some authors—such as the anonymous writers of the Philippians' Christ poem and the letter to the Hebrews—presenting a kind of amalgam of the two views."[6]

What are we to make of this? Certainly, his argument is not entirely original. Charles Talbert has made an oddly similar case, though his, too, is deeply problematic.[7] But more needs to be said. In chapter 6, I outlined problems associated with Ehrman's terminology and interpretative categories, all of which function determinatively in his arguments at this point. As I now turn to Ehrman's claims set out in his chapter 7, this will mean spending much time on his reading of Paul. As we will see, Ehrman fails to offer a serious analysis of Paul's letters altogether and therefore twists the actual shape of Paul's Christology entirely out of shape to fit his wider scheme.

I choose my words carefully here: Ehrman has botched his reading of Paul so entirely that his whole project collapses. It is as misleading as suggesting that the plane is a stone monster. To show this, I will first advance in a more constructive direction. I will show how Paul is to be better understood by actually engaging with the dominant language in his letters, something Ehrman fails to do. This will lead, second, to a critique of Ehrman's portrayal. Third, I will finally offer a few critical thoughts on Ehrman's readings of John and Hebrews.

PAUL'S DIVINE CHRISTOLOGY

In order to best grasp Paul's "divine Christology," one must meet a number of explanatory conditions. We don't have time to discuss all of them, but here are a few for starters. First, one should offer an accurate account of first-century Jewish monotheism, both that in non-Christian Jewish sources as well as that evidenced within Paul's own letters. This will then drive the key question: *What* is "divine" about Christology? Second, one's portrayal of Paul's Christology — his understanding of Christ — ought to cohere with Paul's "way of knowing," the style of his theological conceptualizing. In other words, if we want to speak of Paul's Christo*logy*, we need to think about Paul's epistemology. This point may seem a little abstract right now, but it should become clear. Third, any portrayal of a Christology that claims to be Pauline, of course, needs to explain the data we find in Paul's letters. Examining all of these issues, by the way, is what is involved in doing the work of a good *historian*.

Explanatory Condition 1: Monotheism

First, then, we return once again to the question of monotheism. Biblical scholars have proposed at least four different models for understanding Jewish faith in one God in the New Testament period. There are three minority positions. (1) Some argue that because first-century Jewish monotheism was so "strict" or "exclusive" Christ *cannot* be divine. The strict boundary between God and everything else must, so the argument goes, exclude Christ from "inclusion."[8] (2) Other scholars doubt that first-century Jewish faith in God was monotheistic at all.[9] (3) The group to which Ehrman belongs argues that first-century Jewish faith in God was indeed monotheistic, but it was *inclusive*.[10]

But the majority position, as I outlined in the previous chapter, seeks a more inductive approach in conceptualizing the nature of Jewish faith in the one God.[11] God is "transcendently unique," so not on a par with other "divinities" and different only in being more exalted. This, then, raises the key question that Ehrman's position must problematically ignore: *How was God's transcendent uniqueness understood in distinction from the many divine entities such as angels and demons, exalted human agents, and so on?* That is to say, what distinguishes "God Almighty" from the "gods" (to use Ehrman's language—though it is not that of the New Testament, by and large)? And this introduces us to a number of key scholarly positions that Ehrman did not tackle.

As Mike Bird helpfully noted in chapter 2, distinguishing the "transcendent uniqueness" of God means, for many, focusing on *worship*. The one God is the one who is worshiped, and no other beings can be. So, for example, Hurtado argues that it is "in the area of worship that we find 'the decisive criterion' by which Jews maintained the uniqueness of God over against both idols and God's own deputies."[12] This is certainly a better position than Ehrman's, which relies on an argument from silence.[13]

However, even this position is not without problems. Certain texts cited by Ehrman, such as the *Similitudes of Enoch*, describe the worship of figures other than God, namely, Enoch's "Son of Man." To explain this, Hurtado, for example, needs to insist that true God worship is not simply a literary phenomenon (as with Enoch's "Son of Man"), but the actual activity of cultic communities.[14] But care is needed here, or one is in danger of missing the heart of what worship was for first-century Jews and Christians altogether, as well as of misunderstanding New Testament Christology.

Why is this so? As Schrage notes: "God's praise does not only have its place in the church service ... but the entire bodily existence should be for the glorification of God.... True monolatry mobilizes and involves the whole."[15] Likewise, "cultic worship" could be scorned by the prophets (e.g., Isa 58:1–14; Amos 5:21–27; Zech 7–8) unless it reached into the whole of life (see Deut 6:4–9). Besides, Diaspora life meant that the "home and family replaced the temple and community as the focus of worship."[16] So, too, was Paul's understanding of worship in Rom 12:1 about the whole of life.[17]

It follows that this should inform conversations that try to define God's "transcendent uniqueness" in terms of religious devotion.[18] For if one is not careful, focusing too much on worship may lead us to think that certain worshiped figures (like Enoch's "Son of Man") are more important than they really are (as Ehrman clearly holds). What is more, one may also then end up finding that their analysis of New

Testament texts is too restricted. And let us be clear: Paul doesn't have too much to say about the (cultic) worship of Christ, which is why some, like James Dunn and Maurice Casey, push back on Hurtado and arguably give Ehrman interpretative space for his views.[19]

Bauckham's approach could be seen as an improvement. He has offered his own analysis of what constitutes the "divine identity" of the one God of Israel. He focuses on the relation in which God stands to all reality (God alone is "eternal," "creator," "sovereign ruler," etc.). But some of his categories have been challenged from various quarters.[20]

I suggest another way forward, building especially on Bauckham's insights. As noted in my previous chapter, and as all those engaged in these debates recognize, central to first-century Jewish faith in God is the *Shema*. There we see a confession of God's "oneness" ("Hear, O Israel: The LORD our God, the LORD is one," Deut 6:4) allied to an expression of loving commitment to the one God ("Love the LORD your God with all your heart and with all your soul and with all your strength," 6:5). As I pointed out earlier, Ehrman ignores the Shema altogether, which is enough to make whatever he says about Jewish monotheism almost redundant.

But let me press on with my more constructive argument. The *Shema* introduces the key way first-century Judaism conceived of the transcendent uniqueness of God. God's uniqueness was understood in an undoubted variety of ways, with different names for God and different emphases. But central to them all, threading throughout, was a pattern of language that spoke of a unique relationship between Israel and YHWH.[21] As Nathan MacDonald has brilliantly argued, the "primary significance of the *Shema* is the *relationship* between YHWH and Israel. YHWH is to be Israel's one and only."[22] In terms of the New Testament, Erik Waaler argues in a book examining the *Shema* in Paul, "to know that 'God is the only God' or that 'he is one' implies that one *relates* to one God only."[23]

Indeed, rather significantly, such an understanding of monotheistic faith in God sums up nicely what one finds in Paul's letters. So Dunn argues:

> To know God is to be known by him, a two-way relationship of acknowledgment and obligation (Gal. 4.9). As in the (Jewish) scrip-

tures, the "knowledge of God" includes experience of God's dealings, the two-way knowing of personal relationship.[24]

Precisely this kind of faith in God is found in such passages as 1 Cor 8–10; 1 Thess 1:9 (Christ-followers "*turned to God* from idols, *to serve* a living and true God," italics added); 2 Cor 6:16 (with its echoes of Lev 26:11–12 and Ezek 37:27),[25] Gal 4:8–9, Rom 1:23, 25 etc.[26]

Hence, as faith in God was so expressed, it is sensible to think that God's transcendent uniqueness was also understood in relational terms.[27] This is indeed what we find. Although certain figures, who were not the one God, could be worshiped in astonishing ways (the "Son of Man" in the *Similitudes of Enoch* being the most important example), the pattern of themes associated with relation to God was unique to the one God. Relation to God, and God alone, was described and lived in terms of this relational pattern, whether in the entire Old Testament or in any other texts from the Second Temple period. This includes the *Similitudes of Enoch* and all of the other texts Ehrman refers to in his second chapter, which he ill-advisedly cites to support an "inclusive" monotheism.

That relation-to-God-pattern often includes descriptions of cultic worship, but also a lot more besides, indeed necessarily so. It typically includes expressions of a human's ultimate goals and motivations, and it describes the passionate nature of religio-ethical commitment to God in typical ways. It contrasts typical themes with this devotion. It presents the experienced presence of God (through the Spirit) as well as his absence. It speaks of a variety of communications between God and Israel/individual Israelite, personal and corporate. It tends to call God certain things and characterize him in habitual ways, and so on. This relation to YHWH can have different emphases, use different names for God, and incorporate a wide range of other heavenly beings, but the uniqueness of this pattern of language describing relation to YHWH is always maintained and remains much the same shape, whether in *1 Enoch*, Deuteronomy, Isaiah, or Paul.[28]

Explanatory Condition 2: Paul's "Way of Knowing"

Second, studies examining the shape, nature, and structure of Paul's "way of knowing" (i.e., his epistemology) are also revealing. So Dunn argues that "whereas in Greek thought the term ['to know'] characteristically denotes a rational perception, the Hebrew concept also embraced the knowing of personal relationship."[29] Ian Scott's study, as well as the collection of essays in the Healy and Parry edited volume, point in the same direction.[30] So Scott submits that "knowledge of God" in the Old Testament is "most often a passionate devotion to Yahweh."[31] And in Paul, "knowledge of God" involves, at its heart, "a harmonious *relationship* with the Creator."[32] As Mary Healy argues, for Paul, knowledge can be expressed as relationship.[33] To understand this better, ask yourself how we know theological truth. It tends to involve ticking the right set of boxes next to a set of propositions (i.e., sentences on a page). For Paul, theological truth involved a living relationship with God and Jesus. If this was missing, so was the truth.

All of this clarifies what one must look for in examining whether Paul's Christology is "divine" and inform what we mean by that word. For Ehrman, "divine" is a nebulous concept, as we noted in my previous chapter. On the basis of the argument here, the question becomes sharp. It isn't even simply whether Christ, in the New Testament, is "on the divine side of the line which monotheism must draw between God and creatures," though it includes this.[34] Rather, it should run: Is the pattern of language that describes the relation between Jesus and his followers, Christ and the church, analogous to or different from Israel's unique relation to YHWH? This gets us to the heart of the matter and accords with Paul's monotheism and "way of knowing."

Explanatory Condition 3: Paul's "Christ" Language

These two conditions dovetail nicely with the third explanatory issue. Any portrayal of a Christology that claims to be Pauline needs to explain the data we find in Paul's letters. Sounds obvious, doesn't it, but Ehrman seems to ignore it. In approaching matters with this explanatory condition addressed, things fall into place as it means accounting for the things Paul actually wrote. Of course, it will be about relation to Christ because all of Paul's letters were in one way or another concerned with the relation between Christ-followers and Christ. Paul, in writing his many letters, sought to strengthen this vital relationship to the risen Lord. Crucially, this also corresponds to the language of Paul's *Christology*.

These three explanatory conditions come together in 1 Corinthians 8–10, where Paul tackles problems associated with eating idol food.[35] There, Paul makes recourse to the *Shema* as part of his argument against Christian participation in idolatry in Corinth.[36] In 1 Cor 8:1–3, importantly, Paul does this by framing his entire discussion (which will continue until 11:1) by distinguishing between the (merely propositional) knowing of the "knowledgeable," and the necessary knowing associated with loving God and being known by him.[37] Here we see Paul's "way of knowing" in action! Plus, Paul makes an argument on the basis of precisely the kind of relational monotheism we have summarized already.[38]

What is remarkable, however, is how the rest of Paul's argument unfolds in relation to idol food. Instead of speaking of the relation between Christians and *God* over against idolatry, Paul instead speaks of the relation between Christians and the *risen Lord* over against idolatry. And what is more, Paul describes this Christ-relation with the themes and language traditionally used to describe the relation between Israel and YHWH (this is the heart of God's "transcendent uniqueness" for Jews like Paul). For example, in 1 Cor 8:6, the Deuteronomic "Lord" (*kyrios*) is, for Paul, the risen Lord.[39] For many, this verse is a clincher, showcasing a "christological monotheism," *including* Christ in the Shema. All the Greek words of the *Shema* in the Greek translation of the Bible used by the earliest Christians are repeated by Paul in 8:6. The "God" and "Lord" of the *Shema*, which both identify the one God of Israel, are now split between "God" the Father and the "Lord" Jesus Christ. But the full significance of this verse becomes clearer in Paul's wider argument, as hopefully is becoming obvious.

So 1 Cor 8:12 then speaks of "sin against [the brothers]," which is ultimately "sin against Christ" (cf. Gen 39:9; 2 Sam 12:9, 10, 13; Ps 51:6; Prov 14:31; 17:5). After what most commentators understand as the rhetorical digression of 1 Corinthians 9, this Christ-relation finds more developed expression in 10:4, 9, and 14–22. There, drawing on scriptural YHWH-Israel relation themes, Paul speaks of "testing Christ" ("as some of them did"), faithful fellowship (*koinōnia*) with the risen Lord over against the same with idols/demons, and of the (risen) Lord's jealousy in 10:22. In other words, in a context in which Paul clearly understands monotheism as the relational commitment of Christ-followers to the one God over against idolatry, Paul speaks of the relation between Christians[40] *and the risen Lord.*

Paul does this using language and categories drawn from the complex of interrelated themes and concepts that describe the relation of Jewish believers with YHWH. Compare, for example, Deut 6:14– 16. Remember, it is precisely this that constitutes the "transcendent uniqueness" of the one God of Israel, the God to whom Jews owe covenant allegiance. The stories told and retold in the scriptural narratives that affirm, express, and explain this relation with all of its thematic interrelations are retold by Paul, and rethought around the relation between risen Lord and Christ-followers. Including Christ in the *Shema* in 8:6 is but one part of this. Here we see Jewish-Christian Christology in the making.

This correspondence between God and Christ relational language is found not just in one passage in Paul's letters. We can find it in almost every chapter of every Pauline letter in the canon! It would be cumbersome to go through the entire data of Paul's letters, something I have done elsewhere,[41] but consider 1 Thessalonians, especially because this is the Pauline letter Ehrman considers our "earliest surviving writing."[42]

In this letter Paul describes the relation between Christ and Christians in a number of ways. These Christians "hope in our Lord Jesus Christ" (1 Thess 1:3). They "wait for his [God's] Son from heaven" (1:10). They "glory in the presence of our Lord Jesus when he comes" (2:19). Paul and his team "really live, since" the Thessalonian Christians "are standing firm in the Lord" (3:8). Paul then prays:[43]

> Now may our God and Father himself *and our Lord Jesus* clear the way for us to come to you. *May the Lord* make your love increase and overflow for each other and for everyone else, just as ours does for you. *May he* [i.e., the Lord Jesus] strengthen your hearts so that you will be blameless and holy in the presence of our God and Father when our Lord Jesus comes with all his holy ones. (1 Thess 3:11–13, italics added)

So Paul clearly believed that he could pray to Jesus while wandering the Mediterranean world, and not only expected that Jesus would hear, but also that he could actively change the hearts of these Thessalonian Christians (presumably through the Spirit). In both 4:17 and 5:10 Christ's presence is portrayed as *the* great encouragement. The point of salvation is that "we may live together with him [Christ]" (5:10). Thus, although the risen Lord is in some sense *absent* (they also wait for his "coming," etc),[44] Christ is at the same time present and active to answer Paul's prayers. So Paul ends his letter: "the grace of our Lord Jesus Christ *be with you*" (5:28, italics added). And notice how Christ is characterized in this, as "gracious" and as "avenger." Listing the many scriptural parallels with descriptions of the Israel-YHWH relation here would be cumbersome, but anyone with a Bible can see this looks a lot like the way Jews described relation to the one God.

Of course, Ehrman does not consider *any* of this Pauline material in anything like the depth it needed. This is a huge problem because it represents Paul's dominant christological language found across his letter (see our third explanatory condition). In passage after passage one finds a pattern of data that describes, in one way or another, the relation between Christ and Christ-followers (including Paul himself). It is a pattern, which arguably Paul recognized, that regularly corresponds in theme and language with the YHWH-Israel relation.

This is just a smattering of relevant verses, but for example (you might want to buckle up, here): it includes an array of Christ-shaped goals and motivations[45] and expressions of devotion that extend into the whole of life.[46] It involves descriptions of the Christ-relation as all-consuming, involving great fervency.[47] It contrasts this broad understanding of Christ-devotion with matters reminiscent of Jewish God-language.[48] As part of the Christ-relation, the risen Lord is also present and active in numerous ways,[49] and yet at the same time absent;[50] and in heaven,[51] and so present through the Spirit.[52] To underscore the relational dynamic involved, Christians communicate[53] with this present-by-the-Spirit-yet-also-absent-Lord,[54] and the risen Lord likewise communicates with Christians.[55] And so Christ's character and the nature of his lordship are also described in God-language-analogous ways.[56]

These matters constitute, to a greater rather than lesser extent, an existential reality in Paul's life and so they are not merely a collection of loose, unrelated ideas. The absence and desired presence of Christ was for Paul the force behind his most deeply expressed yearnings (see Phil 1; 2 Cor 5 etc.). These various points are also regularly found together in single arguments in Paul's letters.

In other words, and this is where the rubber hits the road, "the way Second Temple Judaism understood God as unique, through the God-relation pattern, was used, by Paul, to express the pattern of data concerning the Christ-relation."[57] This is a very Jewish(-Christian) way of saying that Jesus isn't merely an exalted being, nor even just some kind of "divine god." It is saying, in such a manner that corresponds neatly with our explanatory conditions, that Jesus is on the divine side of the line, that Jesus is, as other New Testament scholars would say, included in the "unique divine identity." And these conclusions are, crucially, *grounded on dozens of Pauline texts*! Paul's Christ is therefore fully divine, sharing the transcendent uniqueness of the one God of Israel. If this case is to be refuted, a lot of texts need to be "explained away." All I can say is "Good luck with that!"

PICKING APART EHRMAN'S PAULINE CHRISTOLOGY

We are now in a place to make five critical observations about Ehrman's treatment of Paul, and the report is not going to look good.

First, as my above overview of Paul's christological language shows, to claim that "Paul understood Christ to be an angel who became a human," as Ehrman does,[58] requires ignoring masses of the relevant Pauline data that would speak directly against such a claim. Ehrman will need to do a lot more than simply elect Gal 4:14 as the interpretive key, as I noted in my previous chapter. Of course, one may embark on a creative rereading of all of that material (and once again I say, "Good luck with that!"), but Ehrman simply chooses to ignore it. There is no angel or intermediary being of any kind in any text that parallels the way Paul speaks of this Christ-relation. Rather, the way Paul describes the relation between Christ and Christians is analogous only to the relation between Israel and YHWH. As we noted in our explanatory conditions, this is a conclusion of great christological significance.

Second, Ehrman does admit that Paul could speak of Christ as "God" in Rom 9:5. But the significance he attaches to this reveals a much more extensive error of judgment. Who cares if Paul called Jesus *theos* in Romans 9:5? And I'm not entirely convinced that this is the best translation of the disputed syntax either. Paul could speak of *Satan* as *ho theos* ("the god") in 2 Cor 4:4! Simply calling a being "god" is, frankly, not what Ehrman thinks it is. Remember, we need to do the work of *historians* and ask how Jewish faith in the one God ("God Almighty" as Ehrman writes) is distinguishable from language about other divine beings. We have suggested it is through a relational pattern, and this is likewise understood in a relational way.[59]

Third, the only extensive piece of exegetical work Ehrman undertakes in terms of Paul analyses Phil 2:6–11. But his exegesis of these slender few verses involves some highly problematic moves. Here Ehrman would have benefited from a close study of Fee's *Pauline Christology*.[60] Ehrman claims:

> Christ appears to be portrayed here, in his preexistent state, as a divine being, an angel—but not as God Almighty. He is not the Father himself, since it is the Father who exalts him. And he is not—most definitely not—"equal" with God before he becomes human.[61]

A number of problems exist here. (1) Which scholar *ever* claimed that Jesus was "the Father himself"? This is setting up a straw man argument. Jesus is also not portrayed as a Mercedes Benz. It is an irrelevant claim.

(2) Is Christ called "an angel" by Paul here? No. What about anywhere in the whole of Philippians? No. Does this claim not, further, run counter to the christological language that surrounds it? Yes. For instance, what about the christological significance of language in Philippians 1, where Paul states that he would rather die and be with Christ, "which is better by far" (1:23)? Or what about that same chapter's portrayal of Christ as present and active (though also absent and in heaven) by the Spirit (1:19)? Or the language of boasting in Christ, being confident in the Lord and being slaves of Christ,[62] or Paul's desire to exalt Christ in his body (1:1, 14, 20, 26)? And in Philippians 3, Paul speaks of rejoicing and boasting in Christ (3:3–4), and of everything being considered as rubbish "because of the surpassing worth of knowing Christ Jesus my Lord" (3:8).[63] Paul speaks of Christ who has "power that enables him to bring everything under his control" (3:21), and so on. All of this is language of great christological significance, especially when one keeps the matters we discussed earlier in mind about faith in God. You will

not find such language used to describe relation to an angel in any ancient Jewish texts. In Philippians, the way relation to Christ is described and mapped out, and therefore understood, is analogous only to Israel's relation to YHWH. Hence, elucidating the meaning of Phil 2:6–11 through Gal 4:14 is way off target and shows poor exegetical judgment.

(3) Ehrman's claim above, that Christ is "most definitely not" equal with God before he becomes human, is based on a disputed translation of a single word. He refers to one scholar, Samuel Vollenweider, in defense of his reading. But what about the arguments famously proffered by Hoover (not mentioned by Ehrman),[64] endorsed by Wright, Gorman, Fee, and others?[65] They translate the word not as "grasped after" (i.e., that which Christ would have tried to seize, but didn't),[66] but as an idiom meaning "taking advantage of." In this case, Christ was "equal with God" and didn't "take advantage of this," but poured himself out. My beef is not so much with Ehrman's conclusion (my internal jury is still out on this translation issue), but the misplaced confidence of his conclusion (the "most definitely not" bit), especially when he does not refer to or tackle the most recent defenses of the opposing reading (e.g., Fee's and Gorman's).[67] Indeed, Ehrman thinks that the two halves of this "poem" (2:6–8 and 2:9–11) sit uncomfortably together.[68] But is this simply because Ehrman's reading has trouble accounting for the flow of thought in the language?[69] Others, as we have already noted, do not find their readings presenting the same problems.[70]

(4) For his claim that Jesus is not "God Almighty" in this passage, I refer to my previous chapter and the discussion about his use of the words "God" and "Almighty," as well as my examination of monotheism in both of my chapters. Let it be noted that "God the Father" isn't called "God Almighty" in Philippians, either! I also insist that "divine being" is too vague a term to be useful, as Paul will go on and exegete parts of Isaiah 40–55 in 2:9–11, as Ehrman also acknowledges. In this Isaianic text we are told that "I am the LORD; that is my name! I will not yield my glory to another or my praise to idols" (Isa 42:8). Are idols "divine" in the same sense as YHWH? Ehrman's language is too imprecise. As Wright opines in commenting on this verse in his recent slender volume: "The God who refused to share his glory with another has shared it with Jesus."[71] This looks more

like the kind of christological monotheism that Bird summarized in chapter 2 than Ehrman's vaguely defined "inclusive" monotheism.

So one may roughly render the logic of Phil 2:6–11 as follows, although, I note, 2:6–11 involves poetic language not necessarily suitable to a perfect argumentative representation. I therefore strongly urge that we not forget, as most do, the equally important christological language in Philippians 1 and 3!

2:6–8	Because Christ is equal with God, he does not consider this equality as something to be used for his own advantage.
	Being in the form of God, he therefore pours himself out for others, even to death on a cross.
2:9–11	In light of this act of selfless love for others, God publicly vindicates and recognizes Jesus' selfless act as a demonstration of God's true divinity.
	Therefore, Christ is honored as the prophets said only the one God of Israel can be: in universal worship and obeisance, all to the glory of the Father.

The poem is, in this at least plausible reading, all about the graciousness of true divinity. It is about the love of God expressed in Christ giving himself "for us," a position that accords nicely with Paul's theology elsewhere (e.g., Rom 5:8).

So after these critical remarks, Ehrman's original claim would better read as:

"Christ appears to be portrayed here, in his preexistent state ..." *and let's stop there.*

Fourth, and I want this point to sink in, Ehrman's questionable exegesis of Phil 2:6–11 is the *only* extended engagement with Paul's letters in his entire book![72] Ehrman has constructed a case about the nature of Paul's Christology by analyzing in depth only six verses in one passage. Just one passage! Your coffee or tea should be in the process of being spat out over this book in disbelief. Of course, Ehrman could be forgiven: a book the size he wrote covering the scope of material it attempts could not possibly analyze all relevant passages. However, it would then be necessary that the portrayal of Pauline passage chosen for such exclusive focus represents Paul's Christology more generally. And this is not the case. Ehrman's exegesis puts Paul's overall christological language *entirely* out of shape. That plane is starting to look like a flying stone monster.

Fifth, Ehrman does not do the work of a historian in other ways. He does not, for example, consider Paul's way of knowing. Nor does he examine the way *Paul* expressed his faith in God. He makes general points about monotheism, as we saw, and then imports his dubious conclusions onto Paul.

More could be said in criticism of his treatment of Paul. His claim that the apostle represents a trajectory on the way to a Christology that sees Jesus as "a divine being" who "comes from heaven to take on human flesh *temporarily*,"[73] is again evidence of a poorly timed aversion to theological nuance. The logic of his claim that "it is because of this exalted status that Jesus was deemed worthy of worship"[74] should be challenged. And so on. But more centrally, his limited exegesis does little to support a proposal that, indeed, stands in tension with the vast majority of Paul's language. Christ, in Paul, is already understood as Jews understood the transcendent uniqueness of the one God. Ehrman's entire explanatory project, therefore, fails.

MOPPING UP THE PIECES

The heart of Ehrman's chapter on incarnation Christologies was all about Paul, so my response has focused on the same. Space is running out, so I only have room for a couple of comments about his reading of John and his paragraph on Hebrews.

First, apart from his problematic interpretive framework, which I critiqued in my last chapter and which operates throughout his reading of these texts, I was more satisfied. That said, his logic seems to run: John's Christology is "incarnational" and must therefore be late. He may have just thrown away a key historical explanatory aid in one fell swoop.

This is to say, and second, that more nuance was called for in dealing with questions about John and historicity, at least conversing with scholars such as Paul Anderson, Tom Thatcher, Richard

Bauckham, and others.[75] Now *of course* John's Gospel isn't "simple recorded history," but then neither are the Synoptics and for the same reason: they have theological agendas.[76] Of course, Ehrman would agree with this, but the key inference is that John cannot so neatly be bracketed out of historical questions, as Ehrman maintains. Yet he writes: John does not offer "Jesus's words" for the gospel is about "John's words placed on Jesus's lips."[77] And so an unnatural either/or is perpetrated.

Third, Ehrman resorts again to this kind of claim: "Jesus is not God the Father in this Gospel."[78] Who on earth ever claimed that Jesus was "God the Father"? The question is whether Jesus was considered to be "on the divine side of the line" in terms of the first-century Jewish monotheism that most advocate, and which I have discussed in my two chapters. This Ehrman does not do.

Fourth, he claims that the Prologue of John's Gospel (John 1:1–18) is "a very high Christology indeed—higher than that even in the Philippians poem."[79] But this claim assumes the problematic association of decisive christological evaluation with time, as critiqued in my previous chapter. Further, it misses that Paul's Christology is as high as it gets, as I have outlined above. His rhetoric makes up "development" from lower to higher when there is only difference of emphasis (at least in terms of whether there is a fully divine Christology).

Fifth, his reading of John's gospel is one-sided and forced to fit his chronological scheme. What about the subordination language in John, for example when Christ says "the Father is greater than I" (John 14:28)? But by the time we get to John, Ehrman needs an incarnational Christology that has clearly moved on from Paul. But both Paul and John entertain subordination language as indeed both present a fully divine Christ. Once again we see that Ehrman's scheme does not, account well for the data.

Sixth, there is his single paragraph on Hebrews, a text that claims that Christ is *superior to angels.* Here, one would expect, some attempt to wrestle with the potential problem of having suggested that New Testament Christology presented Christ as "an angel." Alas, no such discussion emerges.[80] And so he resorts, out of the blue, to an ethical objection to divine Christology: that it would eventually end in anti-Semitism. Is this a diversion tactic? Are we witnessing a rhetorical ploy to draw attention away from the fact that his theory is destabilized by the data it seeks to explain?

CONCLUSION

Ehrman's thesis has seriously disfigured Paul's Christology. He only spends time in one Pauline passage (Phil 2:6 – 11), and even that is far from a success, as he illegitimately imports interpretative language from outside Philippians ("angel," "God Almighty") and ignores vitally important data within Philippians itself (not to mention the rest of Paul). Let me repeat: *he only spends time in one passage*! But, and this is really where the rubber hits the road, his proposal does not explain the vast majority of the rest of Paul's language across his letters and is actually refuted by them. As a result, his work on this part of early Christology is a serious weakness. He leaves so much out of his thesis and distorts that which it does include, that unfortunately the academic community should have serious reservations about the here discussed aspects of *How Jesus Became God*. In my view, the general public would therefore do well not to take his thesis very serious either.

CHAPTER 8

An Exclusive Religion: Orthodoxy and Heresy, Inclusion and Exclusion

Charles E. Hill

INTRODUCTION

On an unusually temperate December day in 1988, I was digging postholes for a fence to go around our trailer in rural Nebraska. The trailer had been generously loaned by my in-laws, rent free, for as long as my wife and I would need it. It was important to get a fence up right away, though, to keep animals at a safe distance. As I struggled to keep from bending the blades of the post-hole digger on the frozen Nebraska soil, I reflected on the fact that just four days earlier I had been breathing the rarified (and warmer) air of Cambridge, England, nervously defending my dissertation before the two scholars who had the power to decide whether it passed or failed, over a cup of tea. Thankfully, the tea was a token of approval. Now we were back in the USA, jobless but happy to have a roof over our heads and a functioning heating system.

As it happened, the Presbyterian church (PCUSA) in town was without a pastor at that time. They invited me to preach for them and after a few weeks offered me a temporary position as Interim Pastor while their search for a permanent pastor continued. It wasn't long before the chairman of the Committee on Ministry for the presbytery called me up. (In Presbyterian polity, a *presbytery* is the assembly of pastors and elders of all the Presbyterian churches in a given area charged with oversight of the churches.) The committee was about to have a meeting and the chairman wondered if I could come along, just to get acquainted with some of the other pastors and elders. A friendly gesture, I thought. The chairman, having formed the opinion that I might be on the more conservative end of the theological spectrum from himself, thought there was one elder in particular I would enjoy meeting. "She has a fairly high Christology," he said.

The elder with the "fairly high Christology" was mentioned to me because she stood out from the crowd of pastors in the presbytery who, by implication, must have held christological views that were something lower than "fairly high." This did not surprise me. I knew, however, that it would have surprised and deeply distressed most of the people in that presbytery's congregations, and probably ruined their Christmases, to learn that any of their pastors did not believe that the Word ever really did become flesh and dwell among us (John 1:14).

The meeting, as it turned out, was not as friendly as I was expecting. I quickly learned that there was only one item on the agenda. It was an "examination of the candidate" — and I failed. Unanimously! Not even the elder with the fairly high Christology voted for me. My contract was rescinded and a letter of reprimand was written to the local church, whose hiring of me was declared "out of order."

In principle, I certainly do not fault the committee. It was their responsibility to protect their people from influences that, in their opinion, would have been a detriment to the people's spiritual well-being — and I happen to agree with that. I just had not thought of myself as one of those influences. But maybe I was wrong.

One of Bart Ehrman's points, as he begins chapter 8 of his book *How Jesus Became God*, is that Christianity from early on has tended to be an *exclusive* religion — exclusive both in regards to other religions and even in regards to other versions of Christianity itself. Christianity, at some times in its history more than others, has shown a tendency to divide itself up. To most people today, this is not a particularly attractive trait. This exclusivist trait is associated almost "exclusively" with conservative or orthodox churches. One reason I related the personal episode above is simply to illustrate that theological exclusivism is not the sole province of "conservative" churches, or of those who are interested in the survival and proclamation of the historic, orthodox Christian faith.

In any case, it will become clear to anyone who embarks on a study of the early Christian church that it soon engendered a remarkable profusion of groups who held sometimes slightly and sometimes radically differing views of who Jesus was. One thing is for sure: this one man Jesus of Nazareth quickly became a source of fascination for a lot of people! And that fascination shows no signs of letting up even today.

It is the purpose of Ehrman's chapter 8 to chronicle some of the major alternatives to the orthodox affirmation of the full humanity and full deity of Jesus Christ. Thus Ehrman introduces the concepts of orthodoxy and heresy/heterodoxy. Using these terms as a historian, he of course is not endorsing the implication that what is called "orthodox" is true or that what is called "heretical" is not true. These are simply convenient terms historians adopt when speaking of what became, in fact, the majority view and what became any number of minority or rejected views.

I am glad Ehrman has chosen to use these terms and to explain his use of them. This is because in many earlier publications he has promoted the use of the terms "proto-orthodox" and "proto-heresy," etc., when talking about the period before the fourth century. The reason for this nomenclature is his often-stated position that, before the fourth century, Christianity was so diverse and disorderly (no good Committees on Ministry back then) that there was no mainstream, no majority, nothing that could be reasonably termed "orthodoxy," despite what some early Christian leaders wanted to claim. Ehrman's reformed practice in this book recognizes that, without asking whether anybody was right or wrong, there was apparently a "majority" or mainstream in Christianity quite soon after the New Testament books were written. This is certainly an advance over his former practice. I hope he sticks with it.

What we find is that this majority in the early church held to the twin "paradoxical" affirmations: first, that Jesus is God *and* that he is man; second, that Jesus is God *and* that this somehow does not jeopardize the confession that there is only one God. Often Ehrman's explanations of the various alternative systems of beliefs are helpful, and nothing if not clear. He offers the reader a quick and interesting tour of such groups as the Ebionites and (Theodotian) adoptionists, who could not accept Jesus' full divinity. Then there were various groups of Docetists, who could not accept Jesus' true humanity. Finally he describes the Gnostics, who separated Jesus and Christ into two entities. There are some disagreements I would have over how to classify all these alternatives, but these are quibbles. Being the outstanding teacher that he is, Ehrman does more than simply describe. Very much like ancient historians (gospel writers included), who were also teachers, Ehrman tries to draw lessons for his readers from his telling of history. Sometimes these lessons are subtle, sometimes more overt.

HUNTERS OF HERETICS

One lesson that comes through in Ehrman's telling of early Christian history is that many of the Christians who played for the winning side (the orthodox), Christians who believed Jesus was both God and man, were not people to be admired. They did some bad things, most of which you might say have to do with the already mentioned Christian tendency to exclusivism. We'll see this in a big way in the next chapter. Apparently the lesson we are supposed to draw from these examples of exclusivist-tending behavior is that it should cast doubt on the legitimacy of their beliefs.

We begin to see the moral judgments in chapter 8 in the repeated use of the term "heresy hunter."[1] Is this, like "orthodoxy" and "heresy," a value-free term common to the historian's trade? It certainly does not seem like it is. The people labeled as such are said to be "obsessed" with "discerning right and wrong beliefs."[2] They are blamed for "rewriting history" and for "claiming" that views held by some of their contemporaries were never held by the apostles or the majority of Christians, when — according to research conducted centuries later by modern scholars — these views really *were* acceptable to their predecessors. Finally, these "heresy hunters" are implicitly criticized for "trouncing and rejecting" these formerly acceptable views as innovations.[3] They were definitely exclusivists!

This moral judgment is interesting on several levels. If indeed the earliest Christians believed Jesus had been elevated to deity only at his resurrection[4] (a claim we'll have to come back to later), is this something the second-, third-, and fourth-century "heresy hunters" knew? Of course it is not. They did not read the Gospels, Acts, and the letters of Paul and others in the same way modern scholars do, by searching for earlier (and ideally, conflicting) sources embedded in these books, and by dissecting them into various hypothetical earlier and later editions. They had not yet discovered that buried within the words of their favorite books was the revelation that their earliest forebears in the faith did not believe Jesus was by nature divine. Should the "heresy hunters," who didn't know all this, be held responsible for rewriting a history they did not know existed—a history that, by the way, no one really knew existed until modern historians wrote it, using modern presuppositions and methods of study (which means they too are rewriting history)?

In an earlier portion of his book, Ehrman gives helpful instructions on how to do history. History has to be done in conformity with the views of the majority of historians: "it is not appropriate for a historian to presuppose a perspective or worldview that is not generally held";[5] "history, as established by historians, is based only on *shared* presuppositions."[6] This is Ehrman's defense for adhering to the naturalistic assumptions by which he operates as a historian. After all, who would want to suffer "exclusion" from the discipline of History for holding presuppositions contrary to those of the majority of historians? But that is another topic. For our purposes here, if we apply this standard to the early orthodox "historians," who supposedly rewrote history, they appear to have been acting precisely as they were supposed to act, precisely as historians in today's guild act too. They were giving a history that conformed to the historical understanding of a majority of their colleagues who knew anything about history. If the minority had a different view, well, they were the minority and could be dismissed. They were not doing history.[7]

Agree with them or not—and Ehrman obviously thinks we should not—the heresiologists (at least most of them; I'm reserving judgment on Epiphanius of Salamis from the late fourth century) appear to have been sincerely concerned for the souls of the people under their charge. Besides arguing against their opponents, they also prayed for them (e.g., Irenaeus, *Against Heresies* 5.25.7). They were not unlike the caring pastor in Ehrman's story in chapter 3, who wept when he learned of Ehrman's rising doubts about the Bible.

But what about the actual truth of the matter? Were the people Ehrman says the heresiologists were slandering really simply perpetuating views that would have been acceptable among orthodox Christians in a previous era? Were people like Justin, Irenaeus, Hippolytus, and Eusebius in fact rewriting history, when they claimed that the heresies were innovations?

DEAD ENDS AND IRONIES

A main point of chapter 8 of *How Jesus Became God* is to argue that "views that were originally considered 'right' eventually came to be thought of as 'wrong'; that is, views originally deemed orthodox came to be declared heretical."[8] Ehrman even identifies this as "one of the hard-and-fast ironies of the Christian tradition: views that at one time were the majority opinion, or at least that were widely seen as completely acceptable, eventually came to be left behind."[9]

It is, of course, true that among the orthodox we can trace a certain evolution in the depth and precision of christological views and other theological tenets as well. Forms of expression that might once have been tolerable later became unacceptable, as flaws or points of vulnerability came to be exposed in the earlier expressions. It is debatable, however, how radical the shifts were or how regularly views "originally deemed orthodox came to be declared heretical." For at least some of the examples Ehrman cites, I will argue, do not establish the sort of "hard-and-fast" irony he speaks of. One of these, the one Ehrman labels the clearest example, I will argue is not a real example at all. This will emerge, I think, as important not only for teaching the moral lessons Ehrman wants to teach, but for the entire argument of his book. I'll come to some specific examples and some specific theologians in a moment, but first an observation about the general, or at least, ideal orientation of orthodox discussions, which will help to show why some attempts became "dead ends."

Back to the Bible

When it comes to the church's understanding of Jesus and of God, the case can be made that theological evolution among the orthodox in the early centuries always had a fundamental retrospective orientation toward the biblical texts (as they were understood at the time). That is, alongside an increasing sophistication and complexity to the definitions, one can see an increasing effort to understand the implications of the whole of the church's Scripture.

Christian theology, with its backward orientation toward the original, is like other religious phenomena of antiquity. Take, for instance, the translation of the Hebrew Scriptures into Greek. After some of the first bold attempts were made (what is called the Old Greek, or the Septuagint), several later revisions of this text that we know about seem to be revisions toward the Hebrew. In one sense, the first attempts at translation had the potential to be the best, as they were carried out closest to the time of the underlying text. But in another sense, they were often loose or rough and stood open to many improvements. And as improvements were made, they were generally oriented to the original.

Or take the copying of New Testament manuscripts. In one sense, the earliest had the potential to be the best, since the manuscript tradition was less cluttered with variants in the early decades. But in another sense, the earliest copyists may not always have been the best trained ones and they may not have had access to the best exemplars. Later scribes, those responsible for the great fourth-century manuscripts known as Codex Vaticanus and Codex Alexandrinus, at least to some degree were able to "restore" the text to a much earlier form, as text critics still try to do today.[10]

Similarly in Christian theology, the first bold attempts are in some ways potentially better, as they are fresher and executed temporally closer to the original revelation, uncluttered by later admixtures. Later attempts at refinement, at least ideally, could benefit however from the consolidated canon of New Testament Scriptures and from ongoing discussion and the mistakes of the past, as they aimed at a more perfect contemporary expression of the ancient givens of the faith.

The mind-set of early orthodox theologians seems well encapsulated in this statement by third-century writer Hippolytus of Rome, in a treatise written against the modalism of a certain Noetus.

> There is, brethren, one God, the knowledge of whom we gain from the Holy Scriptures, and from no other source. For just as a man, if he wishes to be skilled in the wisdom of this world, will find himself unable to get at it in any other way than by mastering the dogmas of philosophers, so all of us who wish to practice piety will be unable to learn its practice from any other quarter than the oracle of God. Whatever things, then, the Holy Scriptures declare, at these let us look; and whatsoever things they teach, these let us learn; and as the Father wills our belief to be, let us believe; and as He wills the Son to be glorified, let us glorify Him; and as He wills the Holy Spirit to be bestowed, let us receive Him. Not according to our own will, nor according to our own mind, nor yet as using violently those things which are given by God, but even as He has chosen to teach them by the Holy Scriptures, so let us discern them. (*Against Noetus* 9)

Where, and to the extent that, such devotion to the Old and New Testament Scriptures was maintained, most of the theological alternatives to orthodox Christology and theology simply had no chance of long-term survival. This is particularly the case with the Ebionites and adoptionists, those who taught that Jesus was simply a man, perhaps "adopted" by God. One can say the same for the various docetic groups, who taught that Jesus was not fully human, or that he was a man visited by a heavenly Christ. For differing reason, these attempts to understand Jesus did not fully assimilate huge segments of New Testament teaching (in fact, the docetists began to be active before the entire New Testament was written and are specifically refuted in 1 and 2 John). Near the middle of the second century Marcion explicitly rejected most of the New Testament books. Others such as the Valentinians (and some Gnostics), however, made use of at least the majority of our current New Testament books (but other books as well). But they employed interpretative techniques that completely baffled non-Valentinian readers of the texts, techniques that required mastery of a "secret" and complex mythological "code" in order to make sense of the interpretations.

As simple and as popular as they might have been for a time (we'll investigate just how popular below), the various "modalistic" theories ultimately were doomed to the same fate. The idea that Christ was himself the Father (and the Spirit), clearly reported in several sources to have been the position of modalists like Noetus of Smyrna, seems so scripturally nonsensical that some scholars have suggested it could not have been real but was a "polemical invention" of his opponents.[11] Perhaps Noetus's view was a bit more sophisticated than our reports allow — who knows? In any case, Hippolytus, in his tract *Against Noetus*, said the man's followers "make use only of one class of passages" of Scripture, just as he says Theodotus, champion of the view that Christ was a mere man, was also one-sided in his use of Scripture (*Against Noetus* 3).

Origen of Alexandria, with little doubt, possessed the most encyclopedic "biblical" mind of anyone in his day, and he provided the church with an astounding treasure of biblical scholarship. But his theological experimentation was most unsuccessful precisely when it ventured to sail beyond Scripture's teaching, with speculation on the preexistence of the soul, and eternal worlds. The church historian Henry Chadwick famously alluded to one of Longfellow's poems when thinking of the work of Origen.[12]

> There was a little girl,
> And she had a little curl
>   Right in the middle of her forehead.
> When she was good,
> She was very, very good,
>   And when she was bad she was horrid.

The final stanza of the poem ends with little Jemima's mother catching her in the middle of one of her "horrid" deeds: "She took and she did spank her most emphatic" — which is not a bad description of the actions of some in the mother church to the excesses of the great Alexandrian scholar!

You could perhaps say that it was not until the Arian and semi-Arian debates of the fourth century that one really gets a sophisticated and plausible alternative attempt at interpreting all the biblical evidence. At many points the Arian and semi-Arian positions seemed to meet the biblical requirements and seemed to align with the spiritual practice of many Christians. But in the end each position was judged to have failed to attribute to Christ the fullness of deity that Colossians says dwelt in Christ.

The Adoptionism of the Ebionites and Theodotians

Perhaps the most important example Ehrman brings forth for Christianity changing its mind, and the most radical, has to do with the view called adoptionism. This view he attributes to the Ebionites (who flourished in the second century) and the Theodotians (who flourished in the early years of the third century). Each of these groups is said to have believed that Jesus was a mere man who was "adopted by God at his baptism."[13] For someone with views like Ehrman's, discovering the Ebionites or the Theodotians is like discovering gold. Here are people who, whether they had been preserving it all along or had just stumbled upon it, were holding to the very teachings that, according to Ehrman, the earliest Christians held about Christ![14]

In fact, Ehrman reports the view of some scholars that the Ebionites were the remnant of the very first Christians: "Jewish believers who congregated in Jerusalem in the years after Jesus's death around the leadership of his brother James."[15] Ehrman is sympathetic to this view, as he says: "In terms of their Christological views, the Ebionites do indeed appear to have subscribed to the perspective of the first Christians."[16]

We should briefly remind ourselves of what the perspective of the first Christians was, according to Ehrman. He has made it clear that "the earliest believers—as soon as they had visions of Jesus and came to believe that he had been raised form the dead—thought he had been exalted to heaven."[17] In the pre-Pauline creed in Rom 1:3–4 (so he argues), "Christ is said to have been exalted to heaven at his resurrection and to have been made the Son of God at that stage of his existence ... he was the human who was exalted at the end of his earthly life to become the Son of God and was made, then and there, into a divine being."[18] "Sometimes this view is referred to as an *adoptionist* Christology.... He was ... a human being who has been 'adopted' by God to a divine status."[19]

Yet even here there is a bit of confusion or equivocation. For Ehrman repeatedly writes that the "first" or "earliest" Christians believed Jesus had been exalted or adopted to divine status at or because of his resurrection. But when we come to the "adoptionists" of the second and third centuries, we are told they believed Jesus was adopted by God at his baptism. Such a view, according to Ehrman's chronology of christological development, is actually later than the view that he was adopted at the time of his resurrection.[20] So, to be precise, the adoptionist Ebionites and Theodotians should not be hailed as holding the views of the earliest Christians, but perhaps of the second earliest.

Despite that minor clarification, we may still sense the irony Ehrman wants us to sense: how far Christianity has come, to turn from believing in a man who became God, to believing in a God who became man! And then even to turn against those who continued to maintain the original (or second-to-original) Christology, a view of Jesus as adopted by God and exalted to divine status at his resurrection—or was it his baptism? In either case, this turnabout in Christian theology is, Ehrman thinks, the clearest of them all.[21]

But it is only clear if two things are true. First, it can only be clear if, as Ehrman believes he has shown in chapter 6 of *How Jesus Became God*, the first Christians were actually adoptionists, who believed Jesus was a mere man who was exalted to deity at his resurrection (let's just stick with the earliest of the early adoptionist Christologies at this point). In my opinion Ehrman has not shown this. I'll have more to say about the earliest Christians later and will also, of course, recommend you read Simon Gathercole's analysis of "exaltation Christology" in chapter 5 of this book.

Second, the turnabout is only true if indeed the Ebionites taught what Ehrman says they taught, that Jesus had been adopted, exalted to divine, Son of God status, at his baptism (or was it his resurrection?). And the problem is, this is hard to establish.

Our earliest reports of a group known as Ebionites never say they believed Jesus had been exalted to divine status. Ever. Not at his resurrection (supposedly the view of the earliest Christians), nor at his baptism (supposedly the view of the gospel of Mark), nor at his birth (supposedly the view of the gospels of Matthew and Luke). Irenaeus, our earliest source for the teaching of the Ebionites, says that they believed Jesus was the offspring of Joseph and Mary by natural generation and says nothing about them holding that Jesus was ever elevated to divine status (*Against Heresies* 1.26.2; 5.1.3).

Tertullian bluntly claims the Ebionites "refused to think that Jesus was the Son of God" (*Prescription* 33.11). Not even from the time of his baptism? Not according to the report of Tertullian. Hippolytus agrees: "They assert that our Lord Himself was a man in a like sense with all (the rest of the human family)" (*Refutation* 7.22). Not only does Hippolytus's account lack any notice of the Ebionites believing Jesus was exalted to deity, but he reports their claim that Jesus was named "Christ of God and Jesus" because he alone had completely observed the law, and they stated that whoever could keep the law as Jesus did could become a Christ like Jesus was.

It is not until Origen in the third century (*Against Celsus* 5.61) that we have a report of *two* branches of Ebionites, one that believed Jesus was "born of a virgin" and the other that denied this. But Origen's reports are inconsistent, for elsewhere (*Homilies on Luke* 17) he seems to say that all Ebionites deny the virgin birth. The confusion may be based on his reading of Justin Martyr, who wrote many decades earlier. Justin seems to know of two types of Jewish believers in Jesus, but he does not call either of them Ebionites. Each of these groups keeps the Jewish law, but one group does not believe Jesus is divine (*Dialogue* 48) and the other does (*Dialogue* 47). The implication is that those who do believe Jesus is divine believe he preexisted as God, like Justin did.[22] Clearly, if these are Ebionites, then the Ebionites agree that Jesus is divine by nature; if they are not Ebionites, we have no evidence yet that Ebionites believed Jesus was divine in any sense.

Eusebius, in the early fourth century, repeats Origen's report of two branches of Ebionites but asserts that even the group that affirmed Jesus' birth from a virgin by the Holy Spirit did not affirm that he preexisted as God, Word, Wisdom (*Ecclesiastical History* 3.27). We still have no clear report that any Ebionites believed Jesus was divine. We could *hypothesize* that the second branch of Ebionites, those who believed in the virgin birth of Jesus, might have believed he was elevated to deity. But if so, it would only be on the basis of their belief in the virgin birth — no mention is made of whether they believed Jesus rose from the dead. And if they followed the view attributed to one splinter group of the Theodotians (Hippolytus, *Refutation* 7.23), they could have believed in a virginal birth and still not believed Jesus was divine. We have no reason to believe that any group of Ebionites thought Jesus was exalted to deity at his resurrection (or his baptism)—the belief Ehrman asserts they shared with the earliest Christians.

Just as an aside, there is one splinter group that might be a lifeline for Ehrman's claim. One splinter group of the followers of Theodotus of Byzantium, according to Hippolytus (*Refutation* 7.23), taught that Jesus was made God "after the resurrection from the dead." They were apparently an offshoot of the original Theodotians who believed Jesus was made God at his baptism. It appears that the chronology here went in the opposite direction from the way it allegedly did at the beginning of the Christian movement. But other Theodotians, like the Ebionites, denied that Jesus was ever made God.

Postscript

This may be neither here nor there, but I have just learned that there are modern-day Ebionites who claim to be "the living continuation of the Jewish religious movement of Jesus."[23] They apparently have read the ancient testimonies about the Ebionites closely—and they appear to be familiar with historical Jesus studies to boot. As they say on their website:

> We want everyone to know immediately that the Ebionites are not Christians or messianics. Jesus of Nazareth is/was not the messiah, a savior, or part of a godhead. Thinking so is evil and blasphemy. His teachings do not constitute a new or different way to God. It is our goal to show that Judaism is the religion of God, and that worshiping Jesus is a grave sin, but also there is no historically legitimate reason for Christianity. Christian religion was never the intention of Jesus. We see Christianity as a horribly evil religion. We are not a "church" or competing movement within Judaism. Contact a local non-messianic synagogue for regular guidance and worship. Our view regarding theology is based on *historical Jesus* studies. Jesus is dead.

Again, these are modern Ebionites, and I certainly cannot vouch for their claim to be the "the living continuation of the Jewish religious movement of Jesus." At any rate, it doesn't sound like these modern Ebionites and self-professed followers of Jesus of Nazareth believe Jesus was ever exalted to deity, at his resurrection (was he resurrected?), his baptism, or his conception. Nor does it sound as if they are any more tolerant and accepting of the "orthodox" than the orthodox were of the Ebionites in the second and third centuries.

HETERO-ORTHODOXIES AND IRONIES

Modalism

We come now to one christological view that Ehrman dubs a "hetero-orthodoxy," that is, a view that affirmed both Jesus' humanity and his deity, but was still rejected as heretical. Modalism is the view that there is one God who manifested himself at different times in three different modes (Father, Son, and Spirit). By all accounts it was a rising phenomenon in the third century. We know of several teachers associated with it who attracted attention. Ehrman goes so far as to assert that modalism "evidently was held by a majority of Christians at the beginning of the third century—including the most prominent Christian leaders in the church, the bishops of the church of Rome (i.e., the early "popes")."[24] This statement seems to be a generous interpretation of a slim amount of evidence. It is one thing to speculate that the majority of Christians perhaps could not have articulated a clear statement of trinitarian theology; it is quite another to assert that they therefore had specifically a modalist understanding of God.

Ehrman's authority for suggesting that modalism was the majority view of Christians seems to be Tertullian himself in chapter 3 of his work *Against Praxeas*. Here, according to Ehrman, Tertullian "admits that the 'majority of believers' have trouble accepting his own view but prefer the view of the modalists (*Against Praxeas* 3)."[25] Here is what Tertullian says:

> The simple, indeed, (I will not call them unwise and unlearned) who always constitute the majority of believers, are startled at the dispensation (of the Three in One), on the ground that their very rule of faith withdraws them from the world's plurality of gods to the one only true God; not understanding that, although He is the one only God, He must yet be believed in with His own *oikonomia* [economy]. The numerical order and distribution of the Trinity they assume to be a division of the Unity.

The only way to make this say that the majority of Christians are modalists would be to try to make a syllogism out of it: the simple are modalists; most believers are simple; therefore, most believers are modalists. But this only works if there is another hidden element: not just "the simple are modalists" but "*all* the simple are modalists." If only some of the simple are modalists, we don't know if most believers are modalists or not. And in fact, Tertullian doesn't even say that the simple are *modalists*, only that they are startled by the Trinity in Unity because of a confused preunderstanding.

The simple are startled because, when leaving paganism (they may be new converts), they thought they were leaving a plurality of gods for the one true God. They are now being told, in a distortion of the church's teaching, that there are "three gods." But, as Tertullian labors to show, this is not the church's trinitarian teaching.

Tertullian's larger account in his treatise against Praxeas indicates that the swelling number of modalists was a brand new thing. Praxeas, according to Tertullian, was the person who brought these ideas to Rome from Asia, but he had actually recanted his views. For some time, then, these views remained dormant until they recently had sprung up again (*Against Praxeas* 1). Now, it is always possible that Tertullian is stretching the truth or even telling a flat-out lie. But the fact remains that we have no positive evidence for modalism being the majority view even in Rome, let alone in the entire church, as Ehrman implies.

We get another take on the situation in Rome from Hippolytus,[26] and there are similarities to the account of Tertullian. Modalism, according to Hippolytus, was held by two men in Rome who were bishops (Hippolytus does not consider them legitimate): a man named Zephyrinus (bishop 199–217 CE) and a man named Callistus (bishop 217–222) (*Refutation* 9.2). According to Hippolytus, Zephyrinus only adopted these views on the bad advice of Callistus, who was the real ringleader. Like Tertullian, Hippolytus too says this teaching was a newcomer, having "sprung up in our own day" (*Refutation* 9.1). It was introduced by a man named Noetus from Smyrna (some have thought that Tertullian's Praxeas and Hippolytus' Noetus are the same person), but brought to Rome by one of his followers. Interestingly, Hippolytus too, like Tertullian, reports that after surfacing in Rome, it went underground for a time. In Hippolytus's narrative, it was he himself who refuted Zephyrinus and Callistus and forced them "reluctantly to acknowledge the truth." For a short time they confessed their errors, and modalist views were kept at bay in Rome. But now, he laments, they "wallow once again in the same mire" (*Refutation* 9.2).

The bottom line here is that from neither of these writers are we able to conclude that modalism was the majority view even of Christians in Rome, let alone in every place throughout the empire.

Tertullian

But was Tertullian himself, the first Christian theologian to use the word *trinitas*, a heretic in waiting? In a typical Ehrman twist, the hunter (heresy hunter) would later become the hunted. Ehrman says that "Tertullian articulated a view that would later be deemed a heresy."[27]

Ehrman bases this statement on what Tertullian says in *Against Praxeas* 9: "Thus the Father is distinct from the Son, being greater than the Son, inasmuch as He who begets is one, and He who is begotten is another." What is evidently taken to be, by later standards, "completely inadequate" and "heresy" is Tertullian's statement that the Father is not merely "distinct from the Son," but "greater than the Son." Such a view has been called "subordinationism" by theologians and church historians. Christ's subordination to the Father, in this view, would not simply be due to his temporary messianic mission on earth. All Christians would believe that Christ submitted himself to the will of the Father to accomplish his work on earth. There was, as Tertullian says in the passage quoted above from *Against Praxeas* 3, a divine "economy" or arrangement between the three persons of the Trinity.[28]

In this economy or arrangement, while all three persons are one in mind and will, each person is found to exercise certain roles or operations. In relation to these roles, it might be said that the Father is "greater" in that the Son submits to follow the will of the Father while he is on earth as the Messiah.[29] Such an understanding would not be subordinationism. Rather, subordinationism would teach that Christ is intrinsically, essentially, and eternally inferior to the Father, as he would be if he were a "creature" of the Father. A clear statement of this view would be a heresy by Nicene trinitarian standards.

Was Tertullian advocating subordinationism? When we look at a larger context of Tertullian's statement, things look a bit different.

> For the Father is the whole substance, while the Son is an outflow and assignment of the whole, as he himself professes, *Because my Father is greater than I* (John 14:28); and by him, it is sung in the psalm, he has also been made less, *a little on this side of the angels* (Psalm 8:6). So also the Father is other than the Son as being greater than the Son, as he who begets is other than he who is begotten, as he who sends is other than he who is sent, as he who makes is other than he through whom a thing is made. (*Against Praxeas 9*)

Here it becomes plain that Tertullian, writing against those who thought Christ and the Father were the same person, is simply deriving his statement about the Father being greater than the Son from Jesus' words in John 14:28. And it is just as plain that he does not emphasize the word "greater" but simply the distinction; in the next part of the sentence, where he could have repeated the word "greater," he says only "other." While some might think that Jesus' words in John 14:28 themselves should be problematic for trinitarian theology, the great proponents of trinitarian theology themselves certainly did not think so, and they did not avoid these words. In his *Oration against the Arians*, Athanasius affirms that the Son

> is different in kind and substance from originated things and rather is peculiar to the Father's substance and of the same nature. For this reason the Son himself did not say, "My Father is better than I" [cf. John 14:28], lest someone suppose that he is foreign to his Father's nature, but he said "greater," not in some greatness or in time, but because of the generation from his Father. Besides, in the statement, "he is greater" he showed again the particularity of his substance. (*Oration against the Arians 1.58*)[30]

Elsewhere in his treatise *Against Praxeas* Tertullian is specific that the three divine persons are one *substance* or *essence*, speaking as he does of "three coherent Persons, *who are yet distinct* One from Another. These Three are, one *essence*, not one *Person*, as it is said, 'I and my Father are One,' (John 10.30) in respect of unity of substance not singularity of number" (*Against Praxeas 25*). It does not appear, then, that Tertullian should be labeled a subordinationist. As William Rusch says, "Tertullian took an important step in recognizing the

Trinitarian distinction of the three persons. In so doing, he also made a special effort to maintain God's essential unity"; "Tertullian's clear distinction between the three that are of one substance will be an important element in the Nicene formulation."[31]

That eventual Nicene formulation, though it has been accepted by all major branches of historic Christianity, is not without its own controversies. Accordingly we will next look at what Ehrman calls the "Ortho-Paradoxes on the Road to Nicea."

Second-Century Evidence for Jesus as God

Pagan, Early Orthodox, and Gnostic Testimony

Early Christian literature is filled with explicit and implicit references to Jesus as God. Here we give attestations from three different kinds of second-century texts: one from a bishop in the early orthodox tradition, one from a gnostic or semignostic source, and one from a pagan governor.

THE PAGAN: PLINY THE YOUNGER

> But they declared that the sum of their guilt or error had amounted only to this, that on an appointed day they had been accustomed to meet before daybreak and to recite a hymn antiphonally to Christ, as to a god, and to bind themselves by an oath, not for commission of any crime but to abstain from theft, robbery, adultery and breach of faith, and not to deny a deposit when it was claimed. After the conclusion of this ceremony it was their custom to depart and meet again to take food; but it was ordinary and harmless food, and they had ceased this practice after my edict in which, in accordance with your orders, I had forbidden secret societies. (Pliny, *Epistles* 10.96.7, cited from H. Bettenson).

Gaius Plinius Caecilis Secundus (ca. 61–113 CE) was a Roman lawyer and senator who held several important administrative posts in his political career. In Pliny's correspondence with the Roman emperor Trajan, written while Pliny was governor of Pontus-Bithynia in Asia Minor (ca. 111–113 CE), he presents Trajan with the problem of how to act against those who are accused of being Christians. Pliny provides a report as to how he has been conducting interrogations of the accused. He asks the accused three times if they are Christians; if they answer affirmatively, they are either executed or, if Roman citizens, sent to Rome for trial. Those who denied being Christians or said that they were once so but were no longer, were made to prove their innocence by invoking the gods, making offerings of wine and incense to the emperor's image, and then cursing Christ. Pliny is scornful about Christians even calling their religious conduct "a depraved and unrestrained superstition." Interestingly enough, Pliny gives an account of what went on at Christian meetings, and he describes their devotion to Christ through hymns as the veneration of a god.

THE BISHOP: IGNATIUS OF ANTIOCH

> I bid you farewell always in our God Jesus Christ; may you remain in him, in the unity and care of God. I greet Alce, a name very dear to me. Farewell in the Lord. (Ignatius, *To Polycarp* 8.3, trans. M. Holmes).

Ignatius was the bishop of Syrian Antioch (died ca. 110 CE). He wrote a series of letters to several churches while being escorted to Rome en route to his execution. In these letters he makes several striking affirmations about Jesus as God and intimately related to the Father. In some cases, the language seems liturgical, hymnic, and overtures later creedal christological statements (e.g., *Eph.* 7.2; 18.2; 19.3; *Rom.* 3.3; 6.3; *Smyrn.* 10.1; *Trall.* 7.1). There is repeated reference to Jesus Christ as "our God." In the letter to Polycarp, the bishop of Smyrna, the refrain is mentioned in the closing greeting as if it were completely normal for a Christian bishop to talk that way about Jesus. According to Thomas Weinandy: "Ignatius effortlessly and spontaneously wove within his understanding of the relationship between the Father and the Son the simple and unequivocal proclamation that Jesus Christ is God."[32]

THE GNOSTIC: THE INFANCY GOSPEL OF THOMAS

> What kind of great thing he could be—whether a divine being or an angel—I do not know even what to say. (*Infancy Gospel of Thomas* 7.4, trans. B. Ehrman).

The *Infancy Gospel of Thomas*, though its manuscript history is messy, is a second-century account of the childhood of Jesus with an acute emphasis on his great powers. The document may have been known to Irenaeus, who at least considered one of the stories it tells about Jesus to have originated from a Gnostic group known as the Marcosians (Irenaeus, *Against Heresies* 1.20.1). The purpose of the book is probably to underscore that the supernatural power of Jesus goes as far back as his childhood, and he used his miraculous abilities to amaze teachers with his wisdom and to crudely kill off playmates who irritated him. The document bears none of the marks of a fully-blown Gnostic cosmology, where the world was created by an evil demiurge. Nonetheless, it does emphasize the "knowledge" of Jesus and is certainly conducive to a Gnostic interpretation. In the text quoted above, a teacher named Zachaeus takes on Jesus as a pupil, only to be astounded and ashamed that Jesus' allegorical interpretation of the alphabet leaves him looking like an ignorant fool. Zachaeus complains to Joseph about Jesus and then wonders what kind of child he is, stating that Jesus is not of this world, and he must have been born before the world began. In the end, Zachaeus wonders if Jesus is a "god or an angel." For some reason, however, Ehrman translates *theos* as "divine being" rather than "God."

We should not assume that Pliny, Ignatius, and the author the *Infancy Gospel of Thomas* all had the same idea of a god/God in mind in relation to Jesus. What does appear certain, though, is that early in the second century Christians worshiped Jesus in a way ordinarily appropriate for the veneration of a deity (Pliny), Jesus was related to the Father in such a close and intimate way that he could even be considered the God of Christians (Ignatius), and Jesus was a preexistent and supernatural being clearly belonging to the divine realm (*Infancy Gospel of Thomas*).

Second Century Evidence for Jesus as God

The *Nomina Sacra*

O ne of the unique features of early Christian manuscripts is their preference for abbreviated forms for sacred names—hence the Latin term, *nomina sacra*. Typically such abbreviations comprised of combining the first and last letter of a word and omitting all the letters in between. So a name like *Iēsous* for "Jesus" would be contracted to *IS* and the title *Kyrios* for "Lord" would be contracted to *KS*. Added as well is a horizontal line over the letters called a macron, probably to help better identify when a *nomina sacra* is being used.

Hurtado points out that in the earliest observable stage of Christian scribal activity, four words in particular were written as *nomina sacra* with great regularity: God, Lord, Christ, and Jesus. The use of the *nomina sacra* for these names is remarkably widespread and found in early Christian writings, both canonical and noncanonical, from the beginnings of the second century. While the origins and meaning of the *nomina sacra* are debated, the most likely influence was Jewish reverential attitudes toward the writing of the Tetragrammaton, YHWH, which has carried over into Christian usage. The fact that the four earliest Christian *nomina* are key words for God (*Theos* and *Kyrios*) and designations for Jesus (*Iēsous*, *Christos*, and *Kyrios*) leads Hurtado to conclude:

> The *nomina sacra* practice represents an expression of piety and reverence, it is a striking departure from pre-Christian Jewish scribal practice to extend to these designations of Jesus the same scribal treatment

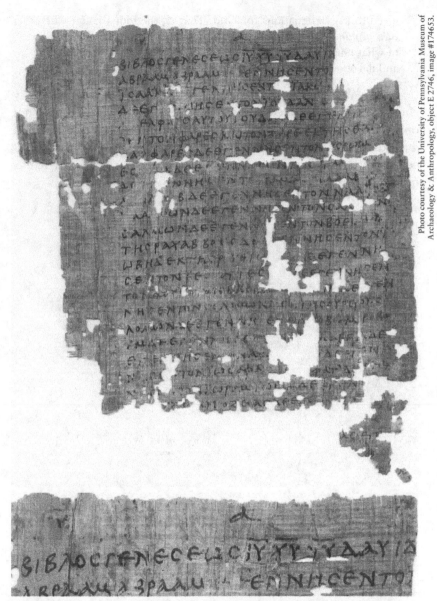

Photo courtesy of the University of Pennsylvania Museum of Archaeology & Anthropology, object E 2746, image #174653.

FIGURE 1 The image shown here is a detail taken from a fragment of the gospel of Matthew copied in the early third century (P. Oxy. 002, also known as 𝔓¹), containing the beginning of the gospel. The first line shows three *nomina sacra* in succession, IY XY YY in Matthew 1:1, meaning "of Jesus Christ the Son [of David]."[33]

given to key designations for God. That is, the four earliest Christian *nomina sacra* collectively manifest one noteworthy expression of what I have called the 'binitarian shape' of earliest Christian piety and devotion."[34]

These abbreviations were used almost universally in the early church. *Nomina sacra* contractions of the name of Jesus appear not only in early Christian manuscripts, but they have been discovered in a third-century floor mosaic at Megiddo in Palestine and in a third-century wall painting in a house church at Dura Europa on the banks of the Euphrates River.

CHAPTER 9

Paradox Pushers and Persecutors?

Charles E. Hill

A CHRISTIAN TELL-ALL

As I write this, networks all over the United States are abuzz with discussion of some pre-release excerpts from former Defense Secretary Robert Gates's new memoir, *Duty: Memoirs of a Secretary at War*. Garnering the most attention are some disconcerting revelations Gates has made about President Obama and Vice President Biden. Political "tell-alls" written by ex-administration insiders of both parties have become common in recent years. As officials quit an administration, it has almost become customary for some of them to spill dirt that those who stay within the fold have to try to clean up. Tell-alls are popular in the celebrity world too. One of the first and certainly most controversial celebrity tell-alls was Christina Crawford's 1978 book about her mother Joan, sarcastically titled *Mommy Dearest*. I can't say I've ever read it or seen the movie, but I have seen the famous clip (you can find it now on YouTube) of Faye Dunaway channeling Mommy Crawford in an emotional rampage, screaming: "No wire hangers!"

Whenever a tell-all comes out, from a one-time insider who has now turned his or her back on the "family," it draws attention. But questions are always asked. Can all those allegations really be true? Is s/he just bitter? Is there a financial motive?

Many readers have likely felt that they are reading a religious tell-all when they read books like *How Jesus Became God* and others of the genre. Here is a former insider (a former fundamentalist, no less), dishing out the scandalous truth about his former love. Like the steady drip of Edward Snowden's revelations about the "information gathering" activities of the NSA, books offering to expose the embarrassing secrets of the Christian faith are appearing these days with seemingly unstoppable regularity.

In the final chapters and in the epilogue of *How Jesus Became God*, we get some tantalizing revelations: contradictions forced Christians to invent paradoxes (with the introduction of a new word, "ortho-pardoxes"); Christians flip-flopped on doctrine; Christians fought with each other; Christians who believed Jesus was God did some bad things to others. The flavor can be seen in one excerpt.

> More specifically, if Christ is God, and God the Father is God, in what sense is there only one God? And if one adds the Holy Spirit into the mix, how does one escape the conclusion either that Christ and the Spirit are not God, or that there are three Gods? In the end, the orthodox settled for the paradox of the Trinity: there are three persons, all of whom are God, but there is only one God. One God, manifest in three persons, who are distinct in number but united in essence. This too became the standard doctrine of the orthodox tradition, and as happened with the Christological ortho-paradox, it also led to further disputes, heretical interpretations, and nuanced refinements.[1]

There we have it. Intractable contradictions constrained the orthodox to "settle" for the paradox of the Trinity—desperate times call for desperate measures! But alas, this settlement did not bring peace. Far from it. The construction of the paradox was followed by "further disputes, heretical interpretations, and nuanced refinements." This is before we even get to the subject of Christian bad behavior.

PARADOXES

There is a strong reliance in chapter 9 of Ehrman's book on the notion that most readers will think the concept of a "paradox" is detrimental to Christianity. Aren't paradoxes simply an admission that your doctrines don't make sense?[2] Ehrman is certainly not the first, nor will he be the last, to think so. Trypho, the Jewish philosopher portrayed by Justin as having an encounter with him in Ephesus sometime between 135–160 CE, said this to his Christian conversation partner:

> Resume the discourse where you left off, and bring it to an end. For some of it appears to me to be paradoxical, and wholly incapable of proof. For when you say that this Christ existed as God before the ages, then that He submitted to be born and become man, yet that He is not man of man, this [assertion] appears to me to be not merely paradoxical, but also foolish. (Justin Martyr, *Dialogue* 48.1)

Justin, who believed and defended the "paradox," was obviously not so embarrassed about it that he would not record and deal with Trypho's challenge. But should he have been?

ORTHO-PARADOXES

If Ehrman is correct, Justin should have been quite embarrassed. In order to show what Justin and his orthodox companions were up against, Ehrman coins a new term for this chapter: "ortho-paradoxes." Of course, as we have just noticed, Christians and even non-Christians like Trypho have always just called these "paradoxes." The reason for calling them "ortho-paradoxes" is that "they are the paradoxes that came to figure so prominently in specifically orthodox Christianity."[3] By analogy, I suppose paradoxes that figured prominently in heterodox Christianity could be called "hetero-paradoxes." I have checked the index of the book *Lost Christianities: The Battles for Scripture and the Faiths We Never Knew*, however, and have found no entry for that term.

These ortho-paradoxes emerged from what Ehrman calls "two brutal facts." I'm not sure why these facts are "brutal," but the adjective surely fits the tenor of Ehrman's presentation. The first brutal fact is that "some passages of scripture appear to affirm completely different views," and the second is that "different groups of heretics stated views in direct opposition to one another, and the orthodox thinkers knew that they had to reject each of these views."[4] It seems to me that these two facts really resolve into one, for how did the orthodox know they had to reject the directly opposing views of different groups of heretics (the second brutal fact)? Mainly because of the first brutal fact. These Christians, as we saw in the last chapter, were committed to following what they found in Scripture, and "some passages of scripture appear to affirm completely different views."

When Ehrman turns to give examples of Scripture appearing to affirm "completely different views," he understandably goes to the Gospel of John and the first epistle of John. Each of these books openly and unabashedly affirms both Jesus' deity and his humanity. But here we have to stop, for this brings up two rather weighty problems for the view Erhman is advocating in the volume. Okay, the first problem is not all that weighty, but the second is. The first problem is that, because the paradox of Christ's humanity and divinity arises first and foremost from the books the early Christians deemed to be Scripture, it was not simply an "ortho-paradox" — one that resulted from the later *orthodox* struggling to come to grips with two apparently irreconcilable affirmations. It was a paradox *from the beginning.* It is not so much an "ortho-paradox" as it is a New Testament paradox — certainly a Johannine paradox, or, as we will soon see, a Pauline paradox or even a pre-Pauline paradox. This simply means that the newly minted term "ortho-paradox" is redundant and might not be one of the words added to the Oxford English Dictionary in 2014. That is not too serious.

The second problem is more serious. For the legitimacy of Ehrman's overall argument in *How Jesus Became God*, it might even be "brutal." The problem, as I see it, is that these "passages of scripture [that] appear to affirm completely different views" are found *integrated* in single books, or in the mind of one and the same person. The writer of the Gospel of John clearly teaches that Jesus Christ is preexistent God, even from the very first verse: "and the Word was God" (John 1:1). Then only a few verses later, the same book and the same author says, "The Word became flesh and made his dwelling among us" (John 1:14).[5]

The writer of 1 John teaches the same two things about Jesus Christ (for our purposes we do not have to decide whether John and 1 John have the same author). We have no indication that the author(s) of these books thought this was embarrassing, that the two ideas about Jesus Christ were "completely different," "contradictory," or "in direct opposition to one another." Instead, to all appearances, this author (or these authors) believed that the facts of Christ's preexistence as God and his incarnation as man were not brutal but amazing and awe-inspiring, and in some wonderful way, harmonious and glorious. "We have seen his glory," the Johannine writer exclaims, "the glory of the one and only Son, who came from the Father, full of grace and truth" (John 1:14).

Nor are these Johannine books alone in affirming and *integrating* these paradoxical ideas about Jesus Christ. Ehrman quotes Col 1:19, "in him all the fullness of God was pleased to dwell," and likens this teaching to the teaching in the Prologue of John, claiming, "We have now moved into an entirely different realm from the earlier exaltation Christologies."[6] But in fact, after mentioning again how the fullness of deity dwelt bodily in Jesus (Col 2:9), the letter goes on to mention Christ's exaltation, when God "raised him from the dead" (2:12; cf. 3:1).

The twin beliefs that Jesus was true man and also true God are combined and assimilated in a massive way in the thought of the author of the letter to the Hebrews. Ehrman rightly says that Hebrews too has "the kind of incarnational Christology found in the Gospel of John.... But a hint of exaltation Christology remains here as well."[7] More than a hint, I would say. But the point is, the "two Christologies" appear not as the uncomfortable concatenation of two originally conflicting Christologies. They are a seamless whole in the thought of the author, who interweaves them naturally and instinctively:

> In the past God spoke to our ancestors through the prophets at many times and in various ways, but in these last days he has spoken to us by his Son, whom he appointed heir of all things, and through whom also he made the universe. The Son is the radiance of God's glory and the exact representation of his being, sustaining all things by his powerful word. After he had provided purification for sins, he sat down at the right hand of the Majesty in heaven. So he became as much superior to the angels as the name he has inherited is superior to theirs. (Heb 1:1–4)

He, God's Son, was "appointed heir," but he was already the agent of creation; he is the radiance of God's glory and sustains the universe, but "became" superior to the angels and inherited a name. No sense of being brutally beaten by two irreconcilable facts here!

I'm suggesting that this is a problem that goes to the heart of Ehrman's book and to the heart of the historical reconstruction of early Christianity as evidenced by Ehrman and others. In order to show this, I'll have to back up to earlier parts of the book to pick up Ehrman's finely constructed but ultimately unsuccessful argument.[8] It is an argument about the development of early Christology.

Ehrman's method, as a historian, is to establish the "earliest" tradition about who Jesus was, then to see how that tradition developed to the end of the New Testament period, and then to see how it developed even further in the post-New Testament period, up to the great symbolic definitions of the councils of Nicea and Constantinople. As he says, he is interested in "how Jesus became God."

But how does one discern where the earliest ideas about Jesus are to be found? The New Testament Gospels, which tell the story of Jesus, are actually not as early as the letters of Paul. So it looks like our earliest source of information for what the earliest Christians believed about Jesus will be found in Paul. But sometimes Paul apparently quotes some earlier compositions—hymns, creeds, confessions, or poems—that already existed before he wrote. These, it is thought, can give us even earlier information about what Jesus' followers believed about him. So far, so good.

But what about the chronological order of these several bits of pre-Pauline tradition? This is more difficult, but it is critically important. For the earliest of these bits of pre-Pauline tradition (so it is argued) present only an *exaltation* Christology. An exaltation Christology, as defined by Ehrman, assumes that Jesus was fully human but only human, as merely human as you and me. Unlike you and me, though, he *became* divine when God is believed to have exalted him to divine status at some pivotal point.

Other bits of pre-Pauline tradition preserved in Paul's letters, however, present an *incarnational* Christology. Sometimes, at least, it is an incarnational theology that does not necessarily reject the exaltation of Jesus to heavenly glory after his resurrection but can even affirm it. How can we tell which bits of pre-Pauline tradition are earlier? For we cannot pick them up, turn them over, and find dates printed on the back. Ehrman seems certain that there is an order to them: the exaltation Christologies came first, and the incarnational Christologies were a later development. But his certainty rests not on historical study but on a predetermined chronological grid that is not provable historically. He gives us this grid, but only late in the book. He presents it as a conclusion, but actually it is a presupposition.

> To use the older terminology, in early Christianity the views of Christ got "higher and higher" with the passing of time, as he became increasingly identified as divine. Jesus went from being a potential (human) messiah to being the Son of God exalted to a divine status at his resurrection; to being a preexistent angelic being who came to earth incarnate as a man; to being the incarnation of the Word of God who existed before all time and through whom the world was created; to being God himself, equal with God the Father and always existent with him.[9]

It is easy for the reader to get the impression that this chronology is a rational "conclusion" of unbiased historical study — instead of what it actually is, a presupposition of historical study — because of the way in which Ehrman presents the evidence.

Here is how he does it. In chapter 4 he introduces the pre-Pauline tradition contained in 1 Cor 15:3 – 5, and in chapter 6 he presents the tradition in Rom 1:3 – 4. Each of these passages is interpreted to mean that Christ only "became" God after his resurrection.[10] These must represent the views of the "earliest" Christians, and, as far as the reader suspects at this point, there are no other "early" traditions out there to compete with them. Meanwhile, waiting in the wings is Phil 2:6 – 11, a passage that is not introduced until chapter 7.[11] Phil 2:6 – 11, containing what Ehrman calls a "Christ poem," is also pre-Pauline. It, however, assumes that Christ existed before his human birth, and existed in the form of God (not simply an angel). Christ was exalted again to heaven after he had humbled himself to take human form and suffer crucifixion in obedience to God. What is more, we now learn there are other pre-Pauline attestations of similar incarnational views of Christ, such as the one Paul uses in 1 Cor 8:6 — "yet for us there is but one God, the Father, from whom all things came and for whom we live; and there is but one Lord, Jesus Christ, through whom all things came and through whom we live."

These pre-Pauline, incarnational traditions, we are told, are *later* than the pre-Pauline traditions that only viewed Jesus as divine based on his exaltation. Ehrman therefore calls the incarnational traditions "amalgams" of earlier traditions.[12] But how do we know this? How do we know that the "exaltation" traditions are not in fact simply *abbreviations* of a fuller incarnational tradition, used to stress Jesus' humanity or his suffering or his fulfillment of prophecies about the coming Messiah?

This is surely how they functioned for Paul, as abbreviations of a fuller Christology. When Paul at the beginning of Romans quoted a tradition that emphasized that Christ was descended from David "according to the flesh," and was set forth as Son of God in power by his resurrection from the dead, he was certainly not thereby denying that Christ was also the preexistent Son of God by nature. When he cited a preformulated creed containing "exaltation" Christology in 1 Cor 15:3–5, this did not cancel out the incarnation Christology he had already expressed earlier in the same letter when he quoted an "incarnation" creed in 1 Cor 8:6. Similarly, when the pre-Pauline author of the Christ poem in Phil 2:6–11 put the poem together, this author too did not see the preexistence of Christ as God as contradicted by his exaltation to heavenly status after the resurrection.

So, how do we know that even the author(s) of the creeds used by Paul in Rom 1:3–4 and 1 Cor 15:3–5 did not also view their creeds as abbreviations of a fuller incarnational Christology? As another example, the author of 1 John writes: "This is how you can recognize the Spirit of God: Every spirit that acknowledges that Jesus Christ has come in the flesh is from God, but every spirit that does not acknowledge Jesus is not from God" (1 John 4:2). Did the author really mean that a spirit from God would not have to believe that Jesus also rose from the dead, or that he also was God "in the beginning" (1 John 1:1)? Of course not. There is an issue at hand, the issue of Jesus Christ's true humanity—"in the flesh"—and the author is specifically addressing that issue. What the spirits must confess here is just one abbreviated summary of a portion of what the author's community believed about Jesus.

The New Testament authors, and Christians ever since, constantly make statements or confessions about Jesus that encompass only a small part of what they believe about him. In fact, they do so whenever they use these words from the Apostles' Creed:

> I believe in Jesus Christ, his only Son, our Lord,
> who was conceived by the Holy Spirit
> and born of the virgin Mary.
> He suffered under Pontius Pilate,
> was crucified, died, and was buried;
> he descended to hell.
> The third day he rose again from the dead.
> He ascended to heaven
> and is seated at the right hand of God the Father Almighty.
> From there he will come to judge the living and the dead.[13]

There is nothing explicit here about Jesus' preexistence or his full deity. True, it is surely *assumed* in the meaning of the words "his only Son" in the first line. But according to Ehrman, such a bare statement could just as well mean that Jesus was *exalted* to Son of God status at his baptism or resurrection, perhaps even at his conception. Or one could say that Christ's full deity is *assumed* by the fact that the creed divides itself in a trinitarian way, with statements about the Father, the Son, and the Holy Spirit. This is no doubt true, but again, this is the *assumption* behind the creed; the creed itself does not spell it out. Creeds are always mere summations of what believers believe; the rest is assumed to be filled in by teaching and preaching and is usually commonly known in the community. The Apostles' Creed has much more to say about Jesus' resurrection and ascension to heaven than about his preincarnate deity. But it was constructed and used by Christians who believed in Christ's preincarnate deity and has been confessed through the centuries by people who believe in his preincarnate deity. Even the Apostles' Creed (like all of the creeds) expresses only a part of what Christians believe.

The only way we know that the pre-Pauline creeds and other expressions of incarnational Christology embedded in his letters are later and the exaltation christological expressions are earlier is by accepting the predetermined chronological grid: Christology *must* have begun from the "lower" and moved to the "higher." But if this is predetermined, how is it "historical" and "scientific," open to testing and falsification?

Here is where the naturalistic assumption makes a *determinative* difference in historical research. For this presupposed theory of christological development determines all of Ehrman's historical/theological judgments throughout the book. And so, the problem of a rigidly applied but unproven chronology of belief about Jesus forms a crack that extends throughout his historical reconstruction of early developments in Christology.

As we saw in the last chapter, the Ebionites and other "adoptionists" in the second and third centuries are said to have held to the Christology of the earliest Christians. This claim is then drawn in to serve as one of the great ironies of Christianity: later Christians rejected as heretics the people who held the first Christian beliefs. We also saw in the last chapter that the Ebionites cannot be shown to have ever believed Jesus became God, let alone that he became God at his resurrection. Now we see that we cannot establish that the earliest Christians believed Christ was a mere man exalted to deity only at his resurrection (or his baptism). Such a view, *if it ever existed*, cannot be shown to be any earlier than a view that recognized Jesus' preexistent deity.

None of the New Testament writers attempted a full articulation of the mysteries of the person of Jesus Christ. We might wish they had, but it is likely that even if they had been both more precise and more expansive, they would not have removed the paradox. As it is, both sides of the "paradox" are clearly held, and they are not clumsily juxtaposed but integrated in the writings of the New Testament authors. As far as we can tell, none of these writers was discomfited by the "seeming contradictions" or the supposed brutality of these two facts, that Jesus was God and that he had come in the flesh. As hard as it may seem to believe, there is no evidence of the kind of hesitation, inner turmoil, or mental torture as is supposed to be experienced by many. These authors had come to the stunning realization that Jesus was both God and man, and none of them thought that either the humanity or the divinity of Jesus, or the humanity and divinity together, rendered faith in him impossible. The "paradox" was accepted as such and did not prevent these authors advocating and commending a full faith in Jesus as the Messiah and Savior to outsiders. It was that faith.

THE ORTHODOX AND THE PARADOXES

So what happens when we step away from the New Testament authors mentioned above and come to early orthodox theologians, like Justin, Irenaeus, Tertullian, Hippolytus, Novatian, and others? Once again we might be led by Ehrman and others to expect to hear panic in their voices. After all, they were left with the unreasonable task of having to reconcile the irreconcilable. But by the time these authors wrote, Christian communities had been reconciled to these irreconcilable realities for a long time.

Orthodox theologians are exercised, no doubt, and sometimes rattled, apparently not by the unnerving contradictions that had been handed them in the muddled testimonies of their Scriptures, but by what they saw as distortions and even blasphemies that were being promoted in their day. Their own attempts at explaining the revelation of Jesus Christ given through the apostles were not always fully consistent, either with themselves or with each other or with Scripture. Their expressions were not always exceptionally well guarded. Some of their efforts were later seen as unsuccessful. They struggled to integrate all the scriptural data and to find the right vocabulary to teach and defend their doctrine. But what Ehrman calls their "ortho-paradoxes" are what they celebrated, not what they tried to cover up and hide from view. And what they were celebrating had been celebrated in their Christian communities for a long time.

Justin Martyr

Justin is an important figure for our knowledge of Christianity in the second century. Ehrman wants to emphasize that for Justin, Christ "did not always exist"[14] and was "brought into existence";[15] for Justin, Christ is "a kind of second God created by God the Father."[16] Justin's language at times has left him open to the charge of holding to some form of "subordinationism," the idea that the Son is a being essentially inferior to God the Father, that he is not fully God. Yet as we will see, this could simply be because Justin did not always fill in the blanks, for, as J. N. D. Kelly has said, Justin's theology "is far from being systematic."[17]

The reason Ehrman's presentation is misleading is that for Justin, Christ, the Logos, is begotten of the Father, and Justin makes a clear distinction between what is begotten of God and what is "created." As Kelly summarizes, for Justin, "while other beings are 'things made' (*poiēmata*) or 'creatures' (*ktismata*), the Logos is God's 'offspring' (*gennēma*), His 'child' (*teknon*) and 'unique Son' (*ho monogenēs*): 'before all creatures God begat, in the beginning, a rational power out of Himself.'"[18] Justin is emphatic on the distinction between being begotten and being created. Christ is not "a kind of second God created by God the Father."[19]

But does the mere fact that he was begotten of the Father mean, as Ehrman concludes, that the Logos "did not always exist"? When Justin says that the Logos, begotten by God, "was with the Father before all the creatures and the Father communed with Him" (*Dial.* 62.4), does this imply that Justin thought, as Arius would later put it, "there was (a time) when he was not"? Is Justin an Arian? The most one could say is that perhaps Justin left some room for an Arian interpretation. But then, such an Arian position had not yet been broached. And the room he left could have been filled the way Athanasius filled it, who countered that God's begetting of the Son is not subject to "time."

What is important for Justin is not the issue of whether there was any "time" before he was begotten, but rather the idea that the Logos and he alone is begotten, not created. This crucial affirmation is echoed in the Nicene Creed itself:

> We believe in one Lord, Jesus Christ.
> The only Son of God,
> Eternally begotten of the Father,
> God from God, Light from Light,
> True God from true God,
> Begotten, not made,
> Of one Being with the Father.

It is sung by advent choirs in one stanza of the hymn, *O Come, All Ye Faithful*:

> God of God,
> Light of Light,
> Lo he abhors not the Virgin's Womb.
> Very God,

Begotten not created.
O come, let us adore him ...
Christ the Lord

At the right time, "through the power of the Word, according to the will of God the Father and Lord of all, He was born of a virgin as a man, and was named Jesus, and was crucified, and died, and rose again, and ascended into heaven" (1 Apol. 46). "Incarnation Christology" and "exaltation Christology" certainly coexist in Justin.

There is also the matter of who it is that Christians worship. Ehrman says Justin indicates "that Christians worship God, the Son, angels, and the Spirit—clearly not a Trinitarian view (1 Apology 13)."[20] The passage in question is not in 1 Apology chapter 13 but chapter 6 (chapter 13 is important, as we will see). The translation in the Ante-Nicene Fathers edition is:

> But both Him, and the Son (who came forth from Him and taught us these things, and the host of the other good angels who follow and are made like to Him), and the prophetic Spirit, we worship and adore...

One way of construing this rather confusing sentence is as a claim that Christians worship angels, along with the Father, the Son, and the Spirit. This is how Ehrman takes it. But this reading is suspect. Not only would it go against all prior (and subsequent) prohibitions against worshiping angels, such as Col 2:18 or Rev 19:10; 22:8–9, but Justin himself clearly says God created the "race of angels" in the beginning along with the race of men (1 Apology 7.5). Unlike the Logos, angels were not begotten but created. Moreover, in chapter 13 Justin offers a sharper and more concise statement that Christians "reasonably worship Him, having learned that He is the Son of the true God Himself, and holding Him in the second place, and the prophetic Spirit in the third." Then in chapter 16 he speaks of baptism "in the name of God, the Father and Lord of the universe, and of our Saviour Jesus Christ, and of the Holy Spirit." In neither of these passages are angels mentioned. Thus, many have thought that the angels in chapter 6 are meant to go alongside "us" as those whom the Son has taught: "the Son (who came forth from Him and taught us and the angels ... these things)." The particular Greek construction in 1 Apology 6 would supports such a reading, as it shows Justin linking together the Father, the Son, and the Spirit by the use of a conjunction (*te*), which is not used for the company of angels.

COMING TO THE "DESIRED RESULT"

While the writings of many more theologians beckon, this will just about have to do for our purposes here. I can agree with Ehrman that the third-century Roman presbyter Novatian articulated a trinitarianism that was bound not to last.[21] Rusch judges that "Novatian's work represents a regression from the levels reached by the Apologists, Irenaeus, and Tertullian."[22] Yet only a few years later, Novatian's contemporary in Rome, a bishop named Dionysius, fared better. In his letter to Dionysius of Alexandria, the Roman Dionysius offers a clear argument that Christ the Son of God is also coeternal with God. The way Ehrman puts it is, "Dionysius reaches the desired theological result."[23]

As we look back on some of the embryonic, pre-Nicene statements of those in the orthodox tradition, such as those catalogued in chapter 9 of *How Jesus Became God*, most Christian readers will likely be inclined toward sympathy for the well-intentioned but not always fully adequate efforts they read about. Let's face it; it is not easy even today, even for those who are familiar with the definitions of Nicea and the writings of Athanasius and others, to make sure they always state everything with correctness and precision. How much more for those Christians writing before Nicea?

Somewhat more annoying is that even in *How Jesus Became God*, while Ehrman certainly can and does use the standard trinitarian terminology, he also often muddies the waters by mixing up the terms "being" and "person." Of the views of Hippolytus and Tertullian he says, "In the divine economy there are three persons—the Father, the Son, and the Holy Spirit. These are three distinct beings,"[24] even though this is not their terminology. Speaking of Justin's view he says, "Christ came forth from God and became his own being,"[25] though Justin does not use that language. For the orthodox, "it was concluded that Christ was a separate being from God the Father."[26] Actually, for the orthodox he was a distinct *person* from God the Father, but the *same being*. Speaking of Dionysius of Rome, "There need to be three divine beings. But the three need to be one, not three."[27] Actually, there "need" to be three divine persons who share the same being or essence.

"Three beings" already gives the impression of three distinct Gods, three Gods that somehow "have to be brought together" to avoid the implication that there are actually three Gods. This is accurate to Ehrman's perception of the predicament of the history of Christian theology, for he seems to perceive it as a confounded logical mess that Christians got themselves into by choosing to submit themselves to the contradictory ideas of their Scriptures. It then becomes a puzzle to solve, to achieve the "desired result." But this is apparently not the way the Christians perceived it, who were trying to speak faithfully about the ineffable God they worshiped.

Trinitarian theology especially from the time of Tertullian, but using terminology formulated at least as early as Justin, speaks of three divine "persons" (Greek *prosōpon*; Latin *persona*), rather than divine beings. The terminology was not taken from some procedure of analytical logic that had nothing to do with Scripture, but instead came directly from the practice of the exegesis of Scripture as relating to theology and Christology.

Michael Slusser points out[28] that Justin, Irenaeus, and Tertullian often spoke of how, in prophetical literature of the Old Testament, such as the Psalms or Isaiah, the reader has to keep in mind the different "persons" doing the speaking, or being spoken to, or being spoken of.[29] For instance, the psalmist says, "The LORD says to my Lord" (Ps 110:1), or "your throne, O God, is forever" (Ps 45:7). As Tertullian states:

> So in these [texts], few though they be, yet the distinctiveness of the Trinity is clearly expounded: for there is the Spirit himself who makes the statement, the Father to whom he makes it, and the Son of whom he makes it. So also the rest, which are statements made sometimes by the Father concerning the Son or to the Son, sometimes by the Son concerning the Father or to the Father, sometimes by the Spirit, establish each several Person as being himself and none other.[30]

Slusser concludes, "It was a method of literary and grammatical analysis of Scripture that provided the early Christian thinkers with a way to talk about God in a Trinitarian fashion."[31] The method and the terminology that these theologians eventually developed were not simply a mechanism by which to solve an abstract puzzle, but were "congruent with both Christian piety and Christian worship."[32]

THE EPILOGUE

Now we come to the bad behavior alluded to earlier. I will admit that I have not looked forward to dealing with this portion of the material, but there is, I think, value in taking it up. In the epilogue Ehrman wants to take us to the aftermath of the long struggle to establish orthodox doctrine about Jesus and about the trinitarian understanding of God. In relation to the pagan world, the conversion of Constantine changed everything for Christianity. Christian readers will probably see this as both bad and good. The long competition between the Christian God and the Roman emperor as god took a new turn. "In the early fourth century, one of the competitors caved in and lost the struggle. With Constantine, the emperor changed from being a rival god to Jesus to be being a servant of Jesus."[33]

How can Christian readers not rejoice? How can anyone not rejoice, unless one thinks the persecution of Christians ought to be a permanent aspect of civilized society? But then "Constantine required the soldiers in his army not to worship him, but to worship the Christian God."[34] The problem here, of course, from our perspective 1,700 years later, is that Constantine *required* the soldiers in his army to worship anyone. The "good thing" that ended the persecution also brought a real, and sad, irony: "Rather than being a persecuted minority who refused to worship the divine emperor, the Christians were on the path to becoming the persecuting majority."[35]

And here is where the story turns sour. The eventual mistreatment of Jews by some Christians, once the church had come into a favored political position in the fourth and later centuries, is a serious matter and is a continual blight on the history of the Christian religion. Entire books have been written, deservedly so, to shine the light on a shameful aspect of Christian history. The puzzling, and I confess, troubling thing is why this topic has to figure so prominently in a book on early Christology.

The ostensible reason is that, in Ehrman's argument, there is a close connection between belief in Christ's deity and violent, Christian anti-Judaism. This is clearly one of the most important lessons he wants readers to learn, as he devotes a section of the epilogue to it and primes the reader for it several times in the last chapters.

The priming starts near the end of chapter 7 in a comment on John 1:11. This text says that Jesus came to his own people and his own people did not receive him. This statement, Ehrman says, has a "clear downside." The downside is not that this rejection of Jesus meant that he would later be killed, or that his followers would bear some of the same abuse he did. The downside of the rejection of Jesus by his people is that, according to the teaching of the gospel of John, Jesus is divine. Thus, if the Jews reject Jesus, they are rejecting God. (This, of course, is true, but it applies to all who reject Jesus, not just to Jews who reject him.) "The far-reaching, and rather horrific, implications of this view," Ehrman promises us, "will be the subject of a later discussion in the epilogue."[36]

Later, after noting that the letter to the Hebrews argues for the superiority of Christ to "simply everything in Judaism," readers are once again "confronted with the discomfiting situation. To make such exalted professions about Christ more or less forced the Christians to drive a wedge between their views and those of Jews, a matter to which we return in the epilogue"[37] — even though both the writer of Hebrews himself and his original audience were Jews themselves. Finally, when considering the Ebionites in chapter 8, Ehrman again puts the reader on notice that Christians' opposition to key aspects of Judaism will be explored "at greater length in the epilogue."[38]

When we finally arrive at the long-anticipated section of the epilogue, Ehrman begins with a sermon on the Passover preached in the late second century by Melito of Sardis. In this sermon "Melito delivers his ultimate charge against his enemies, the Jews."[39] In this highly rhetorical oration Melito charges (is it a "charge" or is it a lament?) that God was murdered at the hand of Israel. Here is the charge of "deicide," the killing of Jesus, who is God. As Ehrman points out, it is the first instance on record of a Christian charging Jews with this crime.[40] Melito himself, as a Christian living in the second century, was far from being in a position to be persecuting anybody, and Ehrman admits this. (This is speculation, but it probably never occurred to Melito to set fire to a synagogue). But it is this one charge of deicide that provides the cover for the remaining account of deplorable conditions that resulted for Jews, once the Christians gained the upper hand.

"Jews came to be legally marginalized under Christian emperors and treated as second-class citizens with restricted legal rights and limited economic possibilities."[41] No one can argue with that ugly historical reality. Two authorities on the subject of Christian anti-Judaism, though, provide a little more of the context.

> Yet orthodoxy's anti-Judaism provided only one small tributary to those Roman legal traditions regarding Jewish rights and practices that had coursed, by Constantine's day, for more than three centuries.... Harsh rhetoric aside ... Christian emperors through the fifth century by and large continued and arguably even extended the policies of their pagan predecessors, granting to Jewish communities a significant degree of autonomy, both religious and social.... By mandate, synagogues were protected from destruction, from appropriation by the military (troops were not to be quartered therein), and from unlawful seizure (in such cases, Jewish communities were to be fairly compensated for their property).[42]

In other words, second-class citizenry for Jews in Roman society, though not undone by Christian emperors, had been a steady condition centuries before any Christian emperor came onto the scene. Modest efforts to enhance Jewish autonomy were extended after Christianity gained influence, and laws protecting synagogues were put in place. Compared to other changes resulting from Constantine's conversion, "the changes that the Christianization of the government worked on the Empire's official legal posture toward Jews and Judaism seem relatively mild."[43]

What was probably more detrimental than official government constraints, according to Fredriksen and Irshai, was the rise in status of the bishops. Christian bishops advanced up the social ladder largely because they were pressed into service by the Roman government to perform various administrative functions. In any case, they sometimes took advantage of their newfound positions of influence and used this influence to the disadvantage of nonbelievers. We have the incident mentioned by Ehrman, in which a bishop was accused of inciting a mob to burn down a synagogue in the city of Callinicum. Fredriksen and Irshai catalogue at least seven similar burnings over the period from about 386 CE and through the reign of Theodosius II (408–450).[44] Despite these incidents, they say:

> Paradoxically, however, the one island of relative safety for religious outsiders remained the synagogue. Jews, like everyone else, could be the occasional object of mob violence. However, Roman legal tradition in general prevailed, and Judaism—unlike paganism or heresy—even when marginalized, was nonetheless never outlawed.... Indeed the hostility of ecclesiastical writers, their repeated efforts to delegitimize and disallow Christian involvement (both clerical and lay) in synagogue activities, and their insistence that Judaism itself represented the ultimate antitype of the true faith, obliquely witness to a positive attitude towards Jews and Judaism on the part of many in their own congregations.[45]

They go on to point out that Judaism never had the same relation to the church as paganism and heresy had:

> ... if only for the reason that Judaism, according to orthodoxy's own self-understanding, was incontrovertibly the source of (true) Christianity. As Augustine observed, although the Church was the bride of Christ, the synagogue was his mother (*Contra Faustum* 12.8). The Church's rise to power did little to resolve the tradition's abiding and intrinsic ambivalence. Thus, from the late fourth century onward, searing hostility and episcopally orchestrated violence—against pagans and contesting Christian churches as well as against Jews—could unpredictably disrupt the comfortable social and religious intimacy that often characterized relations between these various urban communities.[46]

Again, the ostensible reason for the concentration on anti-Judaism is the argument that it can be traced directly to the belief that Jesus is God. The link is forged with iron by Ehrman: "Why not? These were the people who had killed God,"[47] "the bishops ... were using that power in ugly ways against their longtime enemies, the Jews, those who allegedly killed their own God."[48] Yet, without reducing for a moment the tragedy of what happened, may we not ask, is the persecution really traceable in any major way to this belief? It is at least curious that in *none* of the examples of later discrimination and violence cited by Ehrman does the charge of deicide come up as any kind of motivation.

It does not come up in the records of the incident concerning Ambrose of Milan, on which Ehrman expands considerably. Ambrose in 388 CE strove to persuade the emperor Theodosius (379–395) not to order restitution from a certain bishop in Callinicum who allegedly incited his congregation to burn down a synagogue, and not to punish wayward monks who, after being harassed on the road by some Valentinians, retaliated by burning down their meeting house. Ambrose never stipulates that the bishop actually did incite the burning (he does concede that the monks burned the Valentinian building).

In any event, he does not think the bishop or any Christians should be forced to pay for a new synagogue. Why should the Jews be treated better than the Christians?[49] For he cites several examples of Jews burning down churches in the time of the emperor Julian: two at Damascus, one in Gaza, Ascalon, and Berytus, "and in almost every place in those parts" (*Letter* 40.15). Further, "at Alexandria a basilica was burnt by heathen and Jews, which surpassed all the rest" (40.15). What was the response of the Christians to these burnings of their property? Ambrose reminds the emperor that "no one demanded punishment.... The Church was not avenged, shall the Synagogue be so?" (40.15). "The buildings of our churches were burnt by the Jews, and nothing was restored, nothing was asked back, nothing demanded" (40.18). Recently, in Theodosius' own reign, the house of the bishop of Constantinople had been set ablaze (Ambrose does not say who did it). For this deed the Christian bishop explicitly pleaded with the emperor *not* to take vengeance on the perpetrator(s), "for it was worthy of him," says Ambrose, "to forgive the injury done to himself" (40.13).

Ambrose never defends anybody for burning the synagogue, or the monks for burning a Valentinian meeting place. He calls these acts sinful (41.26). It is true that Ambrose more than suggests that the synagogue fire, however it was started (he floats the idea that the Jews may have set the blaze themselves, in order to blame it on the Christians), was in keeping with the judgment of God on the Jews. They had denied and slain the Christ; they received neither the Son nor the Father (40.26). But he most definitely does not see this as any justification for anyone to commit acts of violence against Jews or their properties. And he never charges them with deicide, the specific crime of "murdering their God," and the professed reason for expounding on Christian anti-Judaism in a book on Christology.

I am certainly not claiming that the charge of deicide never functioned as a justification for ill treatment of Jews. Perhaps it did. But if it did, another question is, Would it really have been any different, once political fortunes had shifted, if Jesus had simply been a man elevated to deity as a result of his resurrection? Or adopted as Son of God at his baptism? Or even if he had simply died a forsaken apocalyptic preacher and was later touted as a misunderstood Messiah by zealous followers? I do not believe so, and Ehrman has certainly not shown the likelihood that it would have been.

To reinforce the point, we might be reminded of a certain *non-Christian* religion whose *non-divine* prophet was not executed by Jews or by anybody else. This has sadly not guaranteed benevolent treatment of Jews, or of Christians, from all representatives of this religion.

Come to that, there is one explicitly *anti-Christian* political philosophy that has been responsible in its real-world expressions for mass murder on an almost unbelievable, truly "apocalyptic" scale. Deaths by execution, by manmade famine, and by the imposition of impossible living conditions in slave-labor camps under communist regimes in the twentieth century number in the tens of millions.[50] Yet the multitude of these unconscionable acts has not kept any number of university professors from praising and feting this political philosophy over the years. In the light of so many atrocities perpetrated by representatives of a non-Christian religion and by explicitly anti-Christian, atheist governments, is it really necessary to keep up the heat on Christians today who believe in Christ's deity, as though they should be sentenced to carrying the weight of a long line of anti-Judaism for doing so?

As we have seen, the epilogue of *How Jesus Became God* seeks to consider some of the later historical implications of the orthodox doctrines of Christ and the Trinity. Most of these are not entirely pleasant. So, to end on a more uplifting note, I would like to append a couple of early testimonies from two who saw great societal good as the result of the coming of Christ.

Justin says:

And thus do we also, since our persuasion by the Word ... follow the only unbegotten God through His Son—we who formerly delighted in fornication, but now embrace chastity alone; we who formerly used magical arts, dedicate ourselves to the good and unbegotten God; we who valued above all things the acquisition of wealth and possessions, now bring what we have into a common stock, and communicate to everyone in need; we who hated and destroyed one another, and on account of their different manners would not live with men of a different tribe, now, since the coming of Christ, live familiarly with them, and pray for our enemies, and endeavor to persuade those who hate us unjustly to live conformably to the good precepts of Christ, to the end that they may become partakers with us of the same joyful hope of a reward from God the ruler of all. (*1 Apology* 14)

On the prophecy that the wolf shall feed with the lamb (Isa 11:6), Irenaeus says:

And this has already come to pass, for those who were before most perverse, to the extent of omitting no work of ungodliness, coming to know Christ, and believing Him, no sooner believed than they were changed to the extent of omitting no superabundance, even, of justice; so great is the change wrought by faith in Christ, the Son of God, in those who believe in Him. (*Proof of the Apostolic Preaching* 61)

A great part of the aftermath of the coming of Jesus is that millions of people for nearly two thousand years have found spiritual peace, hope, strength, and even the power to change their natural vices in a Savior who has shared their human woes, yet who is more powerful than all other humans, who is able to save, because he is also God.

Therefore he is able to save completely those who come to God through him, because he always lives to intercede for them. (Heb 7:25)

Third-Century Evidence for Jesus as God

The Alexamenos Graffitio

Israelarchive Alexander Schick (c) www.bibelausstellung.de /Photo by Elke Haas

The Alexamenos Graffito is a famous piece of anti-Christian graffiti that was carved on a wall near the Palatine Hill close to the Circus Maximus in ancient Rome and dates from the third century.

The inscription depicts the figure of a man with the head of a donkey hanging on a cross. Underneath is another man with his arms posed in a gesture of worship. The accompanying inscription reads, "Alexamenos worships his god." The inscription is a wonderful insight into pagan ridicule of Christianity. The insult to Alexamenos is that his god amounts to a half-man half-ass hoisted on a cross. One can scarcely imagine a more visual way of displaying what the apostle Paul called the "foolishness" of the cross to Greeks (1 Cor 1:18–22). What is important to note is how this inscription affirms that Jesus was worshiped by Christians and how Christian communities were perceived by critics as venerating Jesus as a divine being and bestowing divine honors on him.

Third-Century Evidence for Jesus as God

The Inscription at Meggido

Centre for Public Christianity

During the late 1990s construction work in the vicinity of a prison in Tel Meggido in northern Israel uncovered the remains of an ancient church set within a Roman military camp, perhaps the first of its kind in Palestine, datable to the third century, maybe as early as ca. 235 CE.[51] Among the finds include a prayer room with the remains of a broken table and four mosaic panels indicating that the area was probably used for eucharistic celebrations. On one of the panels is an inscription that reads: "The God-loving Akeptous has offered the table to God Jesus Christ as a memorial." Evidently a woman named Akeptous donated the table for use in the Christian community, and the inscription commemorates her generosity as a benefactor to the church. The words "offered" and "memorial," as well as "God Jesus Christ," are sure signs that Jesus is recognized as a divine figure worthy of receiving religious devotion normally appropriate for Israel's God.

CHAPTER 10

Concluding Thoughts

Michael F. Bird

I'm sure you're all familiar with Santa Claus, the obese cola-chugging, cookie-chomping fat man, who commits breaking-and-entering offenses across the world, organized from his crime syndicate HQ in the tax-exempt North Pole, where he keeps little people with pointy ears enslaved in his sweatshop to make cheap merchandise for Toys-R-Us. But that Santa is not the real St. Nicholas. No, the real St. Nicholas of Myra was a bishop in the ancient church known for his care for the poor and his robust affirmation of Jesus' divinity. According to legend, St. Nicholas was a delegate to the Council of Nicea in 325 CE. Nicholas was part of the faction who supported the full and equal divinity of the Son with the Father against the Arians, who denied it. According to some hagiographies, Nicholas was so outraged with Arius's subordinationist view of Jesus as a being less than the Father that he slapped Arius in the face in front of the entire assembly.

Of course, Nicholas was summarily rebuked and had to apologize, but his violent outburst in the cause of orthodox Christology has been memorialized in legends and even in art. I know it's just a story, but we have to ask, "What would St. Nicholas say to Bart Ehrman?" I don't know for sure, but considering his violent encounter with Arius, St. Nicholas might do all his talking with his knuckles. I read on Ehrman's blog that he loves Christmas. Even so, the next time Santa comes to town, Ehrman may want to lock himself in his panic room lest the jolly fat man decides to give him a yuletide body slam as a punishment for being on his naughty list.

Humor aside, out of all the questions someone could conceivably ask about Jesus, a sensible one and an important one is definitely this: "How Did Jesus Become God?" I commend Ehrman for raising it in the public forum and offering a fresh and vigorous engagement with the topic. The reason for the importance of such a question is easy to gauge. The truth of Christ as the revelation of God-in-the-flesh is the load-bearing symbol that bears the weight of the entire symbolic universe of the Christian faith.[1] For Christian devotion rests on two crucial axioms: first, that God was in Christ reconciling the world to himself (2 Cor 5:21); second, that "Jesus is Lord" (1 Cor 12:3). It is not too much to say that for Christians of all types and stripes, their idea of God is bound up with the story of Jesus. It is by looking at Jesus that we see the face of God.

Ehrman is not a Christian, and one must wonder in what sense anyone could be God given Ehrman's agnosticism. He certainly does not think that Jesus is God, and he shies away from the question as to whether it is even possible for God to become a human being. As I read Ehrman's book, I kept hearing the melancholic and mocking lyrics of Joan Osborne's postmodern song, "What if God Was One of Us?" playing in my head. Ehrman's mind is already settled on such matters, and rather than offer religious reflections, he attempts instead to trace how belief in Jesus as God first emerged. Some of his observations about the early church are sound. That said, several of his conclusions as to how devotion to Jesus as a divine figure emerged and what it meant are far from sound. His account of Christian origins smells fishier than shrimp left out for too long in the hot sun.

In this volume, we have attempted to critically engage Ehrman's arguments with a blow-by-blow response to his primary assertions.

Bird argued that, *against Ehrman*, one cannot cut and paste Greco-Roman and Jewish views of intermediary figures onto early devotion to Jesus. That is because, despite some genuine analogies, the early church developed a uniquely cast christological monotheism whereby the person of Jesus was bound up with the identity of the God of Israel. This is why Jesus was considered a fitting object of worship in the early church.

Bird also argued that, *against Ehrman*, Jesus did believe that he was God, since he acted in such a way as to communicate that he embodied God's return to Zion, he shared God's throne, and his deeds could be correlated with God's action in the world. The instantaneous drive to worship Jesus did not result from an extensive period of deliberation; rather, it was a reflexive response to the memory of Jesus carried by his first followers. These followers believed that in Jesus they had met the God of Israel in person.

Evans argued that, *against Ehrman*, the gospel burial traditions are probably historical. Ehrman completely fails to take into account archaeological evidence for victims of crucifixion being buried. In fact, Evans demonstrates that according to Roman custom and law, burial after crucifixion was not unusual. His observation, especially with respect to Roman Palestine, is confirmed by examination of the remains of several victims of crucifixion who were buried according to Jewish law and custom. In addition, what we know about Jewish burial practices makes Jesus' internment by Joseph of Arimathea and the visit of the women to the tomb entirely plausible. On top of that, appearances of Jesus alive to his followers after his death would not itself have generated the belief about resurrection. That is because there was a myriad of ways that his followers could have spoken of his postmortem existence, like his transportation to heaven, seeing his spirit or ghost, or his transformation into an angel. Since resurrection is about the rising of dead bodies, it was the empty tomb and the appearances of Jesus that led them to believe that he was resurrected.

Gathercole argued that, *against Ehrman*, there is a theology of preexistence in the Synoptic Gospels, that a close reading of Mark's gospel does not support a view that Jesus' sonship began at his baptism, and that texts from the "tunnel period" such as Acts 2:36 and Rom 1:4 do not espouse an adoptionist or exaltation Christology. The language of Jesus being "made" and "appointed" in his exaltation pertains not to his identity or relationship to God the Father changing, but to an extension or intensification of his authority over the church and cosmos, in parallel with the fact that God's own reign also extends and intensifies.

Tilling argued that, *against Ehrman*, New Testament Christology cannot be forced into a scheme of development from "exaltation christologies" to "incarnation christologies" simply because the common denominator across the New Testament is that Jesus shares the transcendent uniqueness of the one God of Israel. In addition, Ehrman's reading of Gal 4:14 as supporting an angel Christology, which he makes a central interpretive motif, is steeped in a degree of dubious dubiety higher than Dubai City Tower. Also, Tilling points out that Ehrman's conception of language about God, divinity, and monotheism lacks precision and sophistication and is therefore prone to several category fallacies.

Tilling then argued that, *against Ehrman*, Paul portrays Jesus as possessing the same transcendent uniqueness of the one God of Israel. This case is made, first, by examining certain explanatory conditions that responsible historians should grasp. Second, and in light of these conditions, Paul's language about Christ then comes into sharp focus. It becomes clear that the way Jews distinguished the uniqueness of God is deployed by Paul to speak of Christ. This is to say that Paul describes the relation between Christ and Christ-followers in a way Jews only spoke of God's relation to Israel. And it is in precisely this way that God's transcendent uniqueness was expressed. In other words, Paul constructs a Jewish way of unambiguously including Jesus on the divine side of the line monotheism must draw between God and creatures. Tilling can, in this light, accommodate for dozens of relevant Pauline texts, such as 1 Corinthians 8–10, in such a way that shows a fully divine Christology was central to Paul. This further means that language in Philippians 2 can be better understood, especially in light of material in Philippians 1 and 3. To this end, Tilling explores a number of problems with Ehrman's exegesis of Phil 2:6–11. This is crucial as Ehrman's dubious claims about this passage are the only detailed basis for his construal of Paul's Christology. All of this refutes Ehrman's suggestion that Paul depicts Jesus as a kind of angel. And that is not all. Tilling lists further problems with Ehrman's treatment of John and Hebrews that undermine Ehrman's entire project.

Hill argued that, *against Ehrman*, orthodoxy was not the product of several alleged "heresy hunters" rewriting history. The heterodox deviations that emerged were weighed against the weight of the rule of faith and the Christian Scriptures and found wanting. In addition, Hill also contests Ehrman's account of the Ebionites, Modalists, and Tertullian, in particular as to what they actually believed and why.

Hill then proceeded to argue that, *against Ehrman*, paradox, far from being inimical to orthodoxy, was actually foundational for it. The various paradoxes of the church's faith, such as how Jesus can be human *and* divine or how God can be three *and* one, were simply part of the testimony of the biblical writers, both individually and corporately. While these paradoxes gave inspiration to the rise of beliefs that were eventually regarded as fallacious and inadequate explanations of Christ and God, nonetheless, paradox was ingrained into Christian belief as part of the mystery of the incarnation and God's triune nature. Furthermore, Hill also points out that Ehrman's scheme of christological development might be amiss because several of the texts said to convey an exaltation Christology might in fact be abbreviations of an incarnation Christology. Lastly, while there has been a horrid history of Christian anti-Judaism, it wrong to say that its immediate cause was belief in the deity of Christ.

In closing, I'd like to offer one final thought. Back in 1992, before I came to faith, I attended an Australian production of *Jesus Christ Superstar.* I've since seen several productions of the show in different cities around the world, and this production had many distinctive features. One thing I remember vividly was "Herod's Song." It is a number toward the end of the second act sung by Herod Antipas, where Herod mocks Jesus in a very campish cabaret-style rock song, wonderfully performed by Aussie icon Angry Anderson. In the middle of the song, Herod stops, slaps himself in the face with both hands in frustration at Jesus, points a finger at Jesus, then turns to the audience and says, "He thinks he's God!" The whole audience, myself included, erupted in riotous laughter. How silly for someone to think that he or she is God! And yet, billions of people around the world spend time every day, thinking about, believing in, and praying to Jesus as God.

But is this really a silly belief? I believe it is not. It seems to me that Jesus spoke and acted in such a way as to be claiming that he spoke and acted with, for, and as Israel's God. His self-understanding was not delusional, but was vindicated by his resurrection from the dead, which is why those who encountered the risen Christ worshiped him (Matt 28:17), and even skeptics had to confess him as "My Lord and my God" (John 20:21). Many to this day remain loyal in their worship because of the absolute worshipability of Jesus as the "one who loved me and gave himself for me" (Gal 2:20). And there endeth the lesson!

Endnotes

Chapter 1: The Story of Jesus as the Story of God

1. Bart D. Ehrman, *How Jesus Became God: The Exaltation of a Jewish Preacher from Galilee* (New York: HarperOne, 2014), 353–54.
2. C. F. D. Moule, *The Origins of Christology* (Cambridge: Cambridge University Press, 1977), 2.
3. C. K. Barrrett, *The Gospel according to St. John: An Introduction with Commentary and Notes on the Greek Text* (2nd ed.; London: SPCK, 1978), 156.
4. Ehrman, *How Jesus Became God*, 44.
5. New Testament scholars often speak about "Christology," which is the study of the career, person, nature, and identity of Jesus Christ. There are, of course, many different ways of doing Christology. Some scholars study Christology by focusing on the major titles applied to Jesus in the New Testament, such as "Son of Man," "Son of God," "Messiah," "Lord," "Prince," "Word," and the like. Others take a more functional approach and look at how Jesus acts or is said to act in the New Testament as the basis for configuring beliefs about him. It is possible to explore Jesus as a historical figure (i.e., Christology from below), or to examine theological claims made about Jesus (i.e., Christology from above). Many scholars prefer a socio-religious method by comparing beliefs about Jesus with beliefs in other religions to identify shared sources and similar ideas. Theologians often take a more philosophical approach and look at Jesus' "ontology" or "being" and debate how best to describe his divine and human natures.
6. Martin Hengel, "Christology and New Testament Chronology: A Problem in the History of Earliest Christianity," in *Between Jesus and Paul* (London: SCM, 1983), 31.
7. Martin Hengel, *The Son of God: The Origin of Christology and the History of Jewish-Hellenistic Religion* (London: SCM, 1975), 4. This reminds me also of G. B. Caird's remark (*New Testament Theology* [ed. L.D. Hurst; Oxford: Clarendon, 1994], 343): "the highest Christology of the NT is also its earliest."
8. Hengel, "Christology and New Testament Chronology," 44.

207

9. Larry Hurtado, *One God, One Lord: Early Christian Devotion and Ancient Jewish Monotheism* (2nd ed.; London: T&T Clark, 1998); idem, *Lord Jesus Christ: Devotion to Jesus in Earliest Christianity* (Grand Rapids: Eerdmans, 2003).
10. Hurtado, *Lord Jesus Christ*, 2, 650.
11. Richard Bauckham, *God Crucified: Monotheism and Christology in the New Testament* (Carlisle, UK: Paternoster, 1998), vii–viii; repr. as *Jesus and the God of Israel: "God Crucified" and Other Studies on the New Testament's Christology of Divinity Identity* (Milton Keynes, UK: Paternoster, 2008), ix–x.
12. See, for instance, Chris Tilling, *Paul's Divine Christology* (WUNT 2/323; Tübingen: Mohr Siebeck, 2012), 35–62, and his assessment of Hurtado and Bauckham.
13. Let me add as well that Ehrman would not disagree with all of the approaches and claims of the EHCC. Ehrman believes, with Hengel, that a "major leap was made in those first twenty years" (*How Jesus Became God*, 371), but he disagrees as to what the "leap" was from and to! Ehrman also affirms Hurtado's description of a "binitarian worship" in the early church (ibid., 235), though he has different ideas of the meaning and object of that worship.
14. It is worth noting that an *apocalypse* is a literary genre characterized by other worldly travels, angelic visitations, and periodizing history, and complete with insights into heavenly and future realities. An *apocalyptic worldview* is one that is characterized by a strong sense of dualism (good vs. evil, etc.) and determinism (God has decided how the future will pan out), and it often cultivates a sectarian mindset. What scholars call *apocalypticism* usually means the socio-religious phenomenon of individuals or sects who believe that they are living within the final moments of world history and on the cusp of God's radical intervention in the world.

Chapter 2: Of Gods, Angels, and Men

1. My thanks goes to the Ridley librarian Ruth Millard for finding several books for me at short notice.
2. Ehrman, *How Jesus Become God*, 43.
3. Ibid.
4. Ibid., 17–18.
5. Ibid., 61.
6. Samuel Sandmel, "Parallelomania," *JBL* 81 (1962): 1–13; D. A. Carson, *Exegetical Fallacies* (Grand Rapids: Baker, 1984), 43–44.

7. For a good study on the prologue of the gospel of John, see Craig A. Evans, *Word and Glory: On the Exegetical and Theological Background of John's Prologue* (JSNTSup 89; Sheffield: Sheffield Academic Press, 1993).
8. A passage like Rom 1:3–4 certainly mirrors or parodies the grandiose claims made about the emperor in imperial rhetoric even if it its formulation was drawn from early Jewish Christian tradition. Christian authors were aware of allegations that the story of Jesus' birth was borrowed from pagan accounts of the birth of ancient kings and mythical heroes (see Justin, *Dialogue with Trypho* 67–70; *First Apology* 33; Origen, *Against Celsus* 1.37). Celsus could say that Jesus' elevation to divine status is similar to Trajan's deification of his male lover Antinous (Origen, *Against Celsus* 3.36–38).
9. Ehrman (*How Jesus Became God*, 18–19) seems to admit as much when he says, "I don't know of any other cases in ancient Greek or Roman thought of this kind of 'god-man,' where an already existing divine being is said to be born of a mortal woman. But there are other conceptions that are close." Cf. James Dunn (*Christology in the Making: A New Testament Inquiry into the Origins of the Doctrine of the Incarnation* [2nd ed.; Grand Rapids: Eerdmans, 1996], 22): "There is little or no evidence from the period prior to Christianity's beginnings that the Ancient Near East seriously entertained the idea of a god or son of god descending from heaven to become a human being in order to bring men salvation, except perhaps at the level of popular pagan superstition."
10. Philo, *Embassy to Gaius*, 118. Cf. Dunn (*Christology in the Making*, 18): "Jewish writings tend to be more scrupulous and less free in their attribution of divine sonship and divinity to men."
11. Origen, *Against Celsus* 5.2.
12. See Hurtado, *Lord Jesus Christ*, 134–53; idem, *How on Earth Did Jesus Become God?* (Grand Rapids: Eerdmans, 2005), 46–55.
13. Marinius de Jonge, *God's Final Envoy: Early Christology and Jesus' Own View of His Mission* (Grand Rapids: Eerdmans, 1998), 130. Note also the words of N. T. Wright (*Paul and the Faithfulness of God* [COQG 4; London: SPCK, 2013], 655, 666): "Jesus' first followers found themselves not only (as it were) permitted to use God-language for Jesus, but compelled to use Jesus-language for the One God"; and "He is not a semi-divine intermediate figure. He is the one in whom the identity of Israel's God is revealed, so that one cannot now speak of this God without thinking of Jesus, or of Jesus without thinking of the one God, the creator, Israel's God."
14. Ehrman, *How Jesus Became God*, 43–44, 53–54.
15. Ibid., 39, 49.

16. See Polymnia Athanassiadi and Michael Frede, eds., *Pagan Monotheism in Late Antiquity* (New York: Oxford University Press, 1999); Stephen Mitchell and Peter van Nuffelen, *One God: Pagan Monotheism in the Roman Empire* (Cambridge: Cambridge University Press, 2010).
17. Aristobulus, fragment 4.
18. Augustine, *The Harmony of the Gospels*, 1.22.30.
19. Origen, *Contra Celsus* 5.41.
20. See further, Michael F. Bird, *Crossing over Sea and Land: Jewish Missionary Activity in the Second Temple Period* (Peabody, MA: Hendrickson, 2010), 77–81.
21. James G. Crossley, *Why Christianity Happened: A Sociohistorical Account of Christian Origins (26–50 CE)* (Louisville: Westminster John Knox, 2006), 99.
22. See further, Hurtado, *One God, One Lord*, 17–39; idem, *Lord Jesus Christ*, 29–52; Bauckham, *God Crucified*, 1–24; idem, *Jesus and the God of Israel*, 1–59.
23. Philo, *Decalogue 65* (my own trans.); on Moses as God, see Philo, *Sacrifice of Abel and Cain* 9–10; *Life of Moses* 1.27, 156–58; on the Logos as God, see Philo, *Questions in Genesis* 2.62.
24. Wright, *Paul and the Faithfulness of God*, 620–21.
25. See Bird, *Crossing over Sea and Land*, 79–83.
26. Tacitus, *Histories* 5.5.4.
27. Hurtado, *Lord Jesus Christ*, 151–52.
28. Ibid., 35–36.
29. *Sefer Zerubbabel* (trans. John C. Reeves). In *Old Testament Pseudepigrapha: More Noncanonical Scriptures* (ed. Richard Bauckham, James Davila, Alex Panayotov; Grand Rapids: Eerdmans, 2013).
30. See introduction by Andrei A. Orlove, "Metatron," in *EDEJ* (eds. J. J. Collins and D. C. Harlow (Grand Rapids: Eerdmans, 2010), 942–43.
31. Ehrman, *How Jesus Became God*, 54–55 (italics original).
32. Loren T. Stuckenbruck, *Angel Veneration and Christology: A Study in Early Judaism and in the Christology of the Apocalypse* (WUNT 2/70; Tübingen: Mohr Siebeck, 1995), 200–203.
33. Ibid., 201 (italics original).
34. Bauckham, *Jesus and the God of Israel*, 142; Hurtado, *Lord Jesus Christ*, 592.
35. Ehrman, *How Jesus Became God*, 67.
36. Bauckham, *God Crucified*, 19; idem, *Jesus and the God of Israel*, 16.
37. Hurtado, *One God, One Lord*, 53–54; idem, *Lord Jesus Christ*, 38–39.
38. Hurtado, *Lord Jesus Christ*, 31–35.

39. Bauckham, *God Crucified*, 4, 16–22; idem, *Jesus and the God of Israel*, 3, 13–17.

40. Ehrman, *How Jesus Became God*, 59–61, 252–69.

41. Justin Martyr, *Dialogue with Trypho* 56; 58; 126; *1 Apology* 63.

42. Though such readings are heavily criticized by Andrew S. Malone, "Old Testament Christophanies?" (unpublished PhD thesis, Australian College of Theology, 2012).

43. Dunn, *Christology in the Making*, 154.

44. Peter R. Carrell, *Jesus and the Angels: Angelology and the Christology of the Apocalypse of John* (SNTSSup 95; Cambridge: Cambridge University Press, 1997), 223.

45. Gordon D. Fee, *Revelation* (NCCS; Eugene, OR: Cascade, 2011), 141.

46. Ehrman, *How Jesus Became God*, 61; citing Hurtado, *One God, One Lord*, 82.

47. Hurtado, *Lord Jesus Christ*, 50. Stuckenbruck (*Angel Veneration and Christology*, 272–73) is probably closer to what Ehrman wants to hear said, commenting, "Perhaps the closest analogy to an independent figure coupled with an express retention of a monotheistic framework is evident in some of the sources in which angels are honored alongside God as aligned yet subordinated beings"; yet he points out as well that we "may still be faced with a religio-historical discontinuity as to the kind and intensity of worship between angels and Christ."

48. See discussion in Scot McKnight and Joe Modica, eds., *Jesus Is Lord, Caesar Is Not: Evaluating Empire in New Testament Studies* (Downers Grove, IL: InterVarsity Press, 2013).

49. *Ezekiel the Tragedian* 67–89 (trans. R.G. Robertson). In *Old Testament Pseudepigrapha* (ed. James Charlesworth; Garden City, NY: Doubleday, 1985), 2:811–12.

Chapter 3: Did Jesus Think He Was God?

1. See further, Scot McKnight and Joe Modica, eds., *Who Do My Opponents Say I Am? An Investigation of the Accusations against Jesus* (LNTS 327; London: T&T Clark, 2008); Chris Keith and Larry Hurtado, eds., *Jesus among Friends and Enemies: A Historical and Literary Introduction to the Gospels* (Grand Rapids: Baker, 2011).

2. See further, Raymond E. Brown, "Did Jesus Know He Was God?" *BTB* 15 (1985): 74–79; Craig A. Evans, "The Historical Jesus and the Deified Christ: How Did the One Lead to the Other?" in *The Nature of Religious Language: A Colloquium* (ed. S. E. Porter; Sheffield: Sheffield Academic Press, 1996), 47–67; Michael F. Bird and James Crossley,

How Did Christianity Begin? A Believer and Non-Believer Examine the Evidence (London: SPCK, 2008), 12–17, 28–33.

3. Ehrman, *How Jesus Became God*, 124.
4. Ibid., 111–12.
5. Ibid., 125.
6. Ibid., 127.
7. Bart D. Ehrman, *Misquoting Jesus: The Story behind Who Changed the Bible and Why* (San Francisco: HarperOne, 2007), 10.
8. Ibid., 11.
9. Bart D. Ehrman, *Lost Christianities: The Battles for Scripture and the Faiths We Never Knew* (New York: Oxford University Press, 2005), 219.
10. The session was the "SBL Believers, Scholars and Culture: Assessing the Impact of Two Centuries of Critical Biblical Scholarship," Marriott Marquis Hotel, San Francisco, Friday, November 18, 2011.
11. Bart D. Ehrman, *Jesus, Apocalyptic Prophet of the New Millennium* (New York: Oxford University Press, 1999).
12. Bart D. Ehrman, *Peter, Paul, and Mary Magdalene: The Followers of Jesus in History and in Legend* (New York: Oxford University Press, 2006).
13. I address these issues in Michael F. Bird, "Textual Criticism and the Historical Jesus," *JSHJ* 6 (2008): 133–56.
14. Other methodological problems with Ehrman's radical conclusions are ably documented by Daniel B. Wallace, "Lost in Transmission: How Badly Did the Scribes Corrupt the New Testament Text," in *Revisiting the Corruption of the New Testament: Manuscript, Patristic, and Apocryphal Evidence* (ed. D. B. Wallace; Grand Rapids: Kregel, 2011), 19–55. The chief inconsistencies in Ehrman's method are: (1) Elsewhere, usually in more scholarly writings, Ehrman is more sanguine about New Testament scholarship's ability to reconstruct in some approximation the earliest text of the New Testament; and (2) Ehrman posits both wild and careless copying by untrained scribes and a proto-orthodox conspiracy to tinker with the text to make it more conducive to their religious beliefs about Jesus. The problem is that a conspiracy requires a degree of control, and wild unsupervised alteration of a text is anything but controlled. Both assertions cannot be simultaneously true.
15. Ehrman, *How Jesus Became God*, 88–98. For a fuller account of the origins of the Gospels see Michael F. Bird, *The Gospel of the Lord: How the Early Church Wrote the Story of Jesus* (Grand Rapids: Eerdmans, forthcoming 2014).
16. Dale C. Allison, "The Historians' Jesus and the Church," in *Seeking the Identity of Jesus: A Pilgrimage* (eds. Richard B. Hays and Beverly R. Gaventa; Grand Rapids: Eerdmans, 2008), 84–85.

17. Sean Freyne, *Jesus, A Jewish Galilean: A New Reading of the Jesus-Story* (London: T&T Clark, 2005), 4.

18. I am reminded of the words of Henry Cadbury (*The Peril of Modernizing Jesus* [New York: Macmillan, 1937], 46–47): "When I read a life of Christ that in the most careful approved fashion describes at length the unhistorical character of the gospels and the aspects of their viewpoint which are to be rejected as late and secondary, but then proceeds to construct a portrait of the Master shot through with modern standards of value, I feel like saying, 'Why beholdest thou the mote that is in thy brother's eye, but considerest not the beam that is in thine own eye?'"

19. See I. Howard Marshall, *I Believe in the Historical Jesus* (Grand Rapids: Eerdmans, 1977); Paul Barnett, *Jesus and the Logic of History* (NSBT 3; Leicester, UK: Apollos, 1997); Birger Gerhardsson, *The Reliability of the Gospel Tradition* (Peabody, MA: Hendrickson, 2001); Darrell L. Bock, *Studying the Historical Jesus: A Guide to Sources and Methods* (Grand Rapids: Baker, 2002); Craig L. Blomberg, *The Historical Reliability of the Gospels* (2nd ed.; Downers Grove, IL: InterVarsity Press, 2007); Paul R. Eddy and Gregory A. Boyd, *The Jesus Legend: A Case for the Historical Reliability of the Synoptic Jesus Tradition* (Grand Rapids: Baker, 2007).

20. See Bird, *Gospel of the Lord*, chapters 2–3.

21. Bird and Crossley, *How Did Christianity Begin?* 106–13.

22. See Stanley E. Porter, *The Criteria for Authenticity in Historical-Jesus Research: Previous Discussion and New Proposals* (JSNTSup 191; Sheffield: Sheffield Academic Press, 2000); Dale C. Allison, "How to Marginalize the Traditional Criteria of Authenticity," in *Handbook for the Study of the Historical Jesus* (eds. T. Holmén and S.E. Porter; 4 vols.; Leiden: Brill, 2009), 1:3–30; Rafael Rodríguez, "Authenticating Criteria: The Use and Misuse of a Critical Method," *JSHJ* 7 (2009): 152–67; Chris Keith and Anthony Le Donne, eds., *Jesus, Criteria, and the Demise of Authenticity* (London: T&T Clark, 2012).

23. Dale C. Allison, *Resurrecting Jesus: The Earliest Christian Tradition and Its Interpreters* (New York: T&T Clark, 2005), 76.

24. Ehrman, *How Jesus Became God*, 96–97.

25. See, e.g., Tom Holmén, "Doubts about Double Dissimilarity: Restructuring the Main Criterion of Jesus-of-History Research," in *Authenticating the Words of Jesus* (eds. Craig A. Evans and Bruce D. Chilton; Leiden: Brill, 1999), 47–80; Porter, *Criteria for Authenticity*, 70–79, 113–22; Dagmar Winter, "Saving the Quest for Authenticity from the Criterion of Dissimilarity: History and Plausibility," in *Jesus, Criteria, and the Demise of Authenticity* (ed. Chris Keith and Anthony Le Donne; London: T&T Clark, 2012), 115–31.

26. Craig A. Evans, *Jesus and his Contemporaries: Comparative Studies* (Leiden: Brill 1995), 13–15; N. T. Wright, *Jesus and the Victory of God* (COQG 2; London: SPCK, 1996), 131–33; Gerd Theissen "Historical Scepticism and the Criteria of Jesus Research or My Attempt to Leap Across Lessing's Yawning Gulf," *SJT* 49 (1996): 152–170; Gerd Theissen and Annette Merz, *The Historical Jesus: A Comprehensive Guide* (Minneapolis: Fortress, 1998), 116–18; Gerd Theissen and Dagmar Winter, *The Quest for the Plausible Jesus: The Question of Criteria* (Louisville: Westminster John Knox, 2002).

27. See a good introduction in Anthony Le Donne, *The Historical Jesus: What Can We Know and How Can We Know it* (Grand Rapids: Eerdmans, 2011); also Chris Keith, "Memory and Authenticity: Jesus Tradition and What Really Happened," *ZNW* 102 (2011): 155–77.

28. Dale C. Allison, *Jesus of Nazareth: A Millenarian Prophet* (Minneapolis, MN: Fortress, 1998), 35–36. See similarly Cadbury (*The Peril of Modernizing Jesus*, 191): "That is the task of all history; the evangelic episode is no unique one. First the labor of criticism and research, and then artistic, poetic reconstruction."

29. Joseph Klausner, *Jesus of Nazareth: His Life, Times, and Teachings* (trans. Herbert Danby; London: Allen & Unwin, 1929), 169–70.

30. On Jewish restoration hopes generally, see Emil Schürer, *The History of the Jewish People in the Age of Jesus Christ* (3 vols.; rev. and ed. by G. Vermes, F. Millar, and M. Black; Edinburgh: T&T Clark, 1973–86), 2:514–47; E. P. Sanders, *Judaism: Practice and Belief 63 BCE—66 CE* (London: SCM, 1992), 289–98; N. T. Wright, *New Testament and the People of God* (COQG 1; London: SPCK, 1992), 299–338; James D. G. Dunn, *Jesus Remembered* (CITM 1; Grand Rapids: Eerdmans, 2003), 393–96.

31. Robert L. Webb, *John the Baptizer and Prophet: A Socio-Historical Study* (Eugene, OR: Wipf & Stock, 2006), 222–27.

32. John P. Meir, *A Marginal Jew: Rethinking the Historical Jesus* (ABRL; New York: Doubleday, 1991), 1:452.

33. Matt 3:3; Mark 1:3; Luke 3:4; and 4Q176 1.4–9; 1QS 8.14; 9.19–20.

34. Even Ehrman (*Jesus, Apocalyptic Prophet*, 186) says: "One of the best-attested traditions of our surviving sources is that Jesus chose twelve of his followers to form a kind of inner circle."

35. Ehrman, *How Jesus Became God*, 115–24; see Michael F. Bird, *Are You the One Who Is to Come? The Historical Jesus and the Messianic Question* (Grand Rapids: Baker, 2009).

36. R. T. France, *The Gospel of Mark: A Commentary on the Greek Text* (NIGTC; Grand Rapids: Eerdmans, 2002), 126.

37. Ehrman, *How Jesus Became God*, 127.
38. Jacob Neusner, *A Rabbi Talks with Jesus: An Intermillennial, Inferfaith Exchange* (New York: Doubleday, 1993), cited from N. T. Wright, "Jesus and the Identity of God," *Ex Auditu* 14 (1998): 22.
39. Sigurd Grindheim (*God's Equal: What Can We Know about Jesus' Self-Understanding in the Synoptic Gospels* [LNTS 446; London: T&T Clark, 2011], 220), concludes his study on Jesus' self-understanding by saying: "The Jesus who emerges then is a Jesus who said and did what only God could say and do. His claims are unmatched by Jewish expectations of the Messiah, by Jewish ideas regarding the glorious characters of Israel's past, the most exalted of the angels, and even the heavenly Son of Man. According to the contemporary Jewish sources, these divine agents do not engage Satan directly, and they do not inaugurate the new creation. They do not forgive sins, and they do not autonomously pass the ultimate, eschatological judgment. They do not pit their own authority against the authority of the word of God. Nor do they demand a loyalty that takes precedence over the commandments of God."
40. The Lucan version of the parable in particular looks like a parody about the brief rise to power of Archelaus as the successor to Herod the Great as ruler of Judea, who constitutes an ironic antitype to Jesus' claim to kingship amidst opposition.
41. On reading Luke 19:11–27 this way, see further, Wright, *Jesus and the Victory of God*, 632–39.
42. 1QS 3.18; 4.19; CD 7.9; 8.2–3.
43. Wright, *Jesus and the Victory of God*, 615.
44. On my own attempt to navigate a way through this morass of debate, see Bird, *Are You the One Who is to Come?* 78–98. Also recommended is Hurtado, *Lord Jesus Christ*, 239–306, and the introductory article by Darrell Bock, "Son of Man," in *DJG* (eds. Joel Green, Jeanine Brown, and Nick Perrin; 2nd ed.; Downers Grove, IL: InterVarsity Press, 2013), 894–900. For more extended scholarly discussion I recommend Maurice Casey, *The Solution to the "Son of Man" Problem* (London: T&T Clark, 2009), and Larry Hurtado and Paul Owen, eds., *"Who Is the Son of Man?" The Latest Scholarship on a Puzzling Expression of the Historical Jesus* (London: T&T Clark, 2011).
45. Ehrman, *How Jesus Became God*, 106–9, 121.
46. I have to add that this Semitic idiom for "man" or "humanity" is why some English translations like the Common English Bible render the underlying Greek phrase *ho huios tou anthrōpou* (lit., "the Son of the Man) as "the Human One" and why the mega-liberal Scholars Version translates the Greek phrase as "the Son of Adam."

47. Ehrman, *How Jesus Became God*, 117, 204.
48. *Epistle of Barnabas* 12.9: "Behold again: Jesus is not the Son of Man, but the Son of God, by pattern and as manifested in the flesh" (my own trans.).
49. M. Eugene Boring, *Mark: A Commentary* (Louisville: Westminster John Knox, 2006), 252.
50. See Bird, *Are You the One Who Is to Come?* 136–40.
51. Note that in Matt 26:64 and Luke 22:69, Jesus says, "*from now on* the Son of Man will be seated at the right hand of the mighty God"; this suggests that Jesus' enthronement is already under way (italics added here and in the table, above).
52. *b. Haggigah* 14a; *b. Sanhedrin* 38b.
53. Wright, *Jesus and the Victory of God*, 624; see Ehrman (*How Jesus Became God*, 205): "God had exalted him to a position of *virtually unheard-of status and authority*" (italics added).
54. Ehrman, *How Jesus Became God*, 225.
55. Allison, *Constructing Jesus*, 225, 304.
56. Ehrman, *How Jesus Became God*, 124–26.
57. For a positive evaluation of the Fourth Gospel's historical value, see D. A. Carson, "Historical Tradition in the Fourth Gospel: After Dodd, What?" in *Gospel Perspectives*; vol. 2: *Studies of History and Tradition in the Four Gospels* (eds. R. T. France and David Wenham; Sheffield: JSOT Press, 1981), 83–145; M. M. Thompson, "The Historical Jesus and the Johannine Christ," in *Exploring the Gospel of John* (eds. R. Alan Culpeppar and C. Clifton Black; Louisville: Westminster John Knox, 1996), 21–42; David Wenham, "A Historical View of John's Gospel," *Themelios* 23 (1998): 5–21; Francis J. Maloney, "The Fourth Gospel and the Jesus of History," *NTS* 46 (2000): 42–58; Craig L. Blomberg, *The Historical Reliability of John's Gospel: Issues and Commentary* (Downers Grove, IL: InterVarsity Press, 2002); Richard Bauckham, "Historiographical Characteristics of the Gospel of John," *NTS* 53 (2007): 17–36.
58. See Michael F. Bird, "Synoptics and John," in *DJG*, 920–24. On the sources of John's Christology, see Tom Thatcher, "Remembering Jesus: John's Negative Christology," in *The Messiah in the Old and New Testaments* (ed. Stanley E. Porter; Grand Rapids: Eerdmans, 2007), 173–74.
59. See M. Eugene Boring, "Markan Christology: God-Language for Jesus?" *NTS* 45 (1999): 451–71; Daniel Johansson, "*Kyrios* in the Gospel of Mark," *JSNT* 33 (2010): 101–24.
60. According to Simon Gathercole (*The Pre-existent Son* [Grand Rapids: Eerdmans, 2006], 79): "a heavenly christology is not a distinctively Jo-

hannine phenomenon: there are plenty of thunderbolts through Matthew, Mark, and Luke as well."

61. J. W. Bowman, *The Intention of Jesus* (London: SCM, 1945), 108.

62. Evans, "Historical Jesus and the Deified Christ," 67.

Chapter 4: Getting the Burial Traditions and Evidences Right

1. Ehrman, *How Jesus Become God*, 7, 165.

2. Ibid., 139.

3. Ibid., 141–42.

4. Ibid., 153.

5. Ibid., 142; see 151.

6. Ibid., 154.

7. Scripture references in this essay are taken from the Revised Standard Version.

8. Ehrman, *How Jesus Became God*, 154.

9. The classic survey of crucifixion in Roman late antiquity is Martin Hengel, *Crucifixion: In the Ancient World and the Folly of the Message of the Cross* (London: SCM; Philadelphia: Fortress, 1977). For a current and learned assessment, see G. Samuelson, *Crucifixion in Antiquity* (2nd ed.; WUNT 2/310; Tübingen: Mohr Siebeck, 2013).

10. Ehrman, *How Jesus Become God*, 157.

11. Ibid., 159 (italics original).

12. Ibid. (italics original).

13. From Papyrus Florence 61, lines 59–60 and 64. For text, discussion, and plate, see A. Deissmann, *Light from the Ancient East* (London: Hodder & Stoughton; New York: George H. Doran, 1927; repr. Peabody, MA: Hendrickson, 1995), 269–70.

14. For details, see Deissmann, *Light from the Ancient East*, 269–70 n. 7; W. M. Calder, "Christians and Pagans in the Graeco-Roman Levant," *Classical Review* 38 (1924): 29–31.

15. C. B. Chaval, "The Releasing of a Prisoner on the Eve of Passover in Ancient Jerusalem," *JBL* 60 (1941): 273–78.

16. Helen K. Bond, *Pontius Pilate in History and Interpretation* (SNTSMS 100; Cambridge: Cambridge University Press, 1998), 199–200, and J. S. McLaren, *Power and Politics in Palestine: The Jews and the Governing of their land 100 BC–AD 70* (JSNTSup 63; Sheffield: JSOT Press, 1991), 93 n. 2.

17. "Pilate, astonished at the strength of their devotion to the laws, straightway removed the images from Jerusalem" (Josephus, *Antiquities* 18.59).

18. Bruce Chilton asks, Would Pilate would have exposed the "corpse of an executed Jew beyond the interval permitted by the Torah" and so

allowed "its mutilation by scavengers just outside Jerusalem?" He rightly thinks not. See B. D. Chilton, *Rabbi Jesus: An Intimate Biography* (New York: Doubleday, 2000), 270.

19. Translation based on M. O. Wise, M. G. Abegg Jr., and E. M. Cook, *The Dead Sea Scrolls: A New Translation* (San Francisco: HarperCollins, 1996), 490.

20. Translation based on L. H. Feldman, *Josephus IX: Jewish Antiquities Books XVIII–XX* (LCL 433; London: Heinemann; Cambridge MA: Harvard University Press, 1965), 495, 497. Josephus pronounces the name of the high priest slightly differently, as "Ananus."

21. A. N. Sherwin-White, *Roman Society and Roman Law in the New Testament: The Sarum Lectures 1960–61* (Oxford: Oxford University Press, 1963), 36: "the capital power was the most jealously guarded of all the attributes of government, not even entrusted to the principal assistants of the governors." The point that Sherwin-White makes is that it was most unlikely that the Jewish Sanhedrin held capital power in the period of the Roman governors (i.e., 6–66 CE).

22. Almost all decapitations in antiquity required two (or more) strokes. See J. L. McKinley, "A Decapitation from the Romano-British Cemetery at Baldock, Hertfordshire," *International Journal of Osteoarchaeology* 3 (1993): 41–44; A. Boylston, "Evidence of Weapon-Related Trauma in British Archaeological Samples," in *Human Osteology in Archaeology and Forensic Science* (ed. M. Cox and S. Mays; London: Greenwich Medical Media, 2000), 357–80, esp. 367–68. McKinley and Boylston review a number of cases involving decapitation, observing that multiple strokes were the norm. See also M. Harmon, T. I. Molleson, and J. L. Price, "Burials, Bodies and Beheadings in Romano-British and Anglo-Saxon Cemeteries," *Bulletin of the British Museum of Natural History: Geology 35* (1981): 145–88; R. J. Watt, "Evidence for Decapitation," in *The Roman Cemetery at Lankhills* (ed. G. Clarke; Winchester Studies 3: Pre-Roman and Roman Winchester; Oxford: Clarendon, 1979), 342–44 + plate XVII.

23. J. M. Grintz, "The Inscription from Giv'at ha-Mivtar: A Historical Interpretation," *Sinai* 75 (1974): 20–23; idem, "The Last Way of the Last Hasmonean," *Ha'Umma* 43 (1975): 256–69. Both studies are in Hebrew.

24. I say "confirmed" now, because years ago Patricia Smith called into question the Antigonus identification. She described the skeleton as belonging to a small, elderly woman (not a tall young man), and said the nails had nothing to do with crucifixion. See P. Smith, "The Human Skeletal Remains from the Abba Cave," *IEJ* 27 (1977): 121–24. It is now believed that Smith, who was asked to examine the Abba Cave finds after Haas

was injured and no longer able to work, examined the wrong box of bones and artifacts. On the curious history of this important find and eventual confirmation that the bones really do belong to Antigonus, see Y. Elitzur, "The Abba Cave: Unpublished Findings and a New Proposal Regarding Abba's Identity," *IEJ* 63 (2013): 83–102. Elitzur not only discusses the Antigonus identification, but he also probes the identity of Abba the priest, the man who at considerable personal risk and suffering arranged to have the remains of Antigonus interred in the burial cave in Jerusalem.

25. I thank Professor Israel Hershkovitz of the Sackler Medical Center of the University of Tel Aviv for allowing me to view the nails recovered from the ornate ossuary found in the Abba Cave.

26. Yehohanan's right heel was in fragments and had to be reconstructed. What is seen in the photograph in this book (and in the plastic facsimile in the Israel Museum) is not what the archaeologists and anthropologists saw when the skeletal remains were first examined. Had the nail not been present, imbedded in the bone itself, it is not likely anyone would have suspected crucifixion.

27. This means that John Dominic Crossan's statement that "we have found only one skeleton and one nail" is inaccurate. See J. D. Crossan, *Who Killed Jesus? Exposing the Roots of Anti-Semitism in the Gospel Story of the Death of Jesus* (San Francisco: HarperCollins, 1995), 188. Because of the apparent lack of archaeological evidence, Crossan doubts that Jesus or anyone else executed was properly buried. Instead, the unburied corpses of these unfortunates were left for the birds and dogs. See also Crossan's earlier publication, "The Dogs beneath the Cross," in his *Jesus: A Revolutionary Biography* (San Francisco: HarperOne, 1994), 123–58, here 154. Unfortunately, Ehrman (*How Jesus Became God*, 157, 377 n. 8) bases part of his argument on Crossan's inaccurate claims.

28. Crucifixion nails were valued for magical purposes, a practice debated in rabbinic literature (see *m. Shabbat* 6:10; *y. Shabbat* 6.9; *b. Shabbat* 67a). According to Pliny the Elder, nails used in crucifixion make effective amulets (*Natural History* 28.11: "they take a fragment of a nail from a cross, or else a piece of a halter that has been used for crucifixion, and, after wrapping it in wool, attach it to the patient's neck"). For an inventory of nails and other items found in Jewish tombs and ossuaries in Israel in late antiquity, see R. Hachlili, *Jewish Funerary Customs, Practices, and Rites in the Second Temple Period* (JSJSup 94; Leiden: Brill, 2005), 401–34. She lists some 138 iron nails. There has not yet been a systematic and thorough study of these nails. Hachlili (511–12) reviews the purposes nails placed in tombs and ossuaries may have had, including magical purposes.

29. Again I thank Professor Hershkovitz for allowing me to view a number of nails thought to have been used in crucifixion, as well as a number of photographs of human skeletal remains.

30. As suggested by Chilton, *Rabbi Jesus*, 270–72. Chilton speculates that the tomb Joseph made available may well have been in the very cemetery where the family tomb of Caiaphas was located, thus making his disapproval of Caiaphas keenly and ironically felt. Ehrman doubts that Joseph would have been sympathetic because, after all, "all condemned" Jesus (Mark 15:46; 15:1). Joseph, a member of the council, would therefore have been among the "all" who condemned Jesus, so it is not likely he would so soon have a change of heart. Ehrman's reasoning here is simplistic and hyperliteral. In any case, it is unlikely that the entire council had assembled at the high priest's home the evening Jesus was arrested. In reality, the council was often divided, with the Sadducees and ruling priests demanding harsh punishment and others, often Pharisees, recommending leniency (as Josephus relates). For examples of this in the book of Acts, see Acts 4:1–21; 5:17–41; 6:12–7:60; 22:30–23:10. The New Testament narrative of a dissenting member of council is entirely realistic.

31. J. Magness, "Jesus' Tomb: What Did it Look Like?" in *Where Christianity Was Born* (ed. H. Shanks; Washington, DC: Biblical Archaeology Society, 2006), 212–26, with quotation from p. 224 (italics added). Magness is rightly contradicting Crossan's claim that the burial of Yehohanan was unusual and that Jesus of Nazareth probably was not buried. One should also consult J. G. Cook, "Crucifixion and Burial," *NTS* 57 (2011): 193–213. Cook concludes that the story of Joseph of Arimathea and the burial of Jesus is consistent with Jewish laws of burial, including burial of the condemned and executed, and archaeology.

32. Ehrman, *How Jesus Become God*, 166–68.

33. This point is convincingly argued in J. J. Johnston, "The Resurrection of Jesus in the Gospel of Peter: A Tradition-Historical Study of the *Akhmîm* Gospel Fragment" (unpublished doctoral dissertation; London: Middlesex University, 2012).

Chapter 5: What Did the First Christians Think about Jesus?

1. Ehrman, *How Jesus Became God*, 241.
2. Ibid., 243.
3. S. J. Gathercole, *The Preexistent Son: Recovering the Christologies of Matthew, Mark, and Luke* (Grand Rapids: Eerdmans, 2006).
4. In these Scripture references, all italics are added.
5. Gathercole, *Preexistent Son*, 113–47.

6. Ehrman, *How Jesus Became God*, 243.
7. Ibid., 238.
8. See Gathercole, *Preexistent Son*, 54–77. There is also the work of Richard Bauckham on Christology, which unfortunately is not mentioned by Ehrman in *How Jesus Became God*. See, for example, his *Jesus and the God of Israel*.
9. See especially D. Johansson, "'Who Can Forgive Sins but God Alone?' Human and Angelic Agents, and Divine Forgiveness in Early Judaism," *JSNT* 33 (2011): 351–74.
10. See, e.g., M. D. Hooker, *The Gospel according to Mark* (BNTC; London: Black, 1991), 111.
11. Craig A. Evans, *Mark 8:27–16:20* (WBC; Nashville: Nelson, 2001), 329.
12. See the excellent account in P. Cartledge, *Alexander the Great* (London: Macmillan, 2004), esp. 72–73.
13. Ehrman, *How Jesus Became God*, 90: "Their authors were highly educated, Greek-speaking Christians of a later generation. They probably wrote after Jesus's disciples had all, or almost all, died. They were writing in different parts of the world, in a different language, and at a later time."
14. Ibid., 218.
15. For some of the difficulties, still helpful is J. H. Moulton and W. F. Howard (with C. L. Bedale), "Appendix: Semitisms in the New Testament," in J. H. Moulton and W. F. Howard, *A Grammar of New Testament Greek*, vol. 2, *Accidence and Word Formation* (Edinburgh: T&T Clark, 1929), 411–85. Now more recently, there are M. Wilcox, "Semitisms in the New Testament," *ANRW* 2.25.2 (1984), and J. R. Davila, "(How) Can We Tell if a Greek Apocryphon or Pseudepigraphon Has Been Translated from Hebrew or Aramaic?" *JSP* 15 (2005): 3–61.
16. Ehrman, *How Jesus Became God*, 222.
17. Ibid.
18. Ibid., 222–23.
19. For Jewish parallels, see, e.g., in the Dead Sea Scrolls, 4Q161, fragments 8–10, and 4Q285, fragment 7.
20. Ehrman, *How Jesus Became God*, 224.
21. He notes that it is untenable to take "son of David" and "Son of God" as sharply contrastive; the "in power" is integrally necessary if a contrast is to be seen in the two lines of the formula. See J. D. G. Dunn, *Romans 1–8* (WBC; Waco, TX: Word, 1988), 6. This shows the difficulty with Ehrman's argument that the phrase is "not needed for this correspondence of the two parts" (*How Jesus Became God*, 221).
22. S. Singh, *Fermat's Last Theorem* (London: Fourth Estate, 1997), 71.

23. A further point to note is the slide in Ehrman's argument from something that "may have" been the case, to a conclusion held with a strong degree of certainty. Note the difference between one of the statements in the course of the argument, and the wording of the conclusion to the discussion of Rom 1:3–4. First: "Paul may have wanted to add this phrase because according to his own theology, Jesus was the Son of God before the resurrection, but he was exalted to an even higher state at the resurrection (as we will see more fully in the next chapter). For the original framer of this creed, however, *it may not have worked this way*" (*How Jesus Became God*, 224 [italics added]). Then: "This creed shows why Jesus was the one who deserved this exalted title [viz. 'Son of God']. At his resurrection, God had made him his Son. He, not the emperor, was the one who had received divine status and so was worthy of the honor of being one raised to the side of God" (ibid., 225).

24. Ibid., 226.

25. See the evidence in W. D. Davies and D. C. Allison, *A Critical and Exegetical Commentary on the Gospel according to Saint Matthew*; vol. 1: *Introduction and Commentary on Matthew I–VII* (ICC; Edinburgh: T&T Clark, 1988), 270.

26. Ehrman, *How Jesus Became God*, 226: "'Paul,' in this speech, takes the verse not to indicate what had already happened to the king as the Son of God, but as a prophecy of what would happen to the real king, Jesus, when he was made the Son of God. The fulfillment of the psalm, Paul declares, has happened 'today.' And when is that "today"? It is the day of Jesus's resurrection. That is when God declares that he has 'begotten' Jesus as his Son."

27. Ibid., 228.

28. Compare the Johannine descriptions of the provenance of the Spirit "whom the Father will send in my name" (John 14:26) and "whom I will send to you from the Father—the Spirit of truth, who goes out from the Father" (15:26).

29. C. Mortensen, "Change and Inconsistency," *The Stanford Encyclopedia of Philosophy* (Winter 2012 Edition), Edward N. Zalta (ed.): http://plato.stanford.edu/archives/win2012/entries/change/.

30. Ehrman, *How Jesus Became God*, 264.

31. There are only two places in the canonical Old Testament where this rare word appears. One is in reference to God, in Ps 97:9: "For you, LORD, are the Most High over all the earth; you are 'super-exalted' above all gods" (NIV, adapted). Clearly this is not a reference to God being elevated to a position above his previous station.

Chapter 6: Problems with Ehrman's Interpretative Categories

1. Ehrman, *How Jesus Became God*, 66–67.
2. Ibid., 30.
3. Ibid., 44 (italics original).
4. Ibid., 249.
5. Ibid., 280.
6. Ibid., 237.
7. Ibid., 249.
8. For all of this, see, e.g., ibid., 232, 249–51, 279, etc.
9. Ibid., 272, 281.
10. Ibid., 249.
11. Ibid., 272 (italics added).
12. See also Dunn, *Christology in the Making*; Gordon D. Fee, *Pauline Christology: An Exegetical-Theological Study* (Peabody, MA: Hendrickson, 2007), both of which are problematic for this very reason.
13. E.g., Ehrman, *How Jesus Became God*, 261, 266.
14. This is a specific point about interpreting parts of the New Testament in terms of preexistence. One could object to my claim in general terms and note that the early church doctrines also used language beyond that of the New Testament to construct christological confessions. It should be responded, however, that the creeds arguably did not, thereby, *misshape* the dynamics of New Testament christological language, as Ehrman does. This point will be substantiated in my next chapter.
15. Darrell D. Hannah, *Michael and Christ: Michael Traditions and Angel Christology in Early Christianity* (Tübingen: Mohr Siebeck, 1999); Fee, *Pauline Christology*, esp. 229–31. Fee's analysis not only points to the ways Old Testament "angel of the Lord" texts can be used to identify the agent as YHWH himself, but suggests the Greek intends progression rather than apposition: "we seem in fact to be dealing with progression here rather than identification, which would mean that Christ is a full rung higher than the angelic theophanies of the OT" (231).
16. Ehrman, *How Jesus Became God*, 253.
17. The "divine realm had many levels," he writes. For example, the Roman emperor "was a divine being on a much lower level" (ibid., 20, 40).
18. Ibid., 45.
19. Ibid., 53.
20. Ibid., 55.
21. Ibid., 64.
22. Ibid., 76–84.
23. Ibid., 9.

24. Ibid., 44 (italics original).
25. Ibid., 76.
26. Ibid., 77.
27. Ibid., 78.
28. Ibid., 79.
29. Ibid., 263.
30. Ibid., 272.
31. Some of the modalists Chuck Hill will discuss in chapter 8 might have tried this claim, but they were hardly New Testament scholars!
32. This is a good verse to point out to Jehovah Witnesses, by the way, given their misplaced obsession over the word *Theos* and the question of whether it includes the definite article ("the") or not.
33. For example, key on these issues are Wiard Popkes and Ralph Brucker, eds., *Ein Gott und ein Herr: zum Kontext des Monotheismus im Neuen Testament* (Neukirchen-Vluyn: Neukirchener, 2004); Nathan MacDonald, *Deuteronomy and the Meaning of "Monotheism"* (Tübingen: Mohr Siebeck, 2003); Johannes Woyke, *Götter, "Götzen", Götterbilder: Aspekte einer paulinischen "Theologie der Religionen"* (Berlin: de Gruyter, 2005); Reinhard Feldmeier and Hermann Spieckermann, *God of the Living: A Biblical Theology* (Waco, TX: Baylor University Press, 2011); Erik Waaler, *The Shema and the First Commandment in First Corinthians: An Intertextual Approach to Paul's Re-Reading of Deuteronomy* (Tübingen: Mohr Siebeck, 2008).
34. I refer to Woyke, *Götter*, ch. 3, esp. "Exkurs 3."
35. "This is a view that scholars have called *henotheism*, in distinction from the view I have thus far been calling *monotheism*. Monotheism is the view that there is, in fact, only one God. Henotheism is the view that there are other gods, but there is only one God who is to be worshiped" (Ehrman, *How Jesus Became God*, 53).
36. William Horbury, "Jewish and Christian Monotheism in the Herodian Age," in *Early Jewish and Christian Monotheism* (eds. Loren T. Stuckenbruck and Wendy E. S. North; London: T&T Clark, 2004), 17.
37. Ehrman, *How Jesus Became God*, 83.
38. Bauckham, *Jesus and the God of Israel*, 108.
39. In addition to the work of Bauckham already mentioned, see also N. T. Wright, *The Climax of the Covenant: Christ and the Law in Pauline Theology* (Edinburgh: T&T Clark, 1991); C. F. D. Moule, *The Origin of Christology* (Cambridge: Cambridge University Press, 1977); Max Turner, "'Trinitarian' Pneumatology in the New Testament?—Towards an Explanation of the Worship of Jesus," *AsTJ* 58 (2003): 167–86; Mehrdad Fatehi, *The Spirit's Relation to the Risen Lord in Paul: An*

Examination of Its Christological Implications (Tübingen: Mohr Siebeck, 2000); Paul A. Rainbow, "Monotheism and Christology in 1 Corinthians 8:4–6" (unpublished DPhil, Oxford, 1987); idem, "Jewish Monotheism as the Matrix for New Testament Christology: A Review Article," *NovT* 33 (1991): 78–91; Paul-Gerhard Klumbies, *Die Rede von Gott bei Paulus in ihrem zZeitgeschichtlichen Kontext* (Göttingen: Vandenhoeck & Ruprecht, 1992); Neil Richardson, *Paul's Language about God* (Sheffield: Sheffield Academic Press, 1994); Francis Watson, "The Triune Divine Identity: Reflections on Pauline God-Language, in Disagreement with J. D. G. Dunn," *JSNT* 80 (2000): 99–124; Tilling, *Paul's Divine Christology*; S. Vollenweider, *Horizonte neutestamentlicher Christologie: Studien zu Paulus und zur früchristlichen Theologie* (Tübingen: Mohr Siebeck, 2002); Larry W. Hurtado, "First-Century Jewish Monotheism." *JSNT* 71 (1998): 3–26; Reinhard Feldmeier, "Christologische Theologie," in *Paulus Handbuch* (ed. Friedrich W. Horn; Tübingen: Mohr Siebeck, 2013), 309–14; and so on (to quote Slavoj Žižek).

40. See *m. Berakoth* 1:1–9.

41. This translation (NIV) is disputed, but the point I am making is not affected. Note also that these two sentences form one sentence in the Hebrew.

42. Richard J. Bauckham, "The Worship of Jesus in Apocalyptic Christianity," *NTS* 27 (1981): 335.

43. Larry W. Hurtado, "What Do We Mean by 'First Century Jewish Monotheism'?" *SBLSP* (1993): 348–68.

44. On this, see also the brilliant MacDonald, *Deuteronomy and the Meaning of "Monotheism."*

45. Ehrman, *How Jesus Became God*, 43.

46. Richard J. Bauckham, "Biblical Theology and the Problems of Monotheism," in *Out of Egypt: Biblical Theology and Biblical Interpretation* (eds. Craig Bartholomew, Mary Healy, Karl Möller, and Robin Parry; Milton Keynes, UK: Paternoster, 2004), 210–11.

47. Bauckham, *God of Israel*, 108.

48. Observe the flow of argument in Ehrman, *How Jesus Became God*, 67–69.

49. Ibid., 213.

50. Ibid.

51. Ibid., 224.

52. Murray J. Harris, *The Second Epistle to the Corinthians: A Commentary on the Greek Text* (Milton Keynes, UK: Paternoster, 2005), 959, see also 833.

53. A vision that "took place about A.D. 43 by inclusive reckoning," if Harris' chronological mathematics is to be trusted (ibid., 835).

54. See Martin Hengel and Anna Maria Schwemer, *Paul between Damascus and Antioch: The Unknown Years* (London: SCM, 1997), 14, 28, 98; Seyoon Kim, *The Origin of Paul's Gospel* (Tübingen: Mohr Siebeck, 1984); Timothy W. R. Churchill, *Divine Initiative and the Christology of the Damascus Road Encounter* (Eugene, OR: Pickwick, 2010).

55. Just why some of the verses noted above may be important will probably become clearer in light of my second chapter.

56. Ehrman, *How Jesus Became God*, 282.

57. For more on some of these complex issues, I refer to Chris Keith and Anthony Le Donne, eds., *Jesus, Criteria, and the Demise of Authenticity* (London: T&T Clark, 2012); Jens Schröter, *From Jesus to the New Testament: Early Christian Theology and the Origin of the New Testament Canon* (Baylor-Mohr Siebeck Studies in Early Christianity; Waco, TX: Baylor University Press, 2013), 1–70.

58. Ehrman, *How Jesus Became God*, 2.

59. Ibid.

60. Ibid., 3.

61. Ibid., 49.

62. Alan F. Segal, *Two Powers in Heaven: Early Rabbinic Reports about Christianity and Gnosticism* (Leiden: Brill, 1977).

63. Ehrman, *How Jesus Became God*, 264.

64. Ibid., 277, 281.

65. So Karl Barth (*Church Dogmatics*, 4/1, 166) writes: "The Word did not simply become any 'flesh,' any man humbled and suffering. It became Jewish flesh." See also Douglas A. Campbell, "Paul's Apocalyptic Politics," *Pro Ecclesia* 22 (2013): 129–52.

66. Ehrman, *How Jesus Became God*, 61.

67. I do not. See Tilling, *Paul's Divine Christology*; and the various publications of Bauckham.

68. Adela Yarbro Collins and John J. Collins, *King and Messiah as Son of God: Divine, Human, and Angelic Messianic Figures in Biblical and Related Literature* (Grand Rapids: Eerdmans, 2008). See, e.g., the brief but incisive criticisms of the volume by Nick Norelli, "King and Messiah as Son of God: Divine, Human, and Angelic Messianic Figures in Biblical and Related Literature (2)": http://rdtwot.wordpress.com/2009/10/04/king-and-messiah-as-son-of-god-divine-human-and-angelic-messianic-figures-in-biblical-and-related-literature–2/.

Chapter 7: Misreading Paul's Christology: Problems with Ehrman's Exegesis

1. Ehrman, *How Jesus Became God*, 249.
2. Ibid., 251.
3. Ibid.
4. Ibid., 252.
5. Ibid., 251 (italics added).
6. Ibid., 282.
7. See Charles H. Talbert, *The Development of Christology during the First Hundred Years, and Other Essays on Early Christian Christology* (NovTSup; Leiden: Brill, 2011), and the helpful critical review: Nick Norelli, *"The Development of Christology during the First Hundred Years: And Other Essays on Early Christian Christology.* A Review." http://rdtwot. wordpress.com/2012/12/02/the-development-of-christology-during-the-first-hundred-years-and-other-essays-on-early-christian-christology/.
8. See, e.g., A. E. Harvey, *Jesus and the Constraints of History* (London: Duckworth, 1982); Maurice Casey, *From Jewish Prophet to Gentile God: The Origins and Development of New Testament Christology* (Cambridge: James Clarke, 1991).
9. See, e.g., Peter Hayman. "Monotheism—a Misused Word in Jewish Studies?" *JJS* 42 (1991): 1–15; Margaret Barker. *The Great Angel: A Study of Israel's Second God* (London: SPCK, 1992).
10. See my previous chapter and Ehrman's argumentation in, e.g., *How Jesus Became God*, 52–55.
11. See n. 39 in my previous chapter for a list of representative names.
12. Hurtado, "First-Century," 22.
13. See my earlier discussion on pages 128–29 in chapter 6.
14. For this, see, e.g., Hurtado, *Lord Jesus Chirst*, 32–42.
15. Wolfgang Schrage, *Unterwegs zur Einzigkeit und Einheit Gottes: zum "Monotheismus" des Paulus und seiner alttestamentlich-frühjüdischen Tradition* (Neukirchen-Vluyn: Neukirchener Verlag, 2002), 159, 163 (trans. C. Tilling).
16. Lester L. Grabbe, *Judaic Religion in the Second Temple Period* (London: Routledge, 2000), 179.
17. E. Käsemann, *Commentary on Romans* (London: SCM, 1980), 327.
18. Tilling, *Paul's Divine Christology*, 60.
19. So Ehrman (*How Jesus Became God*, 54) can claim: "other Jews whom we know about ... thought it was altogether acceptable and right to worship other divine beings, such as the great angels."

20. Andrew Chester, *Messiah and Exaltation: Jewish Messianic and Visionary Traditions and New Testament Christology* (Tübingen: Mohr Siebeck, 2007), 20–27; Dale Tuggy, "On Bauckham's Bargain," *TT* 70 (2013): 128–43.

21. As I argue in Tilling, *Paul's Divine Christology*, 63–72.

22. MacDonald, *Deuteronomy and the Meaning of "Monotheism,"* 151 (italics added).

23. Waaler, *Shema*, 202 (italics added).

24. James D. G. Dunn, *The Theology of Paul the Apostle* (Grand Rapids: Eerdmans, 1998), 47.

25. Though this text may be a later, non-Pauline, interpolation.

26. Cf. Woyke, *Götter*, and the arguments in Tilling, *Paul's Divine Christology*, 68–72.

27. "Relational" is used to indicate "the way in which one person or thing is related to another" (Judy Pearsall and William R. Trumble, eds., *The Oxford English Reference Dictionary* [Oxford: Oxford University Press, 1995], 1216).

28. For more on these claims, see various chapters of Tilling, *Paul's Divine Christology*. Also see Rainbow, "Monotheism and Christology in 1 Corinthians 8:4–6" for a useful list of important Jewish "God" texts.

29. Dunn, *Theology*, 46. This distinction between "Greek" and "Hebrew" can, of course, be challenged (Ian W. Scott, *Implicit Epistemology in the Letters of Paul: Story, Experience and the Spirit* [Tübingen: Mohr Siebeck, 2006], 146–47), but exaggerations aside, there is truth to Dunn's claim.

30. Scott, *Epistemology*; Robin Parry and Mary Healy, eds., *The Bible and Epistemology: Biblical Soundings on the Knowledge of God* (Milton Keynes, UK: Paternoster, 2007).

31. Scott, *Epistemology*, 147.

32. Ibid., 150 (italics added).

33. Cf. the section title in Mary Healy, "Knowledge of the Mystery: A Study of Pauline Epistemology," in *The Bible and Epistemology*, 142, 145–56.

34. Bauckham, "Apocalyptic," 335.

35. The following couple of paragraphs are adapted from my essay, "Campbell's Apocalyptic Gospel and Pauline Athanasianism," in *Beyond Old and New Perspectives on Paul: Reflections on the Work of Douglas Campbell* (ed. Chris Tilling; Eugene, OR: Cascade, 2014).

36. See, esp., Waaler, *Shema*.

37. See Tilling, *Paul's Divine Christology*, 78, for a discussion about the variant readings in other early manuscripts.

38. See esp. Volker Gäckle, *Die Starken und die Schwachen in Korinth und*

in Rom: Zu Herkunft und Funktion der Antithese in 1 Kor 8,1–11,1 und Röm 14,1–15,13 (Tübingen: Mohr Siebeck, 2005), 108, 189–90, 200–204.

39. See also Fee, *Christology*, 585.
40. Yes, we all know this is an anachronistic term. If it causes problems, mentally insert "Christ-followers" in its place.
41. See Tilling, *Paul's Divine Christology*, chapters 5–8.
42. Ehrman, *How Jesus Became God*, 213.
43. And remember, in this letter he instructs Christians to "pray continually" (5:17). This is how Paul's models it in his letter.
44. The Greek word translated as "coming" is *parousia* and simply means "presence" as opposed to "absence."
45. See Rom 1:5; 14:9; 1 Cor 6:13; 7:35; 2 Cor 4:5, 8, 10–11; 5:9–10; 8:19; 12:7–10; Gal 2:20; Phil 1:20, 23; 2:9–11; 3:8; 1 Thess 4:17; 5:10; Philem 6.
46. See Rom 14:6–8; 16:5; 1 Cor 1:7; 1:31; 2:2; 6:16–17; 7:25–38; 11:23–26; 12:3; 15:19; 16:22; 2 Cor 3:16–18; 5:15; 8:5; 10:7; 10:17; 11:2–3; Gal 2:20; 3:29; Phil 2:6–11; 3:1, 8; 1 Thess 1:2–3; 3:8.
47. See Rom 12:11; 1 Cor 1:7; 2:2; 7:32–35; 15:58; 2 Cor 11:2–3; Phil 1:20; 3:8; 4:4, 10; 1 Thess 3:11–13; 5:17.
48. Rom 16:18; 1 Cor 6:13; 7:32–34; 8:12; 10:9; 10:20–22; 11:30–32; 2 Cor 4:4; 5:15; 11:2–3; Gal 1:10; Phil 2:21.
49. See Rom 1:7; 8:9–10; 14:4; 15:18–19, 29; 16:20; 1 Cor 1:3; 3:5; 4:19; 7:17, 25; 16:17, 23; 2 Cor 1:2; 2:10, 12; 3:3; 12:7–10; 13:3–5, 13; Gal 2:20; 4:6; 6:18; Phil 1:2, 19; 3:21; 1 Thess 3:11–13; 5:28; Philem 3, 25.
50. See 1 Cor 11:26; 15:23; 2 Cor 5:6–8; Phil 1:20–24; 1 Thess 2:19; 3:13; 4:17; 5:10, 23. Margaret E. Thrall (*The Second Epistle to the Corinthians* [ICC; London: T&T Clark, 2004], 1:386) writes on these verses that "life in this world means life in exile, life apart from the Lord."
51. See Rom 8:34; 10:6; Phil 3:20; 1 Thess 1:9–10; 4:16. Cf. also 1 Cor 15:47–49; 2 Cor 12:2; Eph 6:9; Col 4:1; 2 Thess 1:7.
52. See Rom 8:9–10; 15:18–19; Gal 4:6; Phil 1:19.
53. Following Karl-Heinrich Ostmeyer's *Kommunikation mit Gott und Christus: Sprache und Theologie des Gebetes im Neuen Testament* (Tübingen: Mohr Siebeck, 2006).
54. Rom 10:9–13; 15:11; 1 Cor 16:22; 2 Cor 12:8; 1 Thess 3:11–13.
55. See 2 Cor 10:18; 12:9; 13:3.
56. See Rom 8:35; 10:12; 14:4, 9; 1 Cor 11:27–30; 15:45; 2 Cor 4:13; 5:14; 10:1; 13:5; Gal 1:1, 11–12; 2:20; Phil 1:8; 3:21; 1 Thess 4:6.
57. Tilling, *Paul's Divine Christology*, 241.
58. Ehrman, *How Jesus Became God*, 252.

59. Compare Ehrman's views expressed in ibid., 268–69.

60. Fee's analysis of this passage is the best part of his entire book, in my view. It ought to be pointed out here that Ehrman does not once mention Gordon Fee's work *Pauline Christology*. Whatever one thinks of Fee's 700+ page book (and I happen to be rather critical), it is a necessary port of call for anyone daring to write on Paul's Christology and be taken seriously by academic peers. Of course, Ehrman's book is meant for a popular audience, so he could be excused from explicitly referencing it, but he has not shown any evidence of having read it; it doesn't inform his argument, and this is just sloppy.

61. Ehrman, *How Jesus Became God*, 263.

62. Murray J. Harris, *Slave of Christ: A New Testament Metaphor for Total Devotion to Christ* (Leicester, UK: Apollos, 1999).

63. See V. Koperski, *The Knowledge of Christ Jesus My Lord: The High Christology of Philippians 3:7–11* (Kampen, Netherlands: Kok Pharos, 1996).

64. R. W. Hoover, "The HARPAGMOS Enigma: A Philological Solution," *HTR* 64 (1971): 95–119.

65. Fee, *Christology*, 381–83; Wright, *Climax*, 62–90; Michael J. Gorman, *Inhabiting the Cruciform God: Kenosis, Justification, and Theosis in Paul's Narrative Soteriology* (Cambridge: Eerdmans, 2009), chapter 1.

66. So Ehrman, *How Jesus Became God*, 263.

67. Ehrman also argues that his view is supported by the fact that Jesus, in the second half of the poem, is exalted even more highly. Thus he couldn't have been equal to God before. But the material does not *have* to be parsed this way at all (see, once again, the discussion in Fee, *Christology*, 372–401; Gorman, *Inhabiting*, 29–32).

68. Ehrman, *How Jesus Became God*, 262–66. I refer again to suspicions I noted in my previous chapter about Ehrman's grasp of historiography.

69. His (implausible) chronological conjecture, that Paul straddles the development from an exaltation Christology to an incarnational one has been challenged in a number of ways already in my previous chapter.

70. See also Richard J. Bauckham, "The Worship of Jesus in Philippians 2:9–11," in *Where Christology Began: Essays on Philippians 2* (ed. Ralph P. Martin and Brian J. Dodd; Louisville: Westminster John Knox, 1998), 128–39.

71. N. T. Wright, *Paul and the Faithfulness of God* (COQG 4; Minneapolis: Fortress, 2013), 683.

72. If, that is, you discount Colossians as Pauline, as Ehrman does. I think he is probably wrong about that, too, especially his claim that material in Colossians 1 is in "an entirely different realm from the earlier exaltation Christologies" (Ehrman, *How Jesus Became God*, 280). It may be slightly

different, but it is no more "advanced" than Paul's christological language found in 1 Thessalonians when understood in the terms advanced in this chapter.

73. Ibid., 249 (italics added).
74. Ibid., 235.
75. See the hotly-debated-yet-worthy-of-discussion papers in Paul N. Anderson, Felix Just, and Tom Thatcher, eds., *John, Jesus, and History*; vol. 1, *Critical Appraisals of Critical Views* (SBLSS; Atlanta, GA: SBL, 2007); idem, *John, Jesus, and History*; vol. 2, *Aspects of Historicity in the Fourth Gospel* (SBLSS; Atlanta, GA: SBL, 2009). Also see Tom Thatcher, ed., *What We Have Heard from the Beginning: The Past, Present, and Future of Johannine Studies* (Waco, TX: Baylor University Press, 2007); Richard Bauckham. *The Testimony of the Beloved Disciple: Narrative, History, and Theology in the Gospel of John* (Grand Rapids: Baker, 2007); Richard Horsley and Tom Thatcher, *John, Jesus, and the Renewal of Israel* (Grand Rapids: Eerdmans, 2013).
76. See also Christopher Tuckett, "The Fourth Gospel and Q," in *Jesus in Johannine Tradition* (eds. Robert T. Fortna and Tom Thatcher; Louisville: Westminster John Knox, 2001), 281–90.
77. Ehrman, *How Jesus Became God*, 271.
78. Ibid., 272.
79. Ibid., 278.
80. Ibid., 281.

Chapter 8: An Exclusive Religion: Orthodoxy and Heresy, Inclusion and Exclusion

1. Ehrman, *How Jesus Became God*, 289, 290, 303.
2. Ibid., 285.
3. Ibid., 289.
4. Ibid., 211–46.
5. Ibid., 146. See also 147.
6. Ibid., 150.
7. To take a cue from Ehrman's discussion (ibid., 147), if every historian were a Mormon (or let's just say if a majority were Mormons), would it be historically true that the angel Moroni appeared to Joseph Smith? Or would it just be that the majority of historians believed it was historically true? Here we get to the question of whether there is anything objective, outside our perception of it—which is a great question. But more to our point here, if the majority of historians believed it to be historically true, could we really disagree with them and still be doing history? By Ehrman's definition, no, we could not.

8. Ibid., 289.

9. Ibid., 308.

10. Witness the title of the book authored by Bruce Metzger, the fourth edition of which was coauthored with Bart Ehrman, *The Text of the New Testament: Its Transmission, Corruption, and Restoration* (Oxford: Oxford University Press, 2005).

11. See John Behr, *The Way to Nicaea* (Crestwood, NY: St Vladimir's Seminary Press, 2001), 148, who also cites Adolf von Harnack, *History of Dogma* (7 vols.; London: Williams and Norgate, 1894–1899), 3:65, for this view.

12. Henry Chadwick, *Early Christian Thought and the Classical Tradition* (Oxford: Oxford University Press, 1984), 95.

13. Ehrman, *How Jesus Became God*, 290.

14. Ibid., 289, 291, 293, 295.

15. Ibid., 291.

16. Ibid., 291.

17. Ibid., 207.

18. Ibid., 218.

19. Ibid., 231.

20. Ibid., 289.

21. Ibid.

22. See the treatment of Ray A. Pritz, *Nazarene Jewish Christianity: From the End of the New Testament Period until Its Disappearance in the Fourth Century* (Jerusalem: Magnes, Hebrew University/Leiden: Brill, 1988), 19–28.

23. See ebionite.org.

24. Ehrman, *How Jesus Became God*, 308–9.

25. Ibid., 311.

26. There is actually a great deal of disagreement over the identity of the author of *The Refutation of All Heresies*, traditionally ascribed to Hippolytus of Rome. I tend to agree with those who think he is not Hippolytus, at least not the same person who wrote the treatise *Against Noetus* and several exegetical works also ascribed to Hippolytus. However, for the purposes of these chapters, I will follow Ehrman's practice and use the name Hippolytus for the author of both of these works, the *Refutation* and the *Against Noetus*.

27. Ehrman, *How Jesus Became God*, 315.

28. This is something Ehrman acknowledges in ibid., 313.

29. Thus, a distinction later came to be made between the "ontological" Trinity, meaning the three persons in their "essential" relations, equal in power and glory, and the "economic" or "functional" Trinity," which

speaks of the way the three persons subsist and act in relation to themselves.

30. Cited from William G. Rusch, ed. and trans., *The Trinitarian Controversy* (Philadelphia: Fortress, 1980), 123.

31. Ibid., 10.

32. Thomas Weinandy, "The Apostolic Christology of Ignatius of Antioch: The Road to Chalcedon," in *Trajectories through the New Testament and the Apostolic Fathers* (eds. A. Gregory and C. Tuckett; New York: Oxford University Press, 2006), 76.

33. Note then that by the early third century, *nomina sacra* were expanded to include *huios* ("Son"). The use of the Greek upsilon (Y) at the end of the nomina sacra in P. Oxy 002 indicates that the nouns are in the genitive case.

34. Larry Hurtado, *The Earliest Christian Artifacts: Manuscripts and Christian Origins* (Grand Rapids; Eerdmans, 2006), 105–6 (esp. 95–134 for wider argument and interaction with scholarly literature on the subject).

Chapter 9: Paradox Pushers and Persecutors?

1. Ehrman, *How Jesus Became God*, 329.

2. A famous paradox of science is the question of whether light is a wave or a particle. Scientists tell us it has the properties of both. Niels Bohr proposed that we cannot use the terms wave and particle at the same time but can only describe how light is behaving at the point at which we observe it. Professor Russell Stannard of the Open University says this about Bohr's attempted solution: "such a solution would mean that we are confined to talking about the way we observe the world. We would forever be denied the possibility of saying anything meaningful about a world that was not being observed—the world as it might be in itself. Einstein was among those who could never accept this limitation. Eighty years on from his famous arguments with Bohr, we seem to be no closer to a resolution. Perhaps we never shall be" (http://www.open.edu/openlearn/science-maths-technology/science/physics-and-astronomy/physics/paradox-wave-particles). I owe this observation to Michael Bird.

3. Ehrman, *How Jesus Became God*, 326.

4. Ibid., 326–27. Again, "The resulting ortho-paradox was driven by the positions that the orthodox were compelled to stake out when opposing the contradictory views of their opponents and the biblical texts" (328).

5. Even those, like Ehrman, who think the prologue is a preexisting poem, regard verses 1 and 14 as belonging to that same integral composition. And, if the author of this poem is different from the final author of the

gospel, then we have two early "Johannine" authors who thought the "paradox" made sense.

6. Ibid., 280.
7. Ibid., 281.
8. To some extent my argument here simply reiterates and expands on what Chris Tilling has said about Ehrman's chronology in chapter 6, to which I refer the reader. Here, however, I'll propose a way to understand the peaceful coexistence of the supposed "exaltation Christologies" and the "incarnational Christologies" and relate this to ongoing developments in the early church.
9. Ehrman, *How Jesus Became God*, 353.
10. See, however, the treatments of these important passages earlier in this book, chapter 4 by Craig Evans and chapter 5 by Simon Gathercole.
11. See the treatment by Chris Tilling in chapter 7 of this book.
12. Ehrman, *How Jesus Became God*, 282.
13. The origins of what is now called the Apostles' Creed go back to early rules of faith, and in particular the Old Roman Creed, from the late second century. These developed from baptismal confessions based on the trinitarian formula given by Jesus in Matt 28:19–20. The first use of the expression "Apostles' Creed" occurs in 390 CE. The creed was modified at various points and reached its final form perhaps in the ninth century. It is widely accepted and used as a subordinate standard in Roman Catholic and Protestant churches throughout the world. The version here is taken from *Ecumenical Creeds and Reformed Confessions* (Grand Rapids: CRC Publications, 1988), 7.
14. Ehrman, *How Jesus Became God*, 334.
15. Ibid., 331.
16. Ibid., 334.
17. J. N. D. Kelly, *Early Christian Doctrines* (rev. ed.; New York: Harper & Row, 1978), 96.
18. Ibid., 97. See also Rusch, *The Trinitarian Controversy*, 5, "To emphasize the essential identity of the Logos with the Father, they [the Apologists] used the biblical image of the Son or Child for the Logos, so they spoke of the Logos not as a creature but as the offspring by generation (Justin *Trypho* 62.105, 125; *1 Apol.* 21)."
19. Ehrman, *How Jesus Became God*, 334.
20. Ibid.
21. Ibid., 337.
22. Rusch, *The Trinitarian Controversy*, 12.
23. Ehrman, *How Jesus Became God*, 339.
24. Ibid., 313.

25. Ibid., 334.
26. Ibid., 326.
27. Ibid., 339.
28. See especially Michael Slusser, "The Exegetical Roots of Trinitarian Theology," *Theological Studies* 49 (1988): 461–76; Stephen O. Presley, "Irenaeus and the Exegetical Roots of Trinitarian Theology," in *Irenaeus: Life, Scripture, Legacy* (ed. Sara Parvis and Paul Foster; Minneapolis: Fortress, 2012), 165–81.
29. Justin, *1 Apology* 36; Irenaeus, *Demonstration of the Apostolic Preaching* 49–50; Tertullian, *Against Praxeas* 11. Scholars have come up with a term for this: "prosopological exegesis."
30. Tertullian, *Against Praxeas* 11. Slusser, "The Exegetical Roots of Trinitarian Theology," 465, observes that Athanasius uses this kind of literary analysis of Scripture as well.
31. Slusser, "The Exegetical Roots of Trinitarian Theology," 475.
32. Ibid.
33. Ehrman, *How Jesus Became God*, 358.
34. Ibid., 359.
35. Ibid., 360.
36. Ibid., 277.
37. Ibid., 281.
38. Ibid., 290.
39. Ibid., 362.
40. Ibid., 360.
41. Ibid., 363.
42. Paula Fredriksen and Oded Irshai, "Christian Anti-Judaism: Polemics and Policies," *Cambridge History of Judaism*; vol. 4, *The Late Roman-Rabbinic Period* (ed. Steven T. Katz; Cambridge: Cambridge University Press, 2006), 977–1034 at 1001.
43. Ibid., 1003.
44. Ibid., 1004, n. 86.
45. Ibid., 1004–5.
46. Ibid., 1007.
47. Ehrman, *How Jesus Became God*, 364.
48. Ibid., 363–64.
49. As William Frend puts it, "Why should heresy and infidelity be favored now?" (W. H. C. Frend, *The Rise of Christianity* [Philadelphia: Fortress, 1984], 624).
50. See Stéphane Courtois, et al., *The Black Book of Communism: Crimes, Terror, Repression* (Cambridge, MA: Harvard University Press, 1999), 7, a total of between 85 million and 100 million deaths "the Communist

record offers the most colossal case of political carnage in history" (from the "Foreword" by Martin Malia).

51. See further Vassilios Tzaferis, "Inscribed 'to God Jesus Christ': Early Christian Prayer Hall Found in Meggido Prison," *BAR*: http://www.bibarch.org/online-exclusives/oldest-church–02.asp. Cited December 10, 2013.

Chapter 10: Concluding Thoughts

1. A point I owe to John Walker, "Paul and the Faithfulness of God: N. T. Wright on Christology," http://freedominorthodoxy.blogspot.com.au /2013/12/paul-and-faithfulness-of-god-nt-wright_27.html, cited December 28, 2013.